Revision Study in Ma

C. H. Hopkins

John Murray

First published 1985
by John Murray (Publishers) Ltd
50 Albemarle Street
London W1X 4BD

Printed in Great Britain at the Alden Press
Oxford London and Northampton

British Library Cataloguing in Publication Data

Hopkins, C. H.
Revision study in mathematics.
1. Mathematics – 1961–
I. Title
510 QA39.2
0–7195–4186–7

Contents

Part 1 Basic Revision

Basic revision is presented broadly in four sections under the headings, Number, Money and Measures, Shapes, and Algebra. The notes at the beginning of each section do not cover every aspect of the subject and are offered only as a guide. The revision exercises which follow each set of notes are designed to test the basic facts contained in examination questions.

Number Revision notes

Fractions

These are *equivalent fractions*: $\frac{2}{3} = \frac{4}{6} = \frac{6}{9} = \frac{8}{12}$ $\quad \frac{3}{4} = \frac{6}{8} = \frac{9}{12} = \frac{12}{16}$

To add and subtract fractions, change to equivalent fractions.
These are *mixed numbers*: $2\frac{1}{3}$ $\quad 4\frac{3}{4}$ $\quad 3\frac{5}{8}$ $\quad 5$.

When written like this: $\frac{7}{3}$ $\quad \frac{19}{4}$ $\quad \frac{29}{8}$ $\quad \frac{5}{1}$, they have become improper fractions. To multiply and divide, change mixed numbers in that way.

Addition	*Subtraction*	*Multiplication*	*Division*
$2\frac{1}{3} + 1\frac{3}{4} + 1\frac{5}{6}$	$4\frac{1}{8} - 1\frac{3}{4}$	$1\frac{1}{5} \times 1\frac{3}{4} \times 2\frac{2}{3}$	$3\frac{1}{8} \div 1\frac{1}{4}$
$= 2\frac{4}{12} + 1\frac{9}{12} + 1\frac{10}{12}$	$= 4\frac{1}{8} - 1\frac{6}{8}$	$= \frac{\cancel{6}^{2}}{5} \times \frac{7}{\cancel{4}_{1}} \times \frac{\cancel{8}^{2}}{\cancel{3}_{1}}$	$\frac{25}{8} \div \frac{5}{4}$
$= 4\frac{23}{12}$	$= 3\frac{9}{8} - 1\frac{6}{8}$	$= \frac{28}{5}$	$= \frac{\cancel{25}^{5}}{\cancel{8}_{2}} \times \frac{\cancel{4}^{1}}{\cancel{5}_{1}}$
$= 5\frac{11}{12}$.	$= 2\frac{3}{8}$.	$= 5\frac{3}{5}$.	$= \frac{5}{2}$
			$= 2\frac{1}{2}$.

Ratio

A ratio is a form of fraction.
The ratio of 10 to 8 can be written $10:8$ or $\frac{10}{8}$.
The simplest fraction equivalent to $\frac{10}{8}$ is $\frac{5}{4}$.
The ratio of 12 to 18 is $\frac{12}{18}$ or $\frac{2}{3}$ $(2:3)$.
When measures of any kind are involved, the units must be the same.
The ratio of 25p to £2 becomes the ratio of 25p to 200p.

This makes the ratio of $\frac{25}{200} = \frac{1}{8}$.
$\frac{3}{4}$ of 76 means $76 \div 4 \times 3$.
$\frac{5}{8}$ of 72 means $72 \div 8 \times 5$.

The same method applies when sharing according to a ratio (see p. 4).

Share £96 in the ratio 2:1:5.
2 + 1 + 5 = 8 equal amounts.
The ratio gives $\frac{2}{8}, \frac{1}{8}, \frac{5}{8}$.
$\frac{2}{8}$ of £96 = £24.
$\frac{1}{8}$ of £96 = £12.
$\frac{5}{8}$ of £96 = £60.
Note: The total is £96.

When an amount is shared in the ratio 2:3:4, the largest share is £32. Find the whole amount.
The ratio gives $\frac{2}{9}, \frac{3}{9}, \frac{4}{9}$.
$\frac{4}{9}$ was £32.
$\frac{1}{9}$ was £8.
The whole amount was £72.

Enlargements are carried out according to a given ratio.

Corresponding sides in similar shapes form equal ratios.
A map or plan is drawn by using a given ratio.
If a scale of 5 cm to 1 metre is used, the ratio is $\frac{5}{100}$ or $\frac{1}{20}$.
All scaled measurements are $\frac{1}{20}$ of the real measurements.
Real measurements are obtained by multiplying scaled lengths by 20.

Factors and Multiples

A *prime* number is only divisible by two positive numbers, itself and 1.

2, 3, 5, 7, 11, 13, 17, 19, 23, . . .

Note: Although 1 is divisible by itself and 1, it is not used as a prime number. The number 2 is the only even number which is prime.
Numbers which are not prime (except 1) are *rectangular* numbers.

4, 6, 8, 9, 10, 12, 14, 15, 16, . . .

Square numbers are formed like this:

1×1	2×2	3×3	4×4.
1	4	9	16.

A number is divisible by any of its factors.
12 will divide by 2, 3, 4, 6 and 12, so 2, 3, 4, 6 and 12 are factors of 12, but only 2 and 3 are *prime factors* of 12.
These numbers have been written as a product of their prime factors:

$$30 = 2 \times 3 \times 5 \quad 12 = 2 \times 2 \times 3 \quad 28 = 2 \times 2 \times 7.$$

Multiples of a number are all divisible by that number.
Multiples of 3: 3, 6, 9, 12, 15, 18 . . .
Multiples of 10: 10, 20, 30, 40, 50 . . .

Square Roots

Since $6 \times 6 = 36$ then $\sqrt{36} = 6$. Since $9 \times 9 = 81$ then $\sqrt{81} = 9$.
The square root of a perfect square is found using prime factors:

$$\begin{aligned} 1764 &= 2 \times 2 \times 3 \times 3 \times 7 \times 7 \\ \sqrt{1764} &= 2 \times 3 \times 7 \\ &= 42. \end{aligned}$$

Approximate square roots, found by trial and error using this list:

$\sqrt{1}$	$\sqrt{4}$	$\sqrt{9}$	$\sqrt{16}$	$\sqrt{25}$	$\sqrt{36}$	$\sqrt{49}$	$\sqrt{64}$	$\sqrt{81}$	$\sqrt{100}$
1	2	3	4	5	6	7	8	9	10

Find an approximate value for $\sqrt{27}$.

$\sqrt{27}$ must lie between $\sqrt{25}$ and $\sqrt{36}$.

$\sqrt{27}$ is between 5 and 6.

Try 5.1	Try 5.2	Try 5.3
× 5.1	× 5.2	× 5.3
= 26.01.	= 27.04.	= 28.09.

The nearest product to 27 in those trials is 27.04.

$\sqrt{27} = 5.2$ approximately.

Note: Since $^{+}6 \times {}^{+}6 = 36$ and $^{-}6 \times {}^{-}6 = 36$, then $\sqrt{36}$ is $^{+}6$ or $^{-}6$.

$\sqrt{25} = \pm 5, \sqrt{49} = \pm 7, \sqrt{100} = \pm 10$ etc.

The facts supplied in an example will decide whether both values are required or if the answer is positive only.

Decimals

When using decimals in any operation, *place value* is important. Figures must be placed in the correct columns.

Addition

1.6 + 5.83 + 29 + 0.047.

```
  1.6
  5.83
 29
  0.047
 36.477
```

Subtraction

53 − 7.28.

```
  53
 −7.28
  45.72
```

Place value affected by multiplication and division

3.57 × 10 = 35.7

6 × 100 = 600

0.037 × 1000 = 37.

3.57 ÷ 10 = 0.357

6 ÷ 100 = 0.06

0.037 ÷ 1000 = 0.000037.

Multiplication

76.8 × 0.19

Multiply 76.8 × 10 = 768

and 0.19 × 100 = 19.

768 × 19 = 14592.

Divide by 1000 (10 × 100).

76.8 × 0.19 = 14.592.

Division

4.512 ÷ 0.12

$$\frac{4.512}{0.12} = \frac{4.512 \times 100}{0.12 \times 100}$$

$$\frac{451.2}{12} = 37.6.$$

4.512 ÷ 0.12 = 37.6.

Fractions and Decimals

$\frac{1}{10} = 0.1 \quad \frac{3}{10} = 0.3 \quad \frac{7}{100} = 0.07 \quad \frac{36}{100} = 0.36 \quad 5\frac{9}{10} = 5.9.$

Fractions	$\frac{1}{5}$	$\frac{3}{5}$	$\frac{7}{20}$	$\frac{19}{25}$	$\frac{27}{50}$	$\frac{5}{8}$.
Changed to equal fractions	$\frac{2}{10}$	$\frac{6}{10}$	$\frac{35}{100}$	$\frac{76}{100}$	$\frac{54}{100}$	$\frac{625}{1000}$.
Changed to decimals	0.2	0.6	0.35	0.76	0.54	0.625.

Correction

Decimal places are counted to the right of the decimal point.
19.3628 corrected to 3 decimal places is 19.363.
19.3628 corrected to 2 decimal places is 19.36.
19.3628 corrected to the nearest ten is 20.

Significant figures commence with the first figure larger than 0.
8.3027 corrected to 4 significant figures is 8.303.
35.08 corrected to 3 significant figures is 35.1.
0.0286 corrected to 2 significant figures is 0.029.

Decimals in standard form
We can write 1372.4 as 137.24×10
or 13.724×100 ($\times 10^2$)
or 1.3724×1000 ($\times 10^3$).
When written as 1.3724×10^3 it is in standard form.
It is in the form $A \times 10^n$, where $1 < A < 10$ and n is an integer.
These are in standard form:

$$56.83 = 5.683 \times 10$$
$$4936 = 4.936 \times 10^3$$
$$0.784 = 7.84 \times 10^{-1} \; (\times \tfrac{1}{10})$$
$$0.0435 = 4.35 \times 10^{-2} \; (\times \tfrac{1}{100}).$$

Number Bases

Number bases provide different methods of writing a number.
The number base decides the value of each number place.

Headings							
	Base 2:	32	16	8	4	2	1
	Base 3:	243	81	27	9	3	1
	Base 5:	3125	625	125	25	5	1
	Base 10:	100 000	10 000	1000	100	10	1

Base 2 number 11011_2 means we must work out

$$(1 \times 16) + (1 \times 8) + (0 \times 4) + (1 \times 2) + (1 \times 1),$$

giving base 10 number 27.

Base 10 number 34 written in base 3 requires headings 27, 9, 3, 1.

(27)	(9)	(3)	(1)
1	0	2	1

When working operations or changing from one base to a different base, you may work through base 10, our normal counting numbers, or use any other method you have been taught.

Bicimals Just as we multiply by 2 to obtain whole number headings in base 2, so we divide by 2 to obtain the headings for bicimals in base 2.

Column headings	8	4	2	1 .	$\frac{1}{2}$	$\frac{1}{4}$	$\frac{1}{8}$	$\frac{1}{16}$	
Fraction $\frac{1}{2}$ as a bicimal:				0 .	1				
$\frac{1}{4}$ as a bicimal:				0 .	0	1			
$\frac{3}{4}$ as a bicimal:				0 .	1	1			$(\frac{1}{2} + \frac{1}{4})$
$\frac{9}{16}$ as a bicimal:				0 .	1	0	0	1	$(\frac{1}{2} + \frac{1}{16})$

Statistics

A set of facts, containing a list of numbers or amounts, may be used to give various items of information. We may use them to obtain diagrams giving an overall picture:

Hours of sunshine

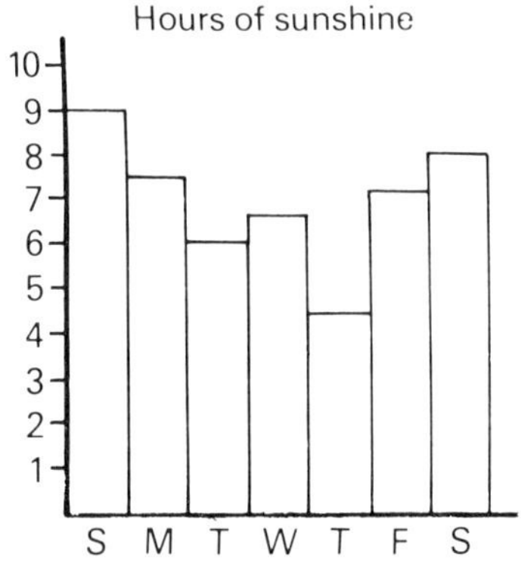

Bar-graph. Largest item decides the vertical scale

Traffic in thousands

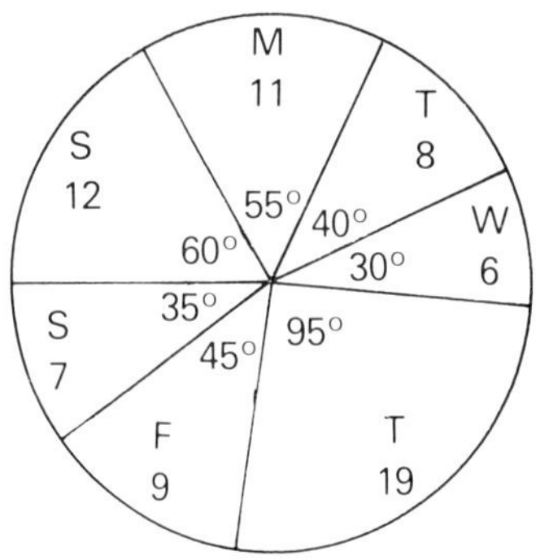

Pie chart. Degrees per unit $= \dfrac{360°}{\text{Total units}}$

Total = 72
One unit = 360 ÷ 72
= 5°

We may obtain average figures:

Mode The number or amount which appears most times.

Median When the list is arranged in ascending order, the middle is the median value.

Mean The mean is obtained by finding the total of the numbers and dividing that answer by the number of amounts.

See later notes in Part 2.

Probability

First find the number of all *possibilities*:	Choosing one from six cards	– 6 possibilities.
	Choosing one from eight people	– 8 possibilities.
	Rolling a die with six faces	– 6 possibilities.

From the total possibilities, find the occurrence of the choice:
In the numbers 1 to 6, the occurrence of an even number is 3.
In the numbers 1 to 10, the occurrence of a square number is 3.

$$\text{The probability} = \frac{\text{The occurrence of the chosen event}}{\text{The total possibilities}}$$

When a die with numbers 1 to 6 is rolled, the probability of

(a) any single number is $\frac{1}{6}$, (b) an odd number is $\frac{3}{6}$ or $\frac{1}{2}$,

(c) a number greater than 4 is $\frac{2}{6}$ or $\frac{1}{3}$.

When the choice is developed to include two or more independent probabilities, the Probability of A *and* B together is: Probability of A x Probability of B.
The Probability of A *or* B is: Probability of A + Probability of B.

See later notes in Part 2.

Sets Notation

{ }	is a set of	A'	complement of A in the universal set	$\emptyset$	empty set
$\in$	is a member of			$\mathscr{E}$	universal set (all)
$\notin$	is not a member of	$\subset$	is contained in (subset)	$n(A)$	number of elements in A
$\cup$	union			$<$	is less than
$\cap$	intersection	$\supset$	contains	$>$	is greater than

This *Venn diagram* illustrates:
$\mathscr{E}$ = {counting numbers < 25}
A = {even numbers < 25}
B = {multiples of 3 < 25}
C = {prime numbers < 25}.

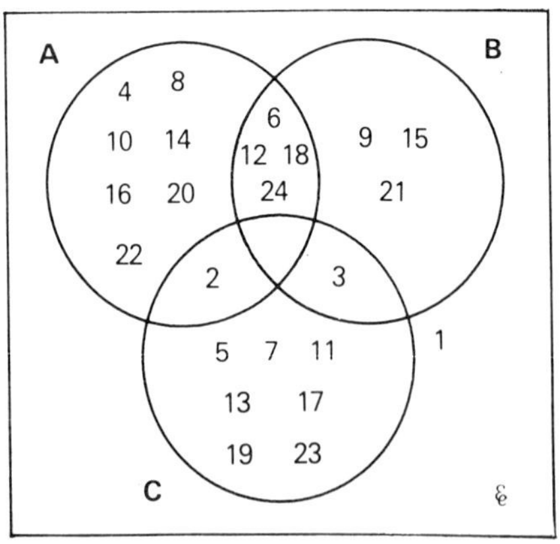

Some facts from the Venn diagram
$A \cap B = \{6, 12, 18, 24\}$ $B \cap C = \{3\}$
$A \cap B \cap C = \{\emptyset\}$ $A \cap C = \{2\}$
$8 \in A$ $21 \in B$ $7 \in C$
$6 \in (A \cap B)$ $3 \notin A$
$(A \cup C)' = \{1, 9, 15, 21\}$
$(A \cup B \cup C)' = \{1\}$
$A \cup B = \{2, 3, 4, 6, 8, 9, 10, 12, 14, 15, 16, 18, 20, 21, 22, 24\}$
$n(A) = 12$ $n(B) = 8$ $n(A \cap B) = 4$ $n(A \cup B)' = 8$.

Estimations

A rough estimate can be used to check some calculations.

38 × 73
Estimate: 40 × 70 = 2800.
Solution: 2774.

2.6 × 38.5 × 35
Estimate: 2.5 × 40 × 35 = 3500.
Solution: 3503.5.

$\frac{3}{8}$ of 78

Estimate: less than half of 78, i.e. 30.
Solution: 29.25.

$\frac{0.2 \times 0.96}{0.6}$

Estimate: $\frac{2 \times 1}{6} = 0.3$.
Solution: 0.32.

An answer should always be assessed according to the terms in the original problem. When an estimate indicates an answer of 7600 and the result is 7.6, check place values throughout the working. In some estimations, it helps to change numbers to standard form.

You may now attempt **Revisions 1** and **2**.

Revision 1. Number

1 Fill the blank spaces to complete these statements:

(a) $\frac{1}{2} = \frac{6}{}$ (b) $\frac{1}{3} = \frac{}{15}$ (c) $\frac{1}{8} = \frac{6}{}$ (d) $\frac{1}{10} = \frac{}{100}$

(e) $\frac{2}{3} = \frac{}{12}$ (f) $\frac{3}{8} = \frac{}{40}$ (g) $\frac{2}{5} = \frac{12}{}$ (h) $\frac{3}{4} = \frac{21}{}$.

2 Calculate how many
(a) eighths in $\frac{3}{4}$ (b) tenths in $\frac{3}{5}$ (c) sixteenths in $\frac{1}{2}$
(d) sixteenths in $\frac{3}{4}$ (e) quarters in $3\frac{3}{4}$ (f) eighths in $5\frac{7}{8}$
(g) fifths in $8\frac{3}{5}$ (h) sixths in $7\frac{5}{6}$.

3 Calculate
(a) $\frac{5}{6} + \frac{3}{4}$ (b) $\frac{3}{4} + \frac{3}{10}$ (c) $\frac{2}{3} - \frac{3}{8}$ (d) $\frac{5}{6} - \frac{3}{8}$
(e) $2\frac{1}{4} + 3\frac{5}{6}$ (f) $4\frac{7}{10} + 3\frac{1}{4}$ (g) $4\frac{3}{8} - 2\frac{2}{3}$ (h) $5\frac{1}{6} - 2\frac{5}{8}$.

4 Calculate
(a) $\frac{1}{4} \times \frac{5}{6}$ (b) $\frac{4}{5} \times \frac{1}{2}$ (c) $\frac{5}{8} \div 10$ (d) $\frac{5}{16} \div 10$
(e) $2\frac{2}{3} \times 2\frac{1}{4}$ (f) $2\frac{2}{5} \times 1\frac{1}{3}$ (g) $2\frac{3}{8} \div 1\frac{1}{4}$ (h) $3\frac{1}{3} \div 1\frac{1}{3}$
(i) $2\frac{1}{2} \times 1\frac{3}{5} \times 1\frac{3}{4}$ (j) $4\frac{1}{2} \times 1\frac{1}{4} \times 2\frac{2}{3}$.

5 Find the ratio of
(a) 20 to 30 (b) 16 to 20 (c) 75p to £1
(d) 10 cm to 15 cm (e) 25p to £2 (f) 5 mm to 2 cm.

6 Share
(a) £15 in the ratio 3:2 (b) £24 in the ratio 5:1
(c) 12 hours in the ratio 18:6 (d) 30 cm in the ratio 7:3
(e) 27 cm in the ratio 4:3:2 (f) £5 in the ratio 2:3:5.

7 Triangle ABC has been enlarged to produce triangle DEF. The ratio of the sides of triangle DEF to the sides of triangle ABC, is 3:1.

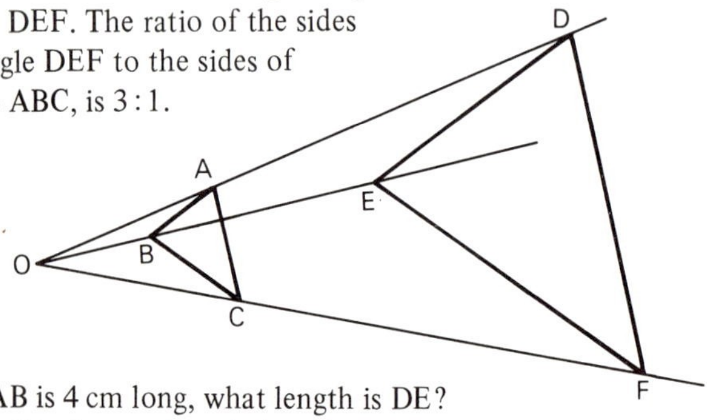

(a) If AB is 4 cm long, what length is DE?
(b) If AC is 6 cm in length, how long is DF?
(c) If EF is $13\frac{1}{2}$ cm, what length is BC?

8 $A = \{\text{positive multiples of } 3 < 24\}$
$B = \{\text{positive factors of } 24\}$
$C = \{\text{square numbers} < 24\}$.
(a) Find (i) $B \cap C$ (ii) $(A \cap B) \cup C$ (iii) $A \cap B \cap C$.
(b) Is it true that (i) $10 \in A$ (ii) $24 \in B$ (iii) $6 \in C$ (iv) $8 \in (A \cap B)$ (v) $4 \in (A \cup C)$?
(c) Show sets A, B and C in a Venn diagram.

9 Work out each number as a product of its prime factors:
(a) 20 (b) 30 (c) 32 (d) 45 (e) 100.

10 Change these base 2 numbers into base 10.
(a) 1101_2 (b) 1011_2 (c) 11000_2 (d) 111011_2 (e) 101111_2
(f) 110011_2.

11 Change these denary numbers to base 2.
(a) 9 (b) 14 (c) 22 (d) 26 (e) 31 (f) 48 (g) 57 (h) 62.

12 These are base 2 operations. Answers should be in base 2.
(a) $111_2 \times 10_2$ (b) $101_2 \times 100_2$ (c) $110_2 \times 10_2$ (d) $1010_2 \times 10_2$
(e) $110_2 \div 10_2$ (f) $1000_2 \div 10_2$ (g) $10100_2 \div 100_2$ (h) $110100_2 \div 100_2$.

13 (a) What number added to 386 gives 679?
(b) If £1000 is shared equally and each share is £125, how many shares are there?
(c) If $3 \times 13 \times 5 \times 11$ is 2145, what is $13 \times 5 \times 3 \times 3 \times 11$?
(d) What is the next term in the series? 1, 5, 13, 29, 61.
(e) What is 762 less than 1423?
(f) Of what number is 327 one-sixth?

14 (a) What is the difference between 729 and 578?
(b) What number can be written in the prime factor form $2 \times 3 \times 3 \times 7$?
(c) In the counting numbers 1 to 20, which is the 10th rectangular number?
(d) Use the figures 4, 2, 3, 7, 6, to make the largest possible number.
(e) Using 5, 3, 7, 9, 2, make the largest number beginning with a 7.

15 (a) Which numbers between 1 and 40 have 6 as a factor?
(b) Which numbers between 1 and 99 are perfect squares?
(c) Which numbers between 1 and 100 have 3 and 4 as factors?
(d) Which even numbers between 1 and 121 have 5 as a factor?

16 Change to decimal form: (a) $\frac{7}{10}$ (b) $\frac{8}{100}$ (c) $\frac{7}{20}$ (d) $\frac{19}{25}$ (e) $\frac{3}{5}$ (f) $\frac{11}{50}$.

17 Change to fractions in their lowest terms
(a) 0.95 (b) 0.8 (c) 0.45 (d) 0.36 (e) 0.46 (f) 0.2.

18 Calculate
(a) $3.72 + 1.8 + 0.62 + 5.01 + 8.45$ (b) $16.25 - 12.09$ (c) $20.04 - 13.9$
(d) $0.273 + 4.3 + 15.92 + 18.6 + 0.412$ (e) $10.46 - 3.98$ (f) $10.05 - 0.96$.

19 Calculate
(a) 1.36×10 (b) 24.7×100 (c) 15.07×10
(d) $38.7 \div 10$ (e) $1.09 \div 100$ (f) $12.4 \div 100$
(g) 15×1.8 (h) 23×4.9 (i) 8.5×35
(j) $82.2 \div 6$ (k) $14.49 \div 9$ (l) $156.1 \div 7$.

20 Divide the length
(a) 3.6 cm by 4 (b) 6.4 cm by 8 (c) 2.1 cm by 7
(d) 12.5 cm by 5 (e) 47.4 cm by 6 (f) 73.8 cm by 9.

Revision 2. Number

1 Replace each letter with a number.

(a) Addition

```
 28A7
  43B
 3C85
   48
 ----
 D134
```

(b) Subtraction

```
 6P73
 Q64R
 ----
  7S5
```

(c) Multiplication

```
   A8B
    79
 -----
  PQ56
 5488
 -----
 RSTUV
```

(d) Division

```
       7A
 2B)CDEF
    P61
    ---
     18Q
     18R
```

no remainder

(e) Magic Square

13	A	B
C	10	12
D	E	7

(f) Magic Square

4	−3	2
A	1	B
C	D	E

(g) Series

1, 4, 9, 16, 25, A
1, 3, 7, 15, 31, B
1, 8, 27, 64, C

2 Find the unknown in the equations
(a) $5 \times 8 \times A = 360$ (b) $15 \times N \times 15 = 1800$
(c) $12 \times B \times 3 \times 2 = 1152$ (d) $14 \times 9 \times M \times 10 = 12600$.

3 (a) Which have 9 as a factor? 83, 126, 567, 834.
(b) Which are prime numbers? 33, 51, 53, 61, 69, 73.
(c) Write 676 as a product of its prime factors.
(d) Give the square root of 676.
(e) Write all the multiples of 9 less than 100.
(f) Two prime numbers total 50. What could those numbers be?

4 Calculate
(a) $9 \times 5\frac{1}{3}$ (b) $2\frac{5}{8} + 1\frac{5}{12}$ (c) $4\frac{1}{6} \div 2\frac{5}{6}$ (d) $(1\frac{1}{4})^2$
(e) $0.572 \div 4$ (f) $5.72 \div 0.4$ (g) 0.073×500 (h) 0.189×3.5.

5 Use the numbers 3, 8, 20, 29, 36, 87.
(a) Which is a perfect square?
(b) Which numbers are prime?
(c) Which is equal to $\sqrt{400}$?
(d) Which is the product of two of the others?
(e) Which is equal to 4×3^2?

6 Calculate by inspection
(a) $\sqrt{81}$ (b) $\sqrt{0.04}$ (c) $\sqrt{1.21}$ (d) $\sqrt{0.49}$ (e) $\sqrt{0.0009}$.

7 Find by trial and error, correct to one decimal place
(a) $\sqrt{39}$ (b) $\sqrt{80}$ (c) $\sqrt{15}$ (d) $\sqrt{8.2}$ (e) $\sqrt{10.4}$.

8 Change these denary numbers to base 5.
(a) 23 (b) 29 (c) 35 (d) 55 (e) 70.

9 Change these base 2 numbers to base 10.
(a) 1111_2 (b) 11011_2 (c) 110101_2 (d) 111011_2 (e) 1100101_2.

10 (a) Share 116 kg of potatoes in the ratio of 3 : 2.
(b) Share £26 in the ratio of 1:3:4.
(c) Share $55.50 in the ratio of 2:3:5.
(d) An alloy is made from copper, tin and zinc in the ratio of 92:5:3. What weight of each metal is required to make 5.5 kg of alloy?

11 What is the value of x in the equations?
(a) $30.624 \times 10^x = 306.24$ (b) $306.24 \times 10^x = 3.0624$
(c) $4.5628 \times 10^x = 0.045628$ (d) $45.628 \times 10^x = 4562.8$
(e) $3.9206 \times 10^x = 3920.6$ (f) $3920.6 \times 10^x = 0.039206$
(g) $0.06345 \times 10^x = 634.5$ (h) $6.345 \times 10^x = 0.06345$.

12 A class of children recorded the number of minutes which elapsed from the time they each left home to the time they arrived at school. These are the thirty times:

15	21	32	15	21	12
26	21	26	20	32	13
13	18	32	26	21	15
10	15	13	18	15	20
32	12	14	18	16	23

Find (a) the modal time,
(b) the median of the times,
(c) the mean time for travelling to school.

13 In a game of cards a pack of twenty is used, containing four Aces, four Kings, four Queens, four Jacks and four Tens. Four players are in the game and each player is dealt four cards, leaving four cards in a pile on the table.
(a) If you are the first player, what are the chances your first card is an Ace?
(b) As the first player, what are the chances your first card will not be a Queen?
(c) The first card dealt is a King, the second is a Ten. What are the chances the third card will also be a Ten?
(d) The four players receive their first cards as follows: Queen, King, Queen, Jack. What are the chances the next card to be dealt will be a (i) Queen (ii) Jack (iii) Ten?

14 (a) Write in figures the number fourteen thousand and four.
(b) Write the number 136.8 in standard form ($A \times 10^n$).
(c) Write all the factors of 28. Write all the factors of 42. From the two lists, pick out the highest common factor of 28 and 42.

15 Give each answer correct to three significant figures.
(a) $36.8 \div 7$ (b) $2.46 \div 1.3$ (c) $18.47 \div 2.9$.
(d) Express 36 grams as a decimal of 190 grams.
(e) What decimal of 23 metres is 129 centimetres?

16 A cricketer has scores of 63, 14, 59, 92 and 67. After his next innings the mean average was 65. How many did he make in his sixth innings?

17 $A = \{3, 6, 9, 12, 15, 18\}$
$B = \{4, 8, 12, 16, 20\}$
$C = \{\text{prime numbers} < 21\}$.
(a) List the members of Set C.
(b) Find (i) $B \cup C$ (ii) $A \cap C$ (iii) $B \cap C$.
(c) If $\mathcal{E} = \{\text{counting numbers} < 21\}$, represent A, B and C in a Venn diagram.
(d) List the sets (i) $(A \cup B)'$ (ii) $(A \cup B \cup C)'$.
(e) Which of these statements is true and which is false?
(i) $20 \in (A \cap B)$ (ii) $C \subset A$ (iii) $(A \cap B \cap C) = \emptyset$ (iv) $9 \in (B \cup C)'$.

18 (a) $11011_2 \times 101_2$. Give an answer in base 2.
(b) What is the denary number 34 in base 3?
(c) Write the fraction $\frac{1}{8}$ as a bicimal in base 2.
(d) If $20 + 20 = 100$, in which base are the numbers written?

19 Place in order of size, smallest first

(a) $\sqrt{81}, \dfrac{61.6}{7}, (0.07 \times 130)$ (b) $11010_2, 100_5, 1001_3, 120_4$

(c) $\dfrac{5}{8}, \dfrac{4}{5}, \dfrac{17}{20}$ (d) $\dfrac{3}{8}, 0.35, 37\%, \left(\dfrac{2}{3}\right)^2$.

20 $\mathscr{E} = \{\text{counting numbers} < 16\}$
$R = \{\text{rectangular numbers} < 16\}$
$T = \{\text{odd numbers} < 16\}$
$S = \{\text{square numbers} < 16\}$.
(a) Draw a Venn diagram to include all elements of $\mathscr{E}$.
(b) List the elements of (i) $T \cap S$ (ii) $R \cap T \cap S$ (iii) $T \cap R'$ (iv) $S \cap (R \cup T)'$ (v) $(R \cup T \cup S)'$.

Money and Measures Revision notes

Measures

60 seconds in 1 minute. 365 days in 1 year. 52 weeks in 1 year.
60 minutes in 1 hour. 366 days in 1 leap year. 12 months in 1 year.
24 hours in 1 day.

Between midnight and midday, a.m.
Between midday and midnight, p.m.
24-hour clock commences 00.00 midnight.

Days per month:

Jan 31	Feb 28 (29)	Mar 31
Apr 30	May 31	June 30
July 31	Aug 31	Sept 30
Oct 31	Nov 30	Dec 31

10 millimetres in 1 centimetre.
100 centimetres in 1 metre.
1000 metres in 1 kilometre.

1000 grams in 1 kilogram.
1000 millilitres in 1 litre.
1 litre occupies 1000 cm^3.

Percentages

Percentage means "per hundred".
To change a fraction or decimal to a percentage, multiply by 100.

$$\frac{3}{5} \times 100 = 60\% \quad \frac{5}{8} \times 100 = 62\tfrac{1}{2}\% \quad 0.27 \times 100 = 27\% \quad 0.08 \times 100 = 8\%.$$

To change a percentage to a fraction or decimal, divide by 100.

$$16\% = \frac{16}{100} = \frac{4}{25} \text{ or } 0.16. \quad 37\tfrac{1}{2}\% = \frac{75}{200} = \frac{3}{8} \text{ or } 0.375.$$

A percentage part

36% of £25

$$= \frac{36}{100} \times 25$$

$= £9.$

Forming a percentage

£2.50 as a % of £30

$$= \frac{250}{3000} \times 100$$

$= 8\tfrac{1}{3}\%.$

A *profit* is the extra when a selling price exceeds a cost price.
A *loss* is made when the selling price is less than the cost price.
A *discount* produces a reduction in the cost of an article. (See p. 16.)

Cost price £80. Selling price £75.

Loss £5.

$$\% \text{ loss} = \frac{5}{80} \times 100 = 6\tfrac{1}{4}\%.$$

Cost £260. Discount 9%.

$$\text{Discount} = \frac{9}{100} \times 260 = £23.40$$

Reduced cost = £236.60.

Interest

Interest is a percentage of an account given periodically by a bank, or it may be the percentage charged on the amount of a loan.

Simple Interest is an equal amount for each year. Principal P, rate of interest r, time t.

$$\text{S.I.} = P \times r \times t.$$

S.I. on £180 for 3 years at 8%.

$$\text{S.I.} = 180 \times \frac{8}{100} \times 3 = £43.20.$$

Compound Interest is worked out and added each year.

C.I. on £250 for 2 years at 12%.

$$\text{Interest 1 year} = 250 \times \frac{12}{100} = £30.$$

New Account = £280.

$$\text{Second Interest} = 280 \times \frac{12}{100} = £33.60.$$

Total Interest = £63.60.

See later notes in Part 2.

Salary and Wages

A salary is an annual income usually paid in 12 equal amounts.
A wage is paid weekly and often depends on the number of hours.

Find the annual salary paid at £395 a month.

Salary = £395 × 12
= £4740.

Find the gross monthly income on an annual salary of £5034.

Monthly income = £5034 ÷ 12
= £419.50.

At £2.68 an hour a man works 40 hours a week. Calculate his week's wage.

Wage = £2.68 × 40
= £107.20.

If a man earns £86.74 for a 38-hour week, what is the rate of pay per hour?

Rate = £86.74 ÷ 38
= £2.23.

When overtime is worked, the rate per hour may be $1\frac{1}{2}$ times the normal rate or may even be double the normal rate per hour. This is often called "time and a half" and "double time".

A woman works 4½ hours' overtime at 1½ times the normal rate of £2.20 an hour. How much is her overtime pay?

Overtime rate = £2.20 × $1\frac{1}{2}$
= £3.30.
Overtime pay = £3.30 × $4\frac{1}{2}$
= £14.85.

A man works a 40-hour week at £2.10 an hour and 5 hours' overtime at "time and a half". Find his full week's wage.

Normal wage = £2.10 × 40
= £84.
Overtime pay = £3.15 × 5
= £15.75.
Total pay = £99.75.

Income Tax

The amount a person earns is the *gross income.*
Income Tax is deducted from the gross income by the employer. Everyone is allowed to earn an amount which is not taxed. That amount is called *Non-taxable allowance* or *Free-pay.*

Taxable income = Gross income minus Free-pay.

A woman earns £315 a month. Her non-taxable allowance is £1545.
Gross annual income = £315 × 12 = £3780.
Income which may be taxed = £3780 − £1545 = £2235.

The government levies a tax rate on taxable income, and that rate may vary each year. Assume the rate is 33p in the £ (33%).

$$\text{Annual tax on £2235} = 2235 \times \frac{33}{100} = \text{£737.55.}$$

Tax each month = £737.55 ÷ 12
= £61.46 approximately.

See later notes in Part 2.

Rates

Each piece of property is given a *Rateable Value.*
The total in a town becomes the town's Rateable Value.
The Council fixes a rate for every £ of the Rateable Value.

Rates collected = Rateable Value × Rate,
or Rateable Value = Rates collected ÷ Rate,
or Rate = Rates collected ÷ Rateable Value.

A house has a rateable value of £280. If the rate is 56p in the £ (56%), how much is paid annually in rates?

$$\text{Rates} = \text{£}280 \times \frac{56}{100}$$
$$= \text{£}156.80.$$

By fixing a rate of 65p in the £, a Council collects £9 750 000. What is the town's rateable value?

$$\text{R.V.} = \text{£}9\,750\,000 \div \frac{65}{100}$$
$$= \text{£}15\,000\,000.$$

Hire Purchase

A *hire purchase* scheme allows a customer to take away the goods by leaving a deposit. The customer then pays a series of equal *instalments*. The customer is really borrowing money and therefore will pay more than the cash price (interest added for the loan). The deposit may be a fixed amount or a percentage of the price.

The cash price is £250. The deposit is 20% of the cash price. On H.P. there are 12 equal instalments of £18.80. What is the H.P. price?

$$\begin{aligned}\text{Deposit} &= 250 \times \frac{20}{100}\\ &= £50.\\ \text{Instalments} &= 12 \times £18.80\\ &= £225.60.\\ \text{H.P. price} &= £225.60 + £50\\ &= £275.60.\end{aligned}$$

The total H.P. price of an article was £150.80 and a deposit of £35 was paid. How much was each of the 12 equal instalments?

$$\begin{aligned}\text{Instalments} &= £150.80 - £35\\ &= £115.80.\\ \text{One payment} &= £115.80 \div 12\\ &= £9.65.\end{aligned}$$

Exchanging Money

Conversion of currency depends on the exchange rate fixed between the two countries.

Assume £1 ≡ $1.10.
How much in dollars can be obtained for £3.50?

$$\begin{aligned}\text{Amount} &= 3.50 \times 1.10\\ &= \$3.85.\end{aligned}$$

Assume £1 ≡ 8.65 francs.
What amount of English money is exchanged for 41.72 francs?

$$\begin{aligned}\text{Amount} &= 41.72 \div 8.65\\ &= £4.80.\end{aligned}$$

A *conversion graph* may also be used.
Draw a graph to represent £1 ≡ 7.50 francs, scaling the horizontal axis 1 mm to 5p up to a value of £4 and the vertical axis 1 mm to 0.50 francs to a value of 30 francs.

How many francs may be obtained for £2.20?

The graph is obtained by plotting the point (£1, 7.50 francs).

From the graph, a reading shows that £2.20 ≡ 16.50 francs.

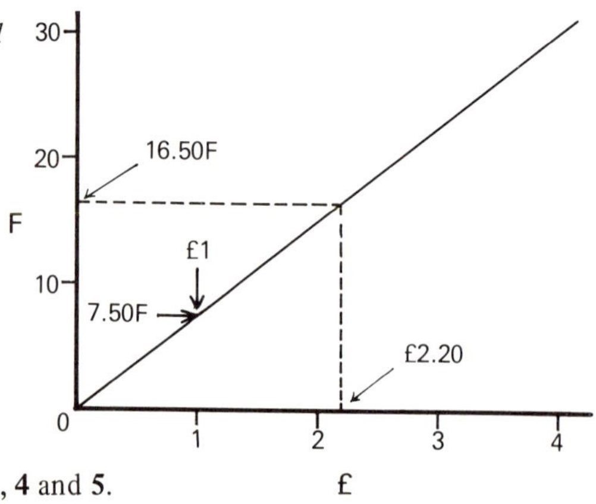

You may now attempt **Revisions 3, 4** and **5.**

Revision 3. Number and Money

1 Calculate
(a) 4.7×10 (b) 9.3×100 (c) 5.26×10 (d) 3.08×100
(e) 22.5×1000 (f) 5.76×10 (g) 4.75×100 (h) 9.82×1000.

2 Calculate
(a) 4.7×3 (b) 9.3×5 (c) 5.26×4 (d) 3.08×7
(e) 22.5×9 (f) 5.76×8 (g) 4.75×6 (h) 9.82×9.

3 By looking at questions 1 and 2, write answers only to these exercises:
(a) 4.7×30 (b) 9.3×500 (c) 5.26×40 (d) 3.08×700
(e) 22.5×9000 (f) 5.76×80 (g) 4.75×600 (h) 9.82×9000.

4 (a) Gas is 21.5p a therm and every bill contains a fixed standing charge of £4.75. How many therms were used when the bill was £30.55?
(b) There is a fixed standing charge of £5.25 on every electricity bill. When 1375 units are used, the total bill is £76.75. Find the cost of one unit.

5 (a) The rateable value of a house was £290 and the general rate was 50p in the £. How much was paid in rates per year?
(b) If the exchange rate in dollars is \$1.04 to the £, how many dollars can be obtained for £2.50?

6 For my own personal writing paper I must pay £1.25 as a standard charge on each order, plus £1.25 for 50 sheets. How much will I pay for an order of
(a) 200 (b) 250 (c) 450 sheets?

7 A man pays £25 000 for a house. What would he receive for the house if he sold it at (a) a 10% profit (b) a 10% loss?

8 Fencing is sold at 3 metres for £6.80. What would be the cost of
(a) 9 metres (b) $10\frac{1}{2}$ metres?

9 (a) The price of all TV sets is to be increased by 7%. What will be the new price of a set which costs £300?
(b) On a bill of £8.20, I am allowed a discount of 10%. How much do I actually pay?

10 How much is earned in one year on an income of
(a) £335 a month (b) £88 a week?

11 The normal rate of pay at a factory is £2.10 an hour. Overtime is paid at double rate. How much can be earned for
(a) a normal 40-hour week without overtime (b) $5\frac{1}{2}$ hours' overtime?

12 Work these divisions, correcting each answer as requested
(a) $14.32 \div 9$ to 2 decimal places (b) $5.273 \div 7$ to 2 significant figures
(c) $5.431 \div 0.8$ to 3 sig. fig. (d) $8.498 \div 1.3$ to 3 sig. fig.
(e) $47.57 \div 2.4$ to 2 dec. pl. (f) $25.7 \div 0.18$ to nearest whole number.

13 Change to percentages

(a) 0.55 (b) $\frac{2}{5}$ (c) $\frac{13}{25}$ (d) 0.07 (e) $\frac{19}{40}$ (f) $\frac{15}{16}$

(g) $\frac{3}{8}$ (h) 0.265 (i) 0.076 (j) $\frac{17}{20}$ (k) $\frac{18}{50}$ (l) $\frac{37}{60}$.

14 What percentage is

(a) £45 of £100 (b) 37p of £1 (c) £16 of £50
(d) 7 kg of 20 kg (e) 16 cm of 25 cm (f) 1 cm of 1 metre
(g) 35p of £1.50 (h) £1.35 of £5 (i) £3.60 of £90?

15 Reduce (a) £5 by 25% (b) £12 by 15% (c) £6.50 by 4%
(d) £250 by 18% (e) £37 by 28% (f) £125 by 16%.

16 If I have £450 in my bank account and the bank allows me £40.50 interest, what is the percentage rate of interest?

17 A store is reducing the price of clothing by 12% and electrical goods by 8%. What will be the new price of each item?

(a) Sports coat £25 (b) Electric iron £15 (c) Electric cooker £185
(d) Suit £60.50 (e) Electric kettle £18.25 (f) Dress £40.75.

18 Calculate the compound interest on

(a) £100 for 2 years at 6% (b) £250 for 2 years at 30%
(c) £550 for 2 years at 10% (d) £2000 for 2 years at 15%
(e) £3500 for 2 years at 20% (f) £10 000 for 2 years at 11%.

19 In one store I can obtain an electric appliance priced at £125 on hire purchase, for a deposit of £35.40 and 9 equal instalments of £10.90 each. At another store the same £125 appliance can be obtained for a deposit of one-fifth of the cash price, plus 12 equal payments of £9.10 each. Find the extra amount over the cash price which I have to pay on hire purchase at each store.

20 (a) The cost of a TV set is £252 but VAT increases the price by 15%. What is the total cash price for the set?

(b) I offer cash for the same TV set and the dealer takes 10% off the total cash price. How much does the set cost me?

(c) If I buy the set on hire purchase, I must pay £60 deposit and 12 equal instalments of £20.90 each. How much extra over the cash price does the set cost me on HP?

Revision 4. Money and Measures

1 Calculate

(a) £4.73 + £2.45 + £0.96 + £3.05 + £8.87 (b) £72.45 − £18.68
(c) £30 − £16.25 (d) £300 − £142.37 (e) 85p × 10 (f) £3.07 × 5
(g) £29.34 ÷ 9 (h) £58.50 ÷ 10.

2 (a) Express in metres the sum 3 m + 5 cm + 8 mm.
(b) Write the length 250 mm in centimetres.
(c) What is the weight 95 grams in kilograms?

3 (a) A trader bought 300 cards at 3p each. How much did he pay?
(b) He sold the cards at 5p each. What was his total profit?

4 State which is cheaper (a) 100 for 60p or 250 for £1.45
(b) 60 for £1.50 or 12 for 36p
(c) 75 for £6.60 or 100 for £9.

5 Work out each item of this bill and find the total cost:
$10\frac{1}{2}$ metres material at £2.80 a metre
9 metres rail at 85p a metre
15 metres tape at 15p a metre
50 hooks at 48p for 10.

6 In one store I would pay £2.70 for 20 metres of flex and at another store I could obtain 50 metres for £6.25. What would I pay at each store for 300 metres of flex?

7 (a) List the months of the year which have only 30 days.
(b) Which are leap years: 1816, 1898, 1936, 1950, 1970, 1976?
(c) How many days from 15 March to 26 August including both dates?

8 How many metres in (a) $\frac{1}{4}$ km (b) 0.9 km (c) $\frac{3}{4}$ km (d) $\dfrac{1}{1000}$ km
(e) 0.7 km (f) 0.35 km (g) $3\frac{1}{10}$ km (h) 2.65 km (i) 5.8 km?

9 How many grams in (a) $\frac{1}{4}$ kg (b) $\dfrac{15}{100}$ kg (c) $\frac{1}{2}$ kg
(d) 0.19 kg (e) $\dfrac{3}{10}$ kg (f) 0.6 kg
(g) 4.75 kg (h) 5.06 kg (i) 3.7 kg?

10 Find the wages for 5 days if in one day a man works
(a) 8 h at 108p an hour (b) 8 h at 1.36 an hour
(c) 9 h at 1.83 an hour (d) 9 h at 192p an hour
(e) $8\frac{1}{2}$ h at £2.70 an hour (f) $7\frac{1}{2}$ h at £2.80 an hour.

11 How much is paid an hour, if a man receives
(a) £66.80 for a 5-day week, 8 hours a day
(b) £78.75 for a 5-day week, 9 hours a day
(c) £74.40 for a 4-day week, 10 hours a day?

12 How much is received each year on these monthly salaries?
(a) £262 (b) £375 (c) £250.50 (d) £416.75 (e) £353.25.

13 Calculate (a) $1\frac{1}{2} \times 184$p (b) $1\frac{1}{2} \times 178$p (c) $1\frac{1}{2} \times$ £1.24 (d) $1\frac{1}{2} \times$ £1.88.

14 How many hours and minutes between
(a) 09.00 and 13.00 (b) 08.30 and 12.15
(c) 08.45 and 13.15 (d) 08.15 and 13.00
(e) 07.45 and 12.30 (f) 07.15 and 14.00?

15 A woman works from 08.30 to 13.15 and from 14.00 to 17.45, Monday to Friday, at £1.66 an hour. She also works from 09.00 to 11.00 overtime on Saturday, at $1\frac{1}{2}$ times the normal rate. What is her week's wage?

16 (a) A watch is 1 hour 16 minutes slow and a clock is 53 minutes fast. What time is the clock showing when the watch shows the time of a quarter to two?
(b) A station clock is 2 hours 24 minutes slow and a town clock is 1 hour 38 minutes slow. What is the time by the town clock when the station clock shows five minutes past ten?

17 The plan of a building is made up of a rectangle BCGI, two equal squares ABJK and CDEF and an equilateral triangle GHI. The length of the rectangle CG is 13.2 m and its breadth BC is one-third of its length. The side of each square is half the rectangle's length.
Find
(a) length AD
(b) length FG
(c) the length DE + EF + FG + GH
(d) the perimeter of the plan.

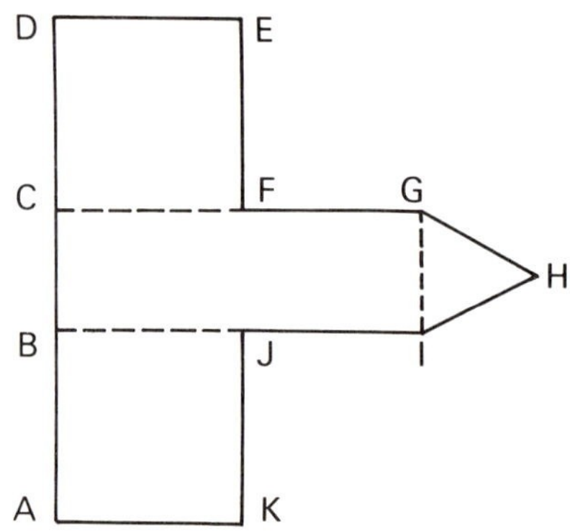

18 (a) What is the cost of 1000 units of electricity at 5.5p a unit?
(b) A mortgage repayment is £86.45 a month. How much is that a year?
(c) A man pays a general rate of £145.52 each half year and a water rate of £18.75 every 6 months. Find his total annual rates bill.

19 The first bus in the morning is 06.35 and buses then run every 20 minutes. I rise at 07.50 and leave the house 50 minutes later. If it takes me 8 minutes to walk to the bus stop, which is the first bus I may take?

20 Which is larger?
(a) $\frac{1}{4}$ km or 300 metres (b) $\frac{1}{2}$ of £7.58 or $\frac{1}{3}$ of £11.25
(c) 0.9 kg or 90 grams (d) $\frac{1}{4}$ of £17.88 or $\frac{1}{5}$ of £22.40
(e) $\frac{3}{10}$ hours or 20 minutes (f) $\frac{1}{10}$ of £85.50 or 170 × 5p.

Revision 5. Money

1 (a) The cost of eggs is 66p for 12. How much would you pay for 100?
(b) What is the price of 750 pencils, each costing 7p?
(c) Share £406 equally among 25 people.

2 Five days a week a man works from 08.30 to 13.00 each morning and 13.45 to 17.30 each afternoon, at a rate of £2.68 an hour. On Saturday for one and a half times the normal rate per hour, he works $3\frac{1}{2}$ hours. What is the weekly wage?

3 (a) A machine costs £313.20 of which £23.20 is VAT. At what percentage is the VAT charged?
(b) The price of a tape recorder costing £91.50, is increased by 6%. Calculate the new price.

Complete the gaps in this table:

	Cost price	Selling price	Profit	% Profit
4	£36	£40.50		
5	£105			15%
6		£43.32	£5.32	
7		£56		60%

8 A school had 55 children involved in a sponsored swimming event for charity. Twelve children each collected £4.65, fifteen raised £3.35 each, eight collected £3.25 each, seven collected £2.75 each, five had £2.55 each and the remainder each brought in £1.15. (a) How much was collected altogether?
(b) What was the average collected per child?

9 The list price of an article was £200.
(a) To that price must be added 15% VAT when it is sold. What is the total cash price?
(b) A woman buys the article for cash and receives 6% discount. How much did she actually pay?
(c) On hire purchase terms, 10% is added to the cash price and a deposit of £73 is required. An equal amount is then paid each month in one year. What is one monthly instalment?

10 (a) By selling a TV set for £315, a store made a profit of 35%. What did the store pay for the set, correct to the nearest penny?
(b) By selling a video outfit for £810 a man made a loss of 25%. What did he originally pay for the equipment?

11 My last quarterly telephone bill showed a rental charge of £18.25. I made 45 calls at 5.2p a call, three calls at 17.5p each, fifteen calls at 12.5p each, eight at 35p each and three at 95p each. VAT at 15% was then added, correct to the nearest penny. What was the total bill?

12 Calculate the Simple Interest on (a) £350 at 5% for 3 years
(b) £104 at 4% for 5 years
(c) $824 at $7\frac{1}{2}$% for 4 years.

13 If the Simple Interest on £780 after 10 years was £507, what rate of interest had been charged?

14 Calculate the Compound Interest on (a) £500 at 6% for 2 years
(b) £600 at 7% for 2 years
(c) £750 at 10% for 2 years.

15 A man borrowed £500 at a compound interest rate of 8%. At the end of the first year he repaid £150 and at the end of the second year he repaid £250. How much did he still owe at the end of the second year?

16 On taxable income, tax is deducted at 35p in the £. How much tax is deducted from a taxable income of
(a) £850 (b) £980 (c) £1360 (d) £3875 (e) £4095?

17 A man earns £460 a month.
(a) What is his annual gross income?
(b) If he pays 4.5% of his gross income in National Health contributions, how much per month is that deduction?
(c) Superannuation is deducted at 6% of gross income. What is his annual superannuation contribution?
(d) His non-taxable allowance is £2470. After his annual superannuation has been taken off his gross income, the non-taxable allowance is also deducted and the remainder is his taxable income. If the rate of tax is 29p in the £, how much tax will he pay in a year? (Only the complete pounds of taxable income are used in calculating tax.)

18 (a) A house has a rateable value of £230 and the rate is 48p in the £. What annual rates does the householder pay?
(b) If a penny rate in a town brings in rates of £360 250, what is the total rateable value?
(c) The rate of a town is 45p in the £ and each year £25 407 225 is collected in rates. What is the town's rateable value?

19 The rate of exchange between the UK and a foreign country is $2.40 to £1.
(a) How much foreign money is worth
(i) £2.60 (ii) £3.45 (iii) £15.75?
(b) How much British money is worth
(i) $12.60 (ii) $30.12 (iii) $285.00?

20 A man has a car which will average 12 kilometres to a litre of petrol and the cost of British petrol is 40p a litre. He travels in a foreign country where the rate of exchange is 12 francs to £1 and petrol costs 5.40 francs for a litre. What is the difference in British money to the nearest penny, between 1000 kilometres of travel in the two countries?

Shapes Revision notes

Construction

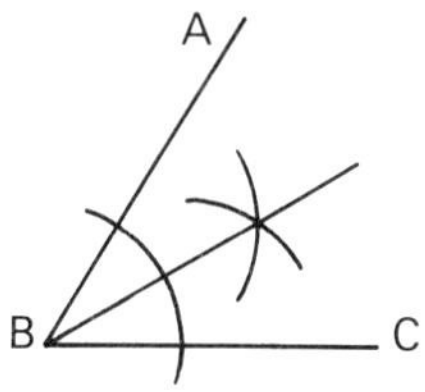

Bisection of $\angle ABC$

Construction

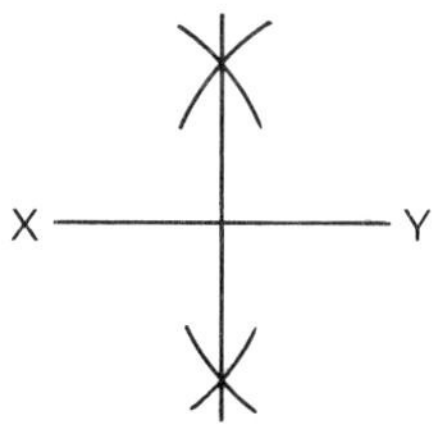

Perpendicular bisector of line XY

Construction

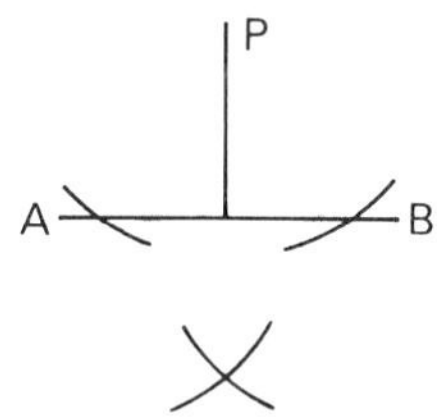

Perpendicular from P to line AB

Construction

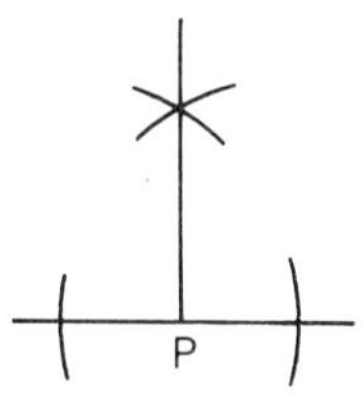

Perpendicular raised at point P

Construction

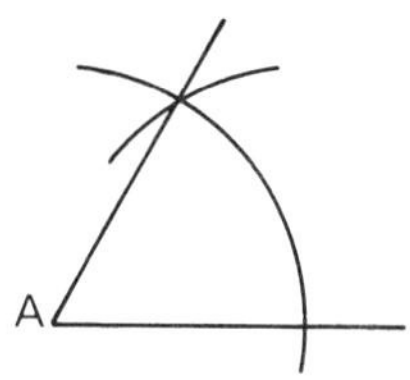

60° at point A

Construction

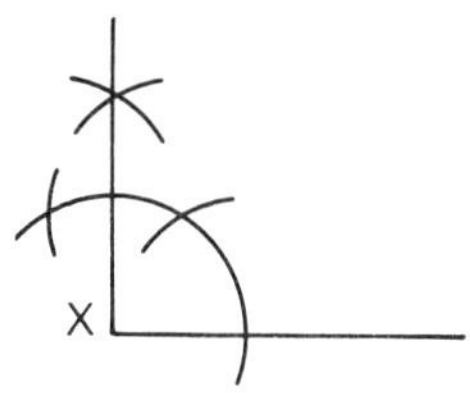

90° at point X

Parallel Lines

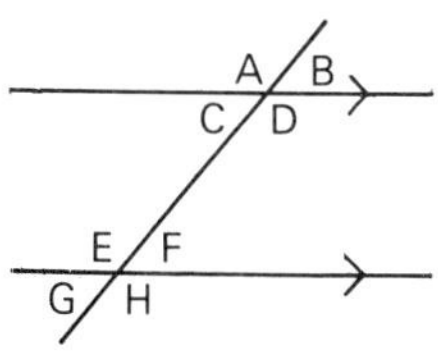

$\angle A = \angle D = \angle E = \angle H$
$\angle B = \angle C = \angle F = \angle G$
$\angle C + \angle E = 180^\circ$

Triangle

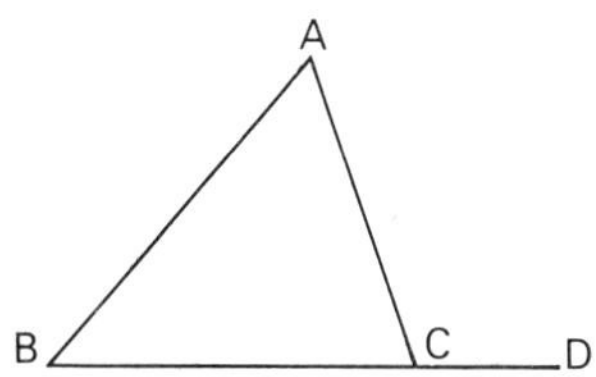

$\angle BAC + \angle ACB + \angle CBA = 180^\circ$
$\angle ACD = \angle BAC + \angle ABC$

Special Triangles

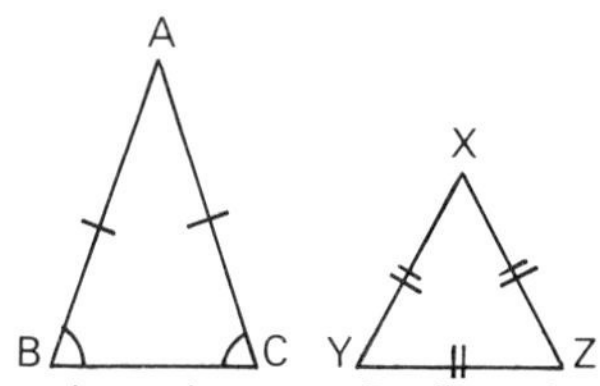

Isosceles — $AB = AC$, $\angle ABC = \angle ACB$

Equilateral — $XY = XZ = YZ$, Each angle is 60°

Supplementary

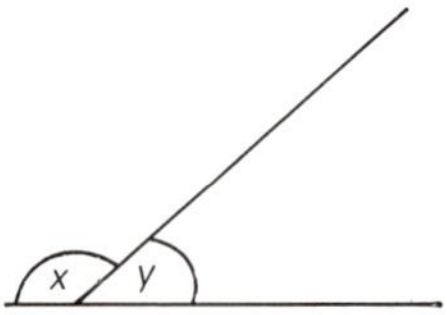

$x + y = 180°$

Complementary

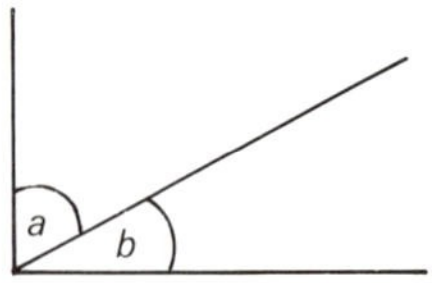

$a + b = 90°$

Vertically Opposite

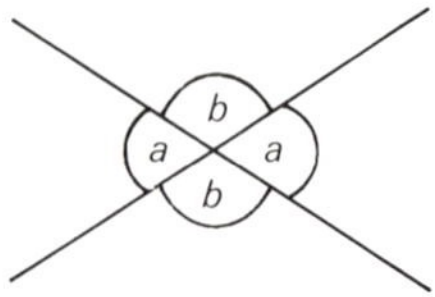

Where $a + b = 180°$, vertically opposite angles are equal

Similarity

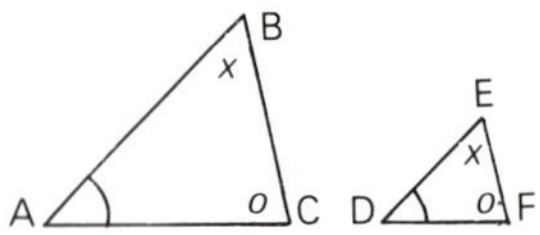

Corresponding sides form equal ratios

$$\frac{AB}{DE} = \frac{BC}{EF} = \frac{AC}{DF}$$

Circumscribed Circle

Centre is at the intersection of the perpendicular bisectors

Inscribed Circle

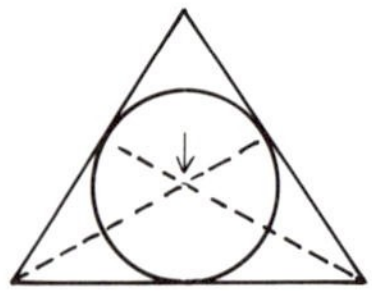

Centre is at the intersection of the angle bisectors

Polygons

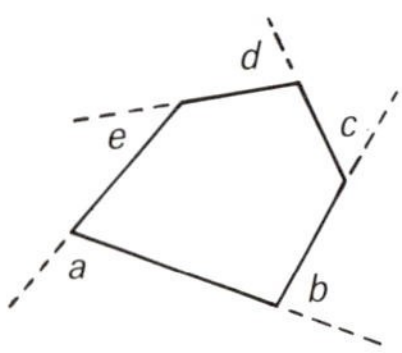

Exterior angles:

$a + b + c + d + e = 360°$

Regular polygons:

Interior angle $= 180 - \dfrac{360}{n}$

Circle

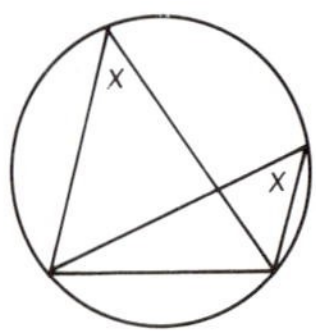

Angles in the same segment are equal

Circle

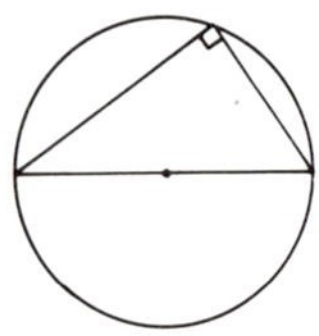

Angle in a semicircle $= 90°$

Circle

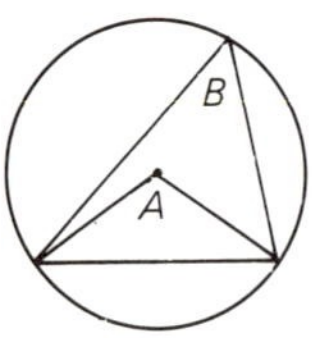

Angle at the centre is twice the angle at the circumference

$\angle A = 2 \times \angle B$

Circle

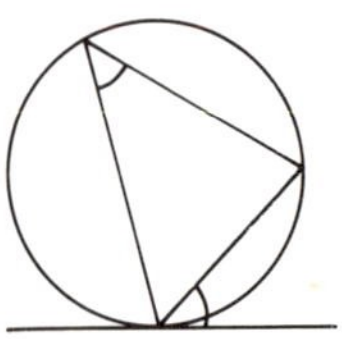

Angle between tangent and chord equals the angle subtended in the alternate segment

Circle

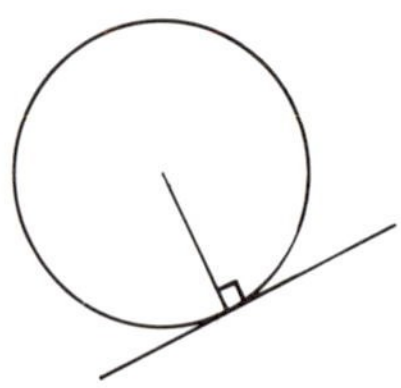

Angle between tangent and radius $= 90°$

Circle

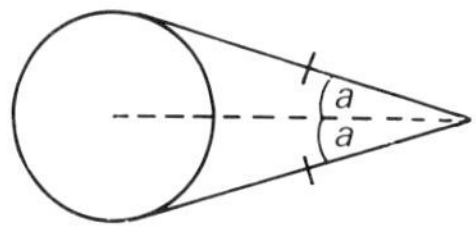

Equal tangents from an external point.
Line to the centre bisects the angle

Circle

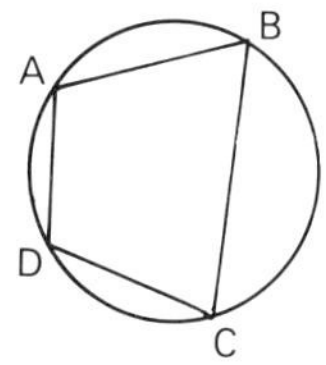

Cyclic quadrilateral
$\angle A + \angle C = 180°$
$\angle B + \angle D = 180°$

Circle

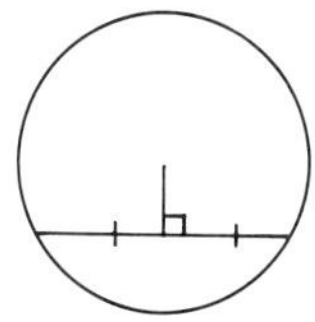

Line from centre to midpoint of chord is perpendicular to the chord

Bearings

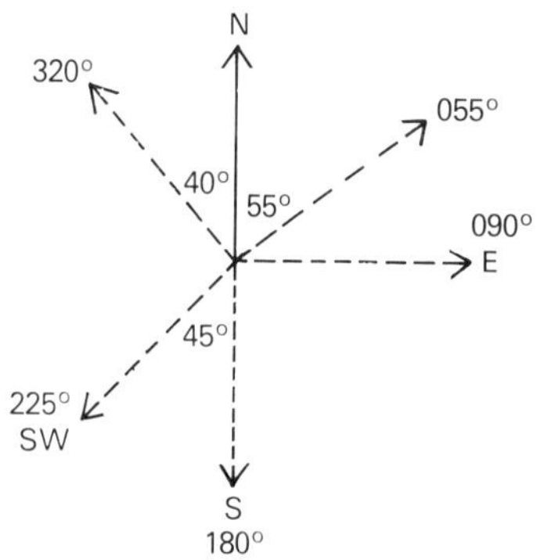

Offset Field Entry

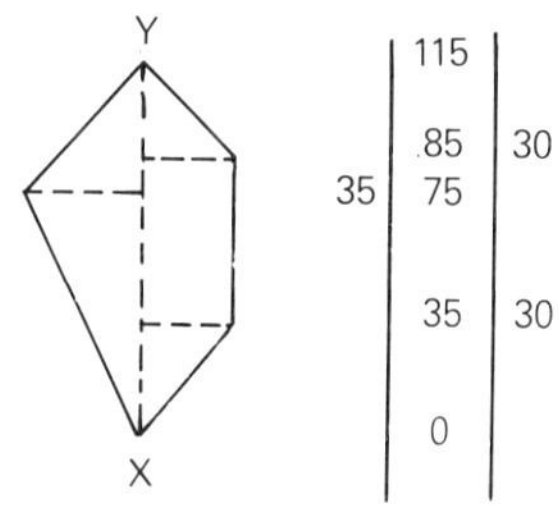

Measurements from X along XY.
Offsets at 90° to XY

Pythagoras

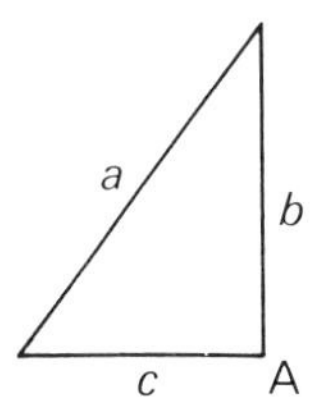

When $\angle A$ is obtuse:
$a^2 > b^2 + c^2$.

When all angles are acute:
$a^2 < b^2 + c^2$.

When $\angle A$ is 90°:
$a^2 = b^2 + c^2$.

When $a = 14$, $b = 8$, $c = 11$, is $\angle A$ acute, obtuse or right?

$$11^2 + 8^2 = 121 + 64 = 185$$
$$14^2 = 196$$
$$14^2 > 11^2 + 8^2.$$

$\angle A$ is obtuse.

When $\angle A = 90°$, $a = 25$, $b = 20$, calculate c.

$$c^2 = a^2 - b^2 = 25^2 - 20^2$$
$$= 625 - 400$$
$$= 225.$$
$$c = \sqrt{225} = 15.$$

See later notes in Part 2.

Position and Transformation

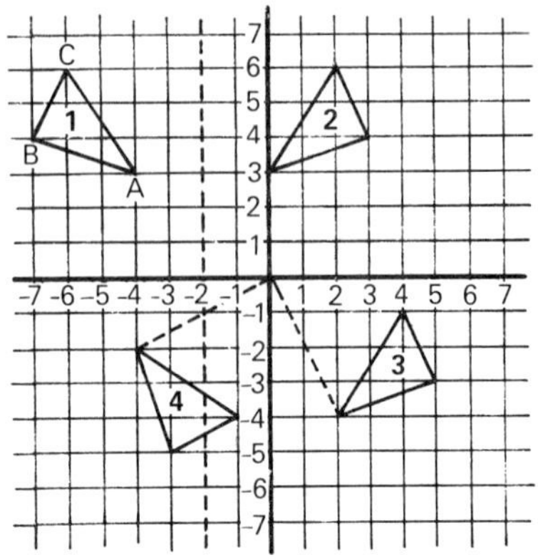

The coordinates for shape 1 are
$(-4, 3), (-7, 4), (-6, 6)$.
Reflection in line $x = -2$. Shape 2
$(0, 3), (3, 4), (2, 6)$.

Shape 2 then translated by vector $\begin{pmatrix} 2 \\ -7 \end{pmatrix}$

gives shape 3 $(2, -4), (5, -3), (4, -1)$.

Shape 3 rotated clockwise $90°$ $(-90°)$ about $(0, 0)$, gives shape 4
$(-4, -2), (-3, -5), (-1, -4)$.

In shape 1: $\overrightarrow{BC} = \begin{pmatrix} 1 \\ 2 \end{pmatrix}, \overrightarrow{CB} = \begin{pmatrix} -1 \\ -2 \end{pmatrix}$. $\quad \overrightarrow{AB} = \overrightarrow{AC} - \overrightarrow{BC}, \quad \overrightarrow{BA} = \overrightarrow{BC} - \overrightarrow{AC}$.

$\overrightarrow{AC} = \begin{pmatrix} -2 \\ 3 \end{pmatrix}, \overrightarrow{CA} = \begin{pmatrix} 2 \\ -3 \end{pmatrix}$. $\quad \overrightarrow{AB} = \overrightarrow{AC} + \overrightarrow{CB}, \quad \overrightarrow{BA} = \overrightarrow{BC} + \overrightarrow{CA}$.

$\overrightarrow{AB} = \begin{pmatrix} -3 \\ 1 \end{pmatrix}, \overrightarrow{BA} = \begin{pmatrix} 3 \\ -1 \end{pmatrix}$.

See later notes in Part 2.

Areas

Rectangle	Area = length × breadth.	$A = LB$
Square	Area = the side squared.	$A = L^2$
Parallelogram	Area = base × perpendicular height.	$A = BH$
Triangle	Area = $\frac{1}{2}$ of base × perpendicular height.	$A = \frac{1}{2}BH$
Trapezium	Area = $\frac{1}{2}$ the sum of the parallel sides × perpendicular distance between them.	$A = \frac{1}{2}H(A + B)$
Circle	Area = π × the radius squared.	$A = \pi r^2$

(Circumference of a circle = $2\pi r$.)

Volumes

All prisms Volume = end area × length.

Rectangular prism:
$V = LBH$.

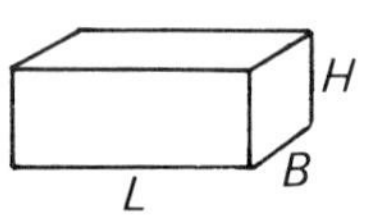

Triangular prism:
$V = \frac{1}{2}bhL$.

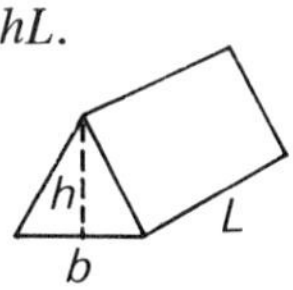

Cylinder:
$V = \pi r^2 L$.

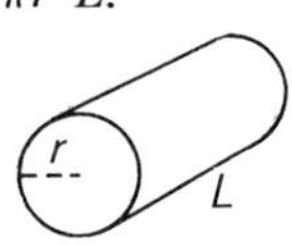

See later notes in Part 2.

Topology

A *node* is the junction of more than two lines or the end of an isolated line.
An *arc* is the line joining two nodes.
A *region* is the area contained by arcs, including the area around the network.

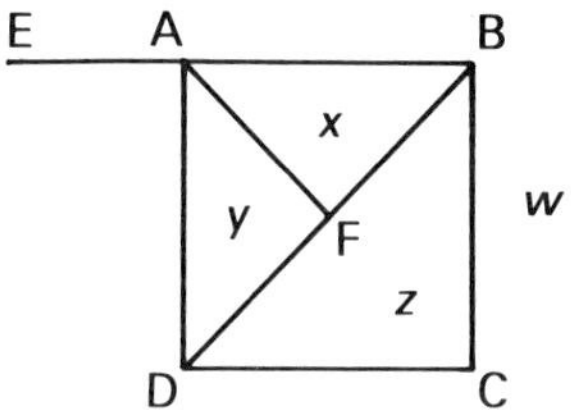

Nodes:		Arcs:	Regions:
A	4-node	AE	*w*
B	3-node	AB	*x*
C	not a node	AF	*y*
D	3-node	AD	*z*.
E	1-node	BF	
F	3-node.	BCD	
		DF.	
Total 5 nodes.		Total 7 arcs.	Total 4 regions.

Euler's relationship $N + R = A + 2.$

Networks are equivalent when nodes and arcs are in similar positions.

Equivalent networks

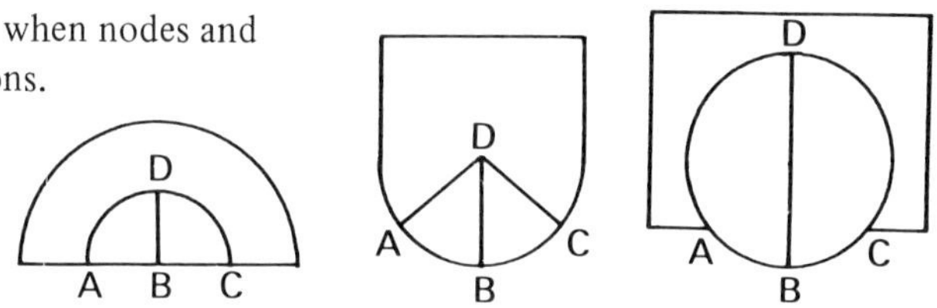

When a network can be drawn in one stroke of the pencil without moving on an arc twice, the network is *traversable.*
If all nodes in the network are even-nodes, it is traversable.
If only two of its nodes are odd-nodes, it is traversable.

Symmetry

Line symmetry

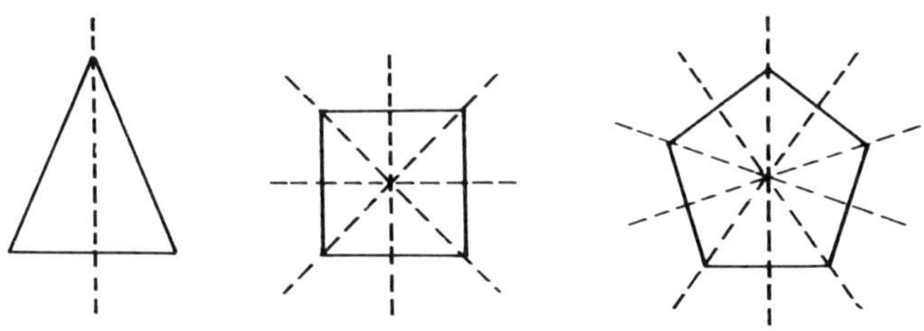

The order of rotational symmetry is the number of times a shape assumes its original position in a rotation of 360°.

Equilateral triangle
Order 3.

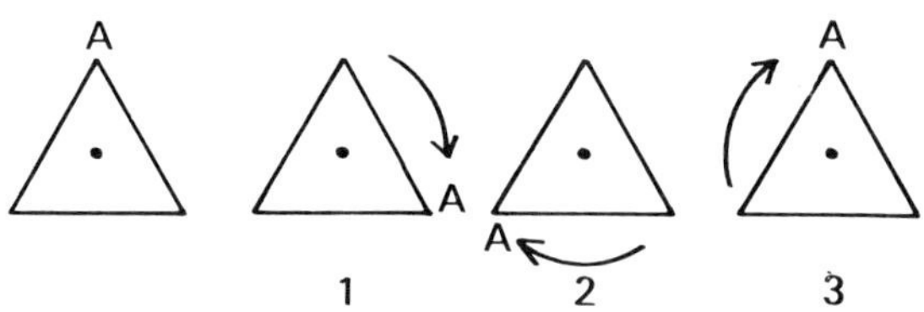

You may now attempt **Revisions 6, 7** and **8**.

Revision 6. Shapes

1 Construct a triangle XYZ in which
(a) XY = 6.5 cm, $\angle$ZXY = 42°, $\angle$ZYX = 38°,
(b) XY = 5.3 cm, XZ = 3.9 cm, ZY = 4.3 cm,
(c) XY = 6.8 cm, $\angle$ZXY = 52°, XZ = 4.1 cm.

2 Calculate each angle marked with a letter.

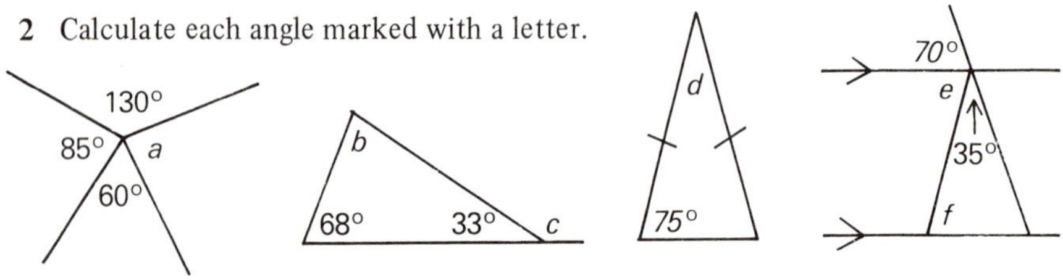

3 (a) Draw a square of 2 cm sides. Enlarge it using a ratio of 3 : 1.
(b) Construct a triangle with sides 2.3 cm, 1.9 cm and 2.4 cm. Enlarge it using a ratio of 4 : 1.

4 (a) Use ruler and compasses only to construct any equilateral triangle.
(b) Using ruler and compasses only, construct a triangle which has angles of 90°, 60° and 30°.
(c) Use ruler and compasses only to construct an isosceles triangle, the largest angle of which is 90°.

5 (a) Construct a triangle ABC so that AB = 6 cm, BC = 7 cm and AC = 6.5 cm.
(b) Use ruler and compasses to drop a perpendicular CD to side AB.
(c) Find the mid-point X of side BC.
(d) Use X as centre and a radius of 3.5 cm to draw a circle. What do you notice?
(e) Is there another circle which will do the same thing?

6 Find the area of
(a) a rectangle, length $2\frac{1}{2}$ cm, breadth $1\frac{1}{5}$ cm,
(b) a square with a side of 25 metres,
(c) a rectangle, length 9.5 cm, breadth 12 cm,
(d) a rectangle, length 18 cm, breadth 6.2 cm,
(e) a parallelogram, base 15 m, height 4.4 m,
(f) a parallelogram, base 10.6 cm, height 20 cm.

7 (a) If the area of a rectangle is 135 m^2 and its breadth is 9 metres, what is the length?
(b) If the area of a parallelogram is 54.6 cm^2 and its base is 7 cm, what is the perpendicular height?

8 Name the quadrilateral which has
(a) two pairs of parallel sides, none of which intersect at 90°, and has adjacent sides of different lengths,
(b) equal diagonals, bisecting each other, but not perpendicular,
(c) diagonals dividing the shape into four 45° isosceles triangles.

9 (a) Through how many degrees do you turn clockwise from South to North-West?
(b) What is the smaller angle between NW and SW?
(c) If the hand of a clock is on the 6, on which figure will it be when it turns clockwise through an angle of
(i) 120° (ii) 180° (iii) 360° (iv) 90° (v) 210°?
(d) Through what angle would you turn clockwise on a clock from
(i) 10 to 4 (ii) 3 to 7 (iii) 5 to 12 (iv) 11 to 7?

10 What are the three-figure bearings of
(a) SW (b) S (c) SE (d) NW (e) NE?

11 Through what angle do you turn clockwise from
(a) West to 330° (b) 035° to 180° (c) South to 280°
(d) 170° to North (e) 260° to 085° (f) 195° to 095°?

12 The lines show the directions of six towns from London, which is at the centre. Town A is due North. Use your protractor to give the 3-figure bearings of towns B, C, D, E and F.

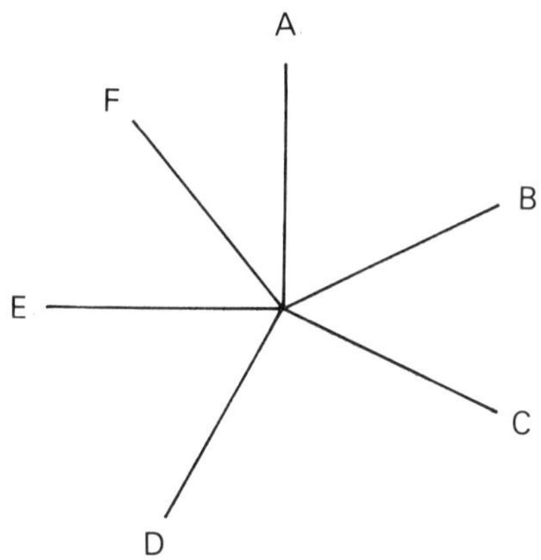

13 (a) The largest angle of an isosceles triangle is 130°. Calculate one other angle.
(b) In an isosceles triangle ABC, $\angle A = \angle B$ and $\angle C$ is twice $\angle B$. Calculate the size of each angle of the triangle.
(c) The angles of an isosceles triangle are in the ratio 4 : 4 : 7. Calculate the size of the largest angle.

14 Find the area of each triangle
(a) Base 18 cm, height 19 cm (b) Base 80 m, height 100 m
(c) Base $2\frac{1}{2}$ cm, height $3\frac{3}{5}$ cm (d) Base 15 m, height $3\frac{2}{5}$ m.

15 Find the height of each triangle
(a) Area 90 cm^2, base 12 cm (b) Area 15.75 cm^2, base 9 cm
(c) Area 64 m^2, base 8 m (d) Area 20 cm^2, base $2\frac{1}{2}$ cm.

16 Calculate the area of each shape.

(a)

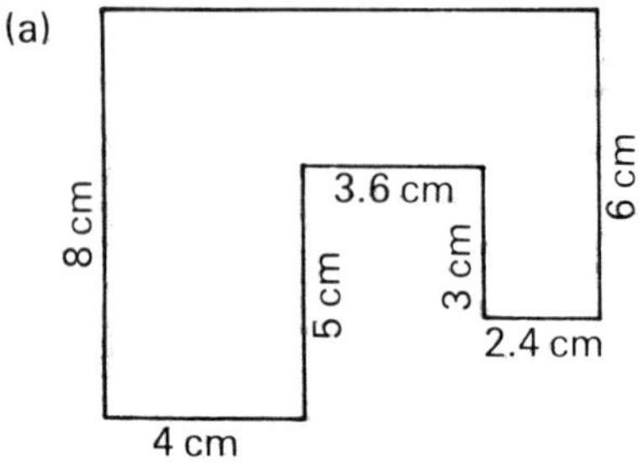

(b)

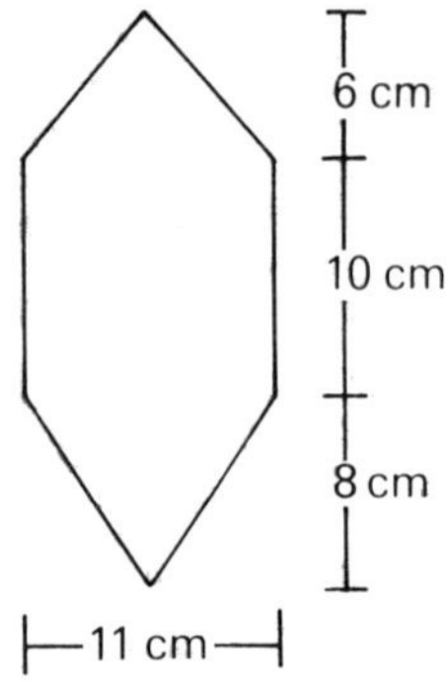

17 (a) List the coordinates of all points from A to H.
(b) Draw your own axes and plot the points.
(c) What is the shape ABFG called?
(d) What is the name of shape ACEF?
(e) What kind of triangle in CDE?
(f) Name the shape ACFH.

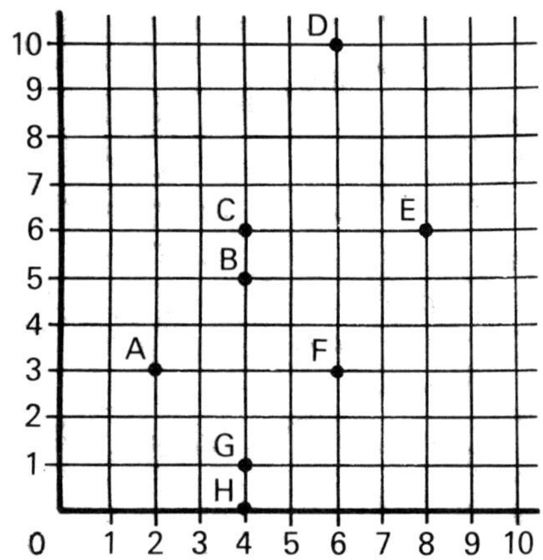

18 If each pair of points were plotted, what would be the coordinates of the centre of the line joining them?

(a) (2, 5), (4, 5) (b) (6, 2), (4, 4) (c) (0, 6), (8, 0)
(d) (0, 3), (5, 7) (e) (3, 5), (4, 2) (f) (4, 7), (7, 6).

19 Draw axes numbered 0 to 15. Imagine a mirror placed vertically through point 7 on the horizontal axis. Give the coordinates of the reflections of shapes formed by joining these points:

(a) A(2, 1), B(1, 6), C(5, 5)
(b) X(1, 2), Y(6, 3), Z(4, 0)
(c) P(2, 12), Q(3, 15), R(6, 10).

20 (a) Draw axes numbered 0 to 10. (b) Plot points A(2, 8), B(3, 4), C(4, 6).

(c) Translate the shape by vector $\begin{pmatrix} 2 \\ 2 \end{pmatrix}$.

(d) By vector $\begin{pmatrix} 1\frac{1}{2} \\ 3 \end{pmatrix}$, a triangle was translated so that its vertices were X(7, 8), Y(5, 4), Z(3, 10). What were the coordinates before the translation took place?

Revision 7. Shapes

1 Here are the takings at a store during one week:

Monday	£7000	Thursday	£8000
Tuesday	£8500	Friday	£12 000
Wednesday	£9500	Saturday	£15 000.

(a) Put the figures into a bar-graph or a pie-chart.
(b) On which day did the store record a quarter of the week's takings?
(c) What percentage of the total takings came in on (i) Friday (ii) Thursday?

2 (a) Draw axes numbered -10 to 10.
(b) Plot points A$(-5, 7)$, B$(-2, 7)$, C$(0, 3)$, D$(-3, 3)$.
(c) Name the shape ABCD.
(d) Transform the shape, first by reflection in line $y = 1$, followed by translation using vector $\begin{pmatrix} 3 \\ 0 \end{pmatrix}$.
(e) Reflect that resulting shape in line $x = -3\frac{1}{2}$.

3 Name the quadrilateral which has
(a) two pairs of parallel sides and unequal diagonals which do not intersect at right-angles,
(b) four equal sides and unequal diagonals,
(c) equal diagonals which bisect each other, but are not perpendicular.

4 Calculate the angles marked with a letter.

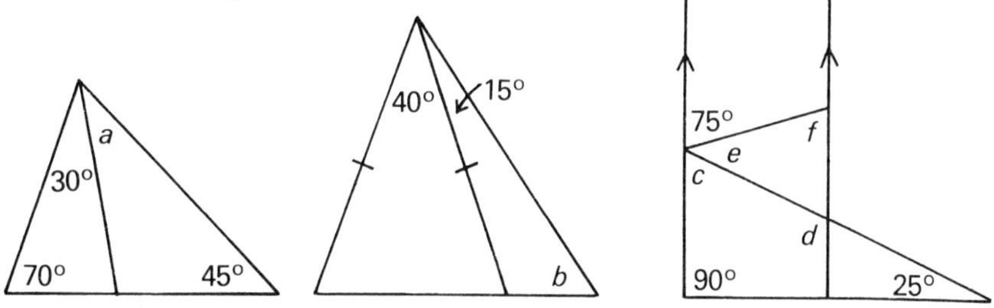

5 For each of the following shapes give
(i) the number of lines of symmetry (ii) the order of rotational symmetry.

(a)

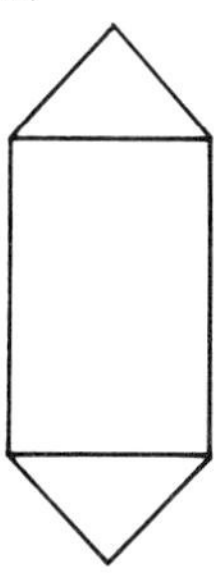

(b)

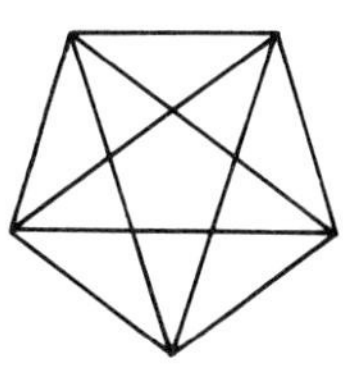

(c)

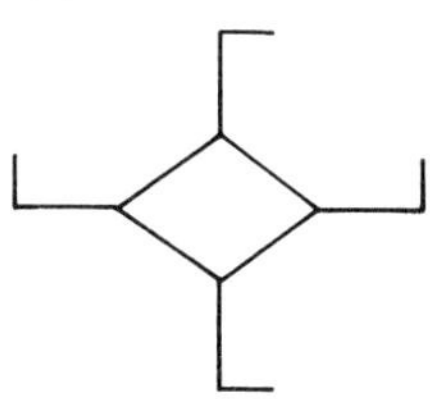

(d)

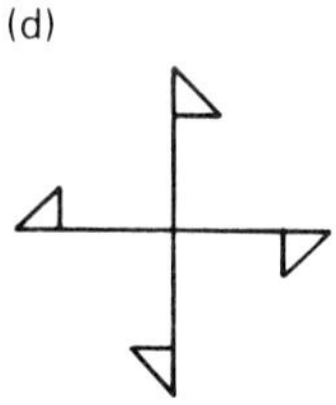

6 Use any instruments to construct each trapezium ABCD.

(a) Parallel sides BC = 4.3 cm, AD = 5.4 cm are 3.1 cm apart. $\angle DAB = 70^\circ$.

(b) AD = 6 cm, $\angle DAB = 90^\circ$, $\angle ADC = 60^\circ$ and BC is parallel to AD with a distance of 3.8 cm between them.

(c) AD = 5.5 cm, $\angle DAB = 110^\circ$, $\angle ADC = 110^\circ$, AB = CD = 2.9 cm.

(d) Side AB is 3 cm and is perpendicular to BC and AD. BC = 4 cm and AD = 5.2 cm.

7 If a and b are the parallel sides of a trapezium and d is the distance between them, find each area.

(a) $a = 16$ m, $b = 12$ m, $d = 7$ m   (b) $a = 50$ cm, $b = 26$ cm, $d = 15$ cm
(c) $a = 39$ m, $b = 23$ m, $d = 30$ m   (d) $a = 9\frac{1}{4}$ cm, $b = 7\frac{1}{4}$ cm, $d = 10$ cm
(e) $a = 5.9$ cm, $b = 8.7$ cm, $d = 20$ cm   (f) $a = 4.5$ cm, $b = 8.3$ cm, $d = 4.5$ cm.

8 Here are four pairs of topologically equivalent networks. Find the pairs.

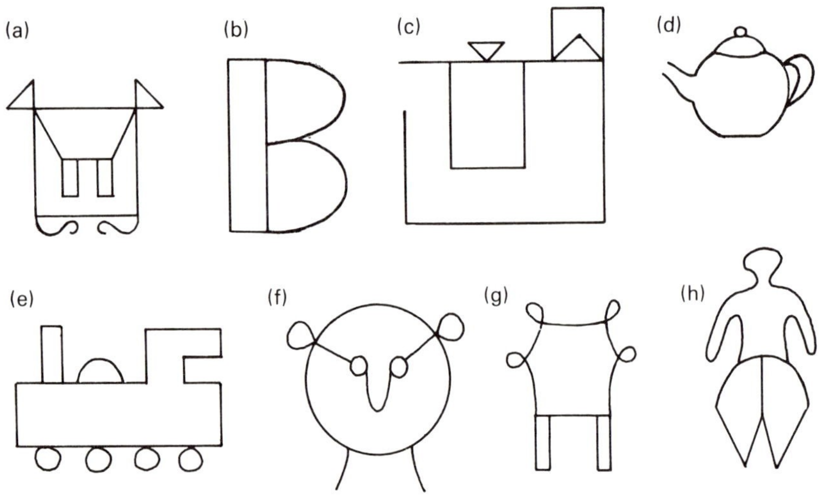

9 Which two triangles are similar?

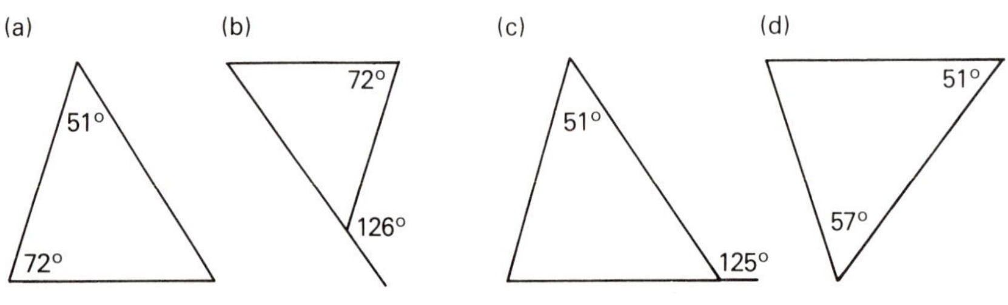

10 Given the vectors $\mathbf{a} = \begin{pmatrix} 2 \\ 4 \end{pmatrix}$ and $\mathbf{b} = \begin{pmatrix} -1 \\ 5 \end{pmatrix}$, find the value of

(a) $\mathbf{a} + \mathbf{b}$ (b) $2\mathbf{b} - \frac{1}{2}\mathbf{a}$ (c) vector $\mathbf{c}$ when $\mathbf{a} + \mathbf{c} = 2\mathbf{b}$.

11 These three triangles are similar, so that $\angle A = \angle X = \angle P$ and $\angle B = \angle Y = \angle Q$.

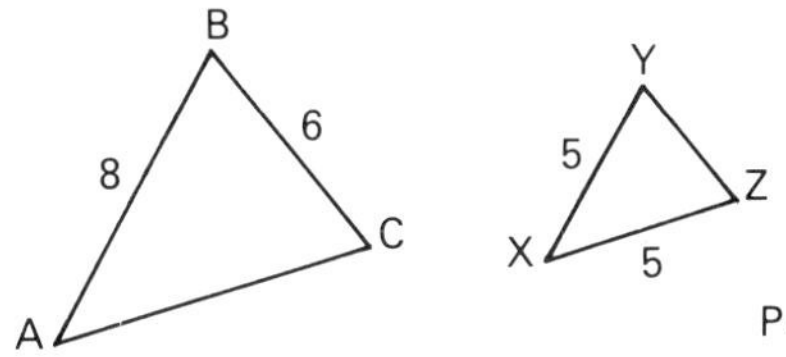

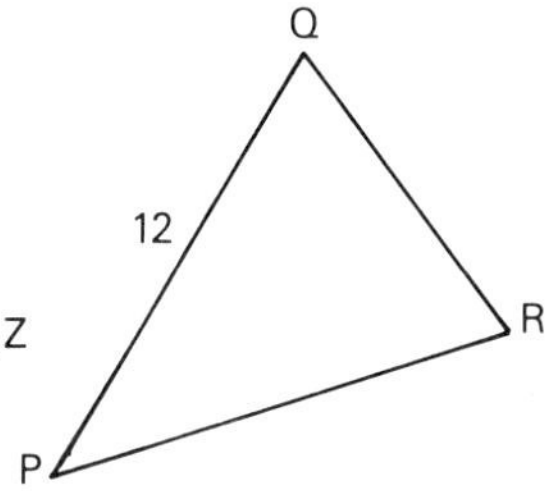

(a) In what ratio are the sides of triangle XYZ to triangle ABC?
(b) In what ratio are the sides of triangle PQR to triangle ABC?
(c) Calculate side YZ.
(d) Find side AC.
(e) Calculate the length of QR.
(f) Find side PR.
(g) If $\angle ABC = 70^\circ$ and $\angle YZX = 67^\circ$, calculate $\angle RPQ$.
(h) Use centimetres to construct triangle ABC and check the angles.

12 Which of these networks are traversable?

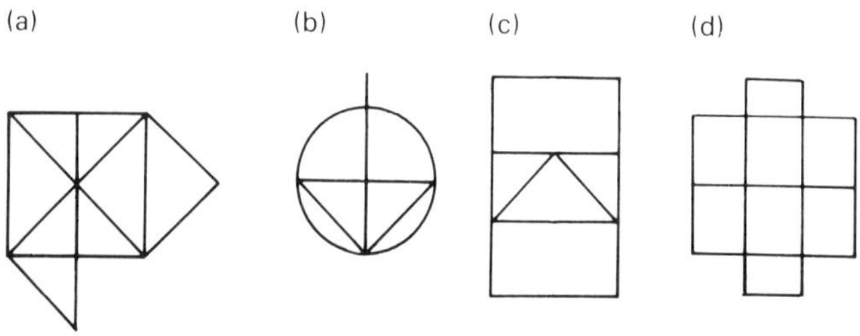

13 Using a scale of 5 mm to 1 km, what lengths on a drawing would represent the following distances?
(a) 18 km (b) 35 km (c) 18.5 km (d) 29.2 km (e) 63.7 km
(f) 125.3 km.

14 Eight landmarks are positioned with these bearings and distances from a central point O. Use a suitable scale to show all points.

Church	2.5 km, 136°	Manor	2.4 km, 326°
School	1 km, 065°	Village Hall	1.8 km, 005°
Inn	0.5 km, 280°	Post Office	1 km, 168°
Crossroads	2.1 km, 215°	Garage	0.6 km, 348°.

15 A plane flies 255 km on a bearing of 155°, then 300 km on a bearing of 195° and finally changes course to fly 325 km on a bearing of 320°, at which point it lands.
(a) Plot the plane's course.
(b) Find the straight line distance from start to finish as accurately as your drawing allows.
(c) On what bearing could it fly to do the same journey in one straight line?

16 (a)

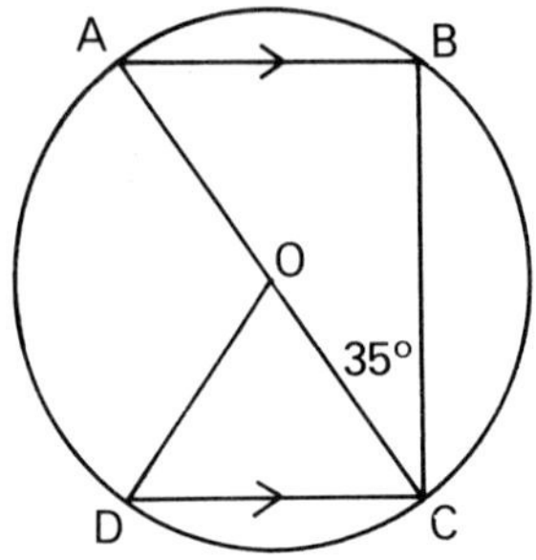

Centre O. AB is parallel to CD.
$\angle BCA = 35^\circ$.
Calculate $\angle ACD$ and $\angle DOC$.

(b)

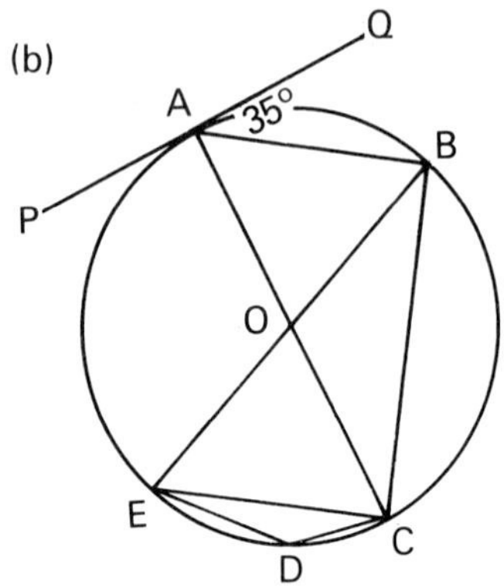

Centre O. PQ is the tangent at A.
$\angle QAB = 35^\circ$.
Calculate $\angle ACE$, $\angle EBC$, $\angle AOE$, $\angle EDC$.

17 Using any instruments
(a) construct triangle ABC so that AB = 6 cm, $\angle CAB = 45^\circ$ and $\angle CBA = 55^\circ$,
(b) construct a circle passing through A, B and C,
(c) construct a circle having AB, BC and AC as tangents.

18 (a) Construct any triangle ABC in which AB is 5 cm and $\angle ACB$ is 90°. What is the radius of the circle passing through A, B and C? Prove your answer by drawing the circle.
(b) Draw a line PQ, 4 cm long. Mark X, the centre of PQ. Draw circles with radii 2 cm, 3 cm and 4 cm, so that PQ is a tangent to all three at point X.
(c) Draw any quadrilateral ABCD so that $\angle A = 76^\circ$, $\angle B = 120^\circ$, $\angle C = 104^\circ$, and $\angle D = 60^\circ$. By drawing the circumscribed circle of triangle ABD, prove that ABCD is a cyclic quadrilateral.

19 (a)

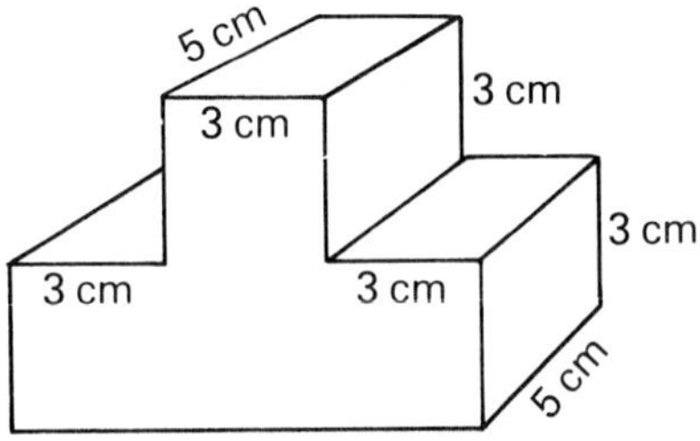

(b)

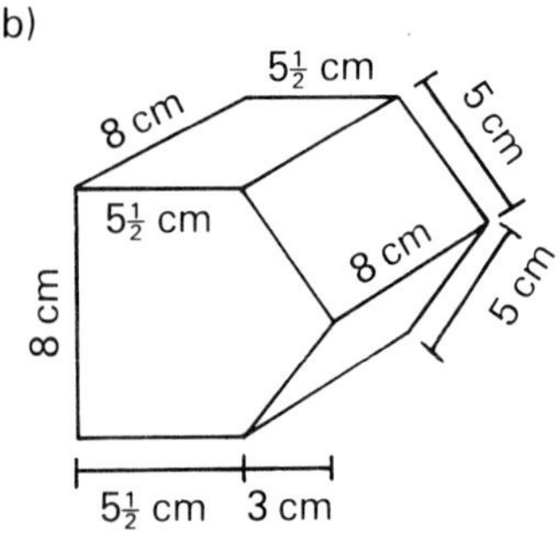

(i) Draw a rough sketch of the net of each solid.
(ii) Find the surface area of each one.
(iii) Calculate the volume of each prism.

20 (a) A pillar is in the shape of a prism 7.3 metres high. The area of the horizontal cross section is 0.25 m^2. Calculate the volume.

(b) A solid platform is a prism 3.6 metres long. Each end is a trapezium whose parallel sides are 2.3 metres and 1.7 metres long, with a depth of 0.8 metres between them. Find the volume of the platform.

(c) A container is in the shape of a triangular prism. The triangular end has a base of $3\frac{1}{5}$ cm and a vertical height of $3\frac{3}{4}$ cm. The prism is $3\frac{1}{3}$ cm in length. Find its volume.

Revision 8. Shapes

1 In each diagram, calculate the angles marked with a letter.

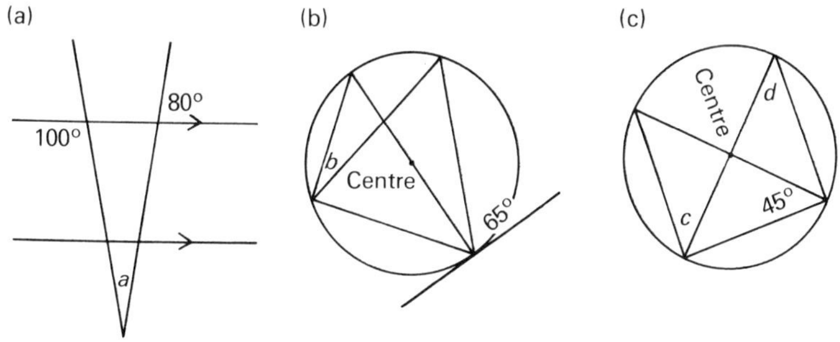

2 Using ruler and compasses only

(a) draw a line $8\frac{1}{2}$ cm long and find its perpendicular bisector,

(b) construct an angle of 90°,

(c) draw triangle ABC in which AB = 5 cm, AC = 6 cm and ∠BAC = 120°. Find the centre of the circle which passes through A, B and C.

3 ABCDE is a regular pentagon inscribed in a circle centre O. X is the centre of side AB. Calculate (a) ∠BOA (b) ∠BAO (c) ∠XOC.

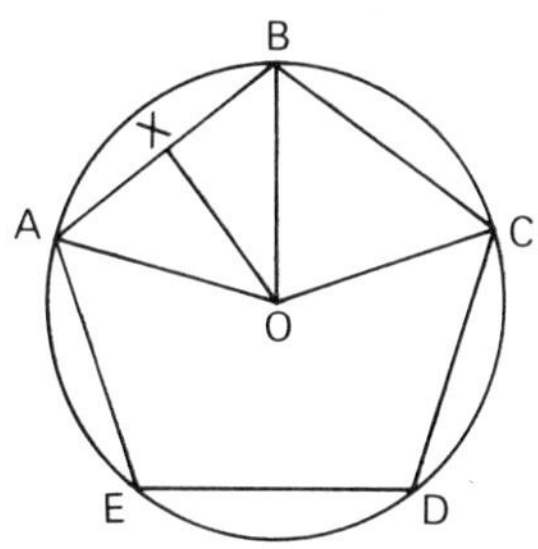

4 Calculate lengths marked with a letter.

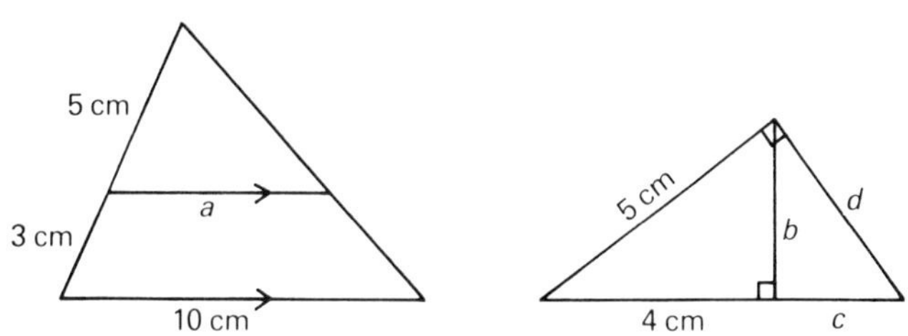

5 If I am looking on a bearing of 035°, in which direction will I face when I turn

(a) 50° clockwise (b) 180°
(c) 90° anticlockwise (d) 230° clockwise?

6 ABCD is a field in the shape of a quadrilateral in which AB = 50 metres. B is due East of A. Corner D is due North of corner B and on a bearing of 035° from A. Corner C is on a bearing 065° from B and 155° from D.

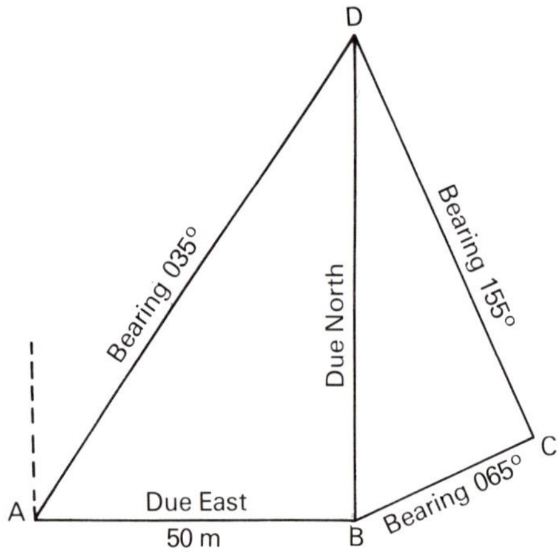

(a) Make a scale drawing of the field.
(b) From the drawing find lengths DB, DC and BC.
(c) Use those lengths to find the area of the field.

7 (a) Calculate the interior angle of a regular polygon with
(i) 8 sides (ii) 24 sides (iii) 9 sides (iv) 36 sides.
(b) How many sides has a regular polygon with an interior angle of
(i) 150° (ii) 144° (iii) 156° (iv) 174°?

8 On this graph,
vector $\overrightarrow{OA} = \mathbf{a} = \begin{pmatrix} 2 \\ 3 \end{pmatrix}$.

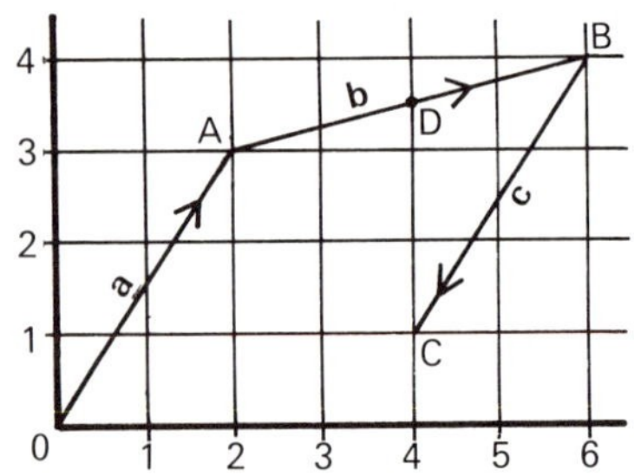

(a) Read off the value of (i) **b** and (ii) **c**.
(b) If D is the midpoint of AB, what is vector $\overrightarrow{AD}$ in terms of **b**?
(c) If AC is joined, what is $\overrightarrow{AC}$ in terms of **b** and **c**?
(d) Find $\overrightarrow{OB}$ in terms of **a** and **b**.
(e) What is $\overrightarrow{OC}$ in terms of **a**, **b** and **c**?

9 ABCHG is a regular pentagon. CDH is an equilateral triangle and EFGH is a square.

(a) How many lines of symmetry has triangle DEH?
(b) Calculate ∠DEH.
(c) Calculate the reflex angle BCD.
(d) What is the obtuse angle AGF?

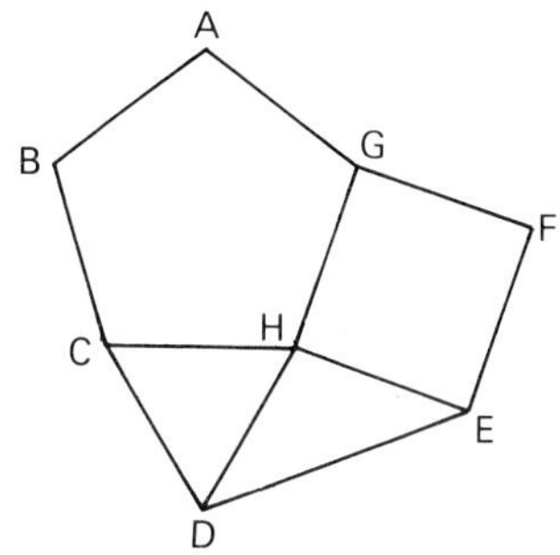

10 State whether the angles at A are right, acute or obtuse.

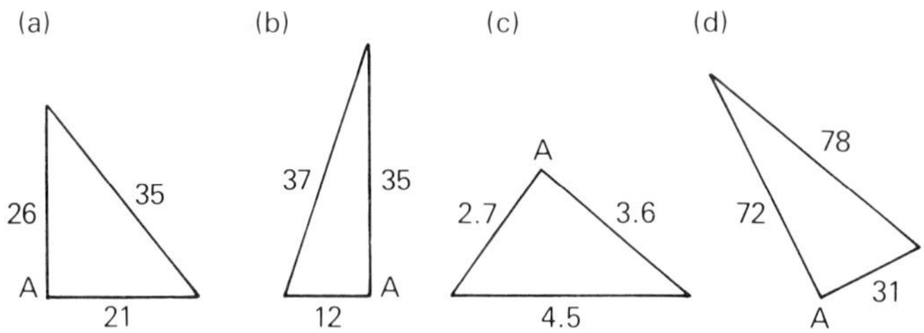

11 ABCD is a metal template with a right-angle at B. AB = 4 cm, BC = 5.8 cm and CD = 3.9 cm. The perpendicular distance of D from AB is 2.2 cm.
Calculate length AD.

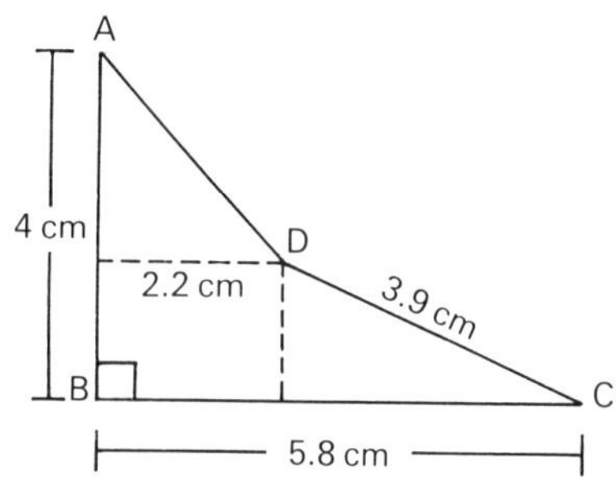

12 In this question, refer to these shapes:

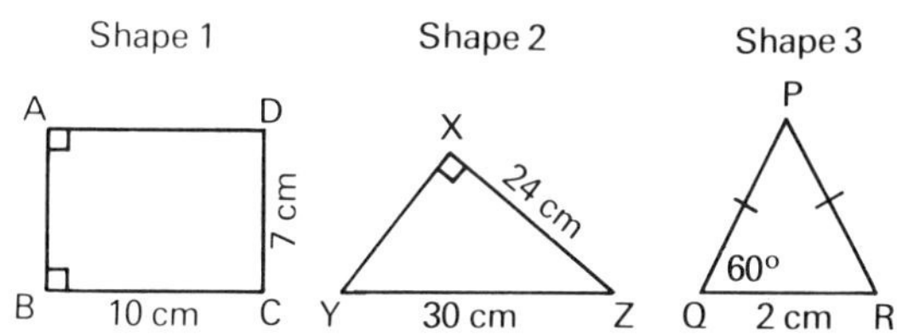

(a) In shape No. 3 calculate ∠QPR.
(b) Calculate the area of shape No. 2.
(c) Calculate the volume of the solid shape created, when shape No. 1 is rotated about side AB. ($\pi = 3\frac{1}{7}$)
(d) If shape No. 3 is the end of a prism which is 5 cm long, find the volume of the prism.

13 From a base line AB, 80 m long, three objects X, Y and Z are surveyed as follows.
X: bearing from A 350°, bearing from B 295°
Y: bearing from A 025°, bearing from B 330°
Z: bearing from A 060°, bearing from B due N
Use a drawing to find distances XY and YZ.

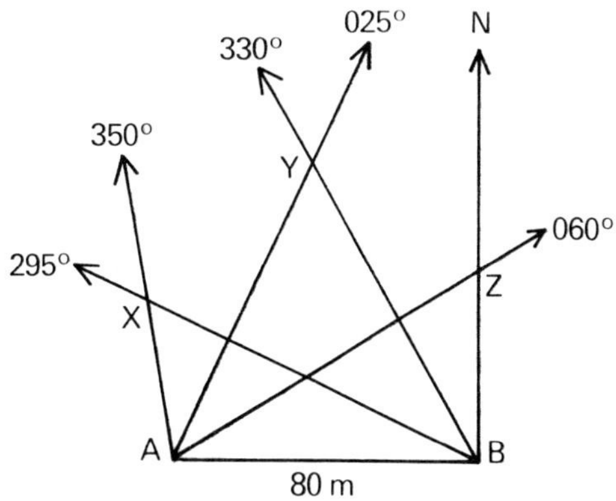

14 A swimming pool is 50 m long with a section as shown in the diagram.

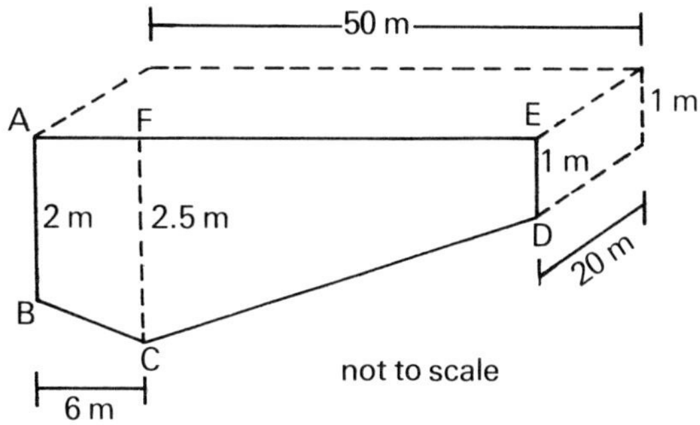

The width of the pool is 20 metres. The two ends are 1 metre and 2 metres deep with a maximum depth of 2.5 metres at FC, which is a horizontal distance of 6 metres from the end AB.

(a) Find the volume of the pool in cubic metres.

(b) How many litres of water will the pool hold if filled to the top?

15 A metal pipe has an end section with outside radius 2.8 cm and inside radius 2.1 cm.
What volume of metal is in 1 metre length of the pipe? ($\pi = 3.14$)

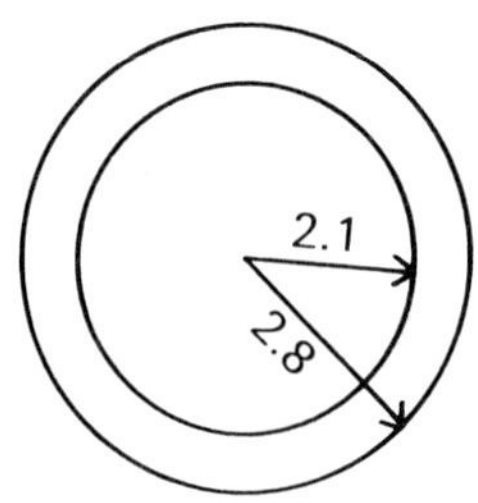

16 The field notes show a rough diagram of a field surveyed along line AB. All figures are in metres.

(a) Make a suitable scale drawing of the field.

(b) Find the area.

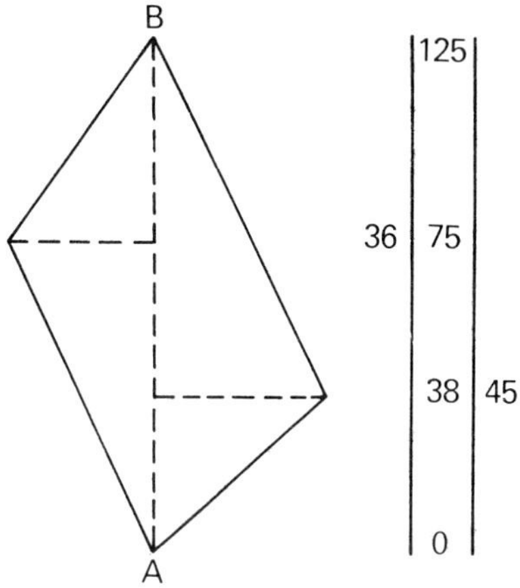

17 Triangle ABC is isosceles with AB = AC. AB = 17 cm and BC = 16 cm. AD is perpendicular to BC and EC is perpendicular to AB. Calculate

(a) length AD,

(b) the area of the triangle,

(c) using your last answer, the length EC correct to 3 significant figures.

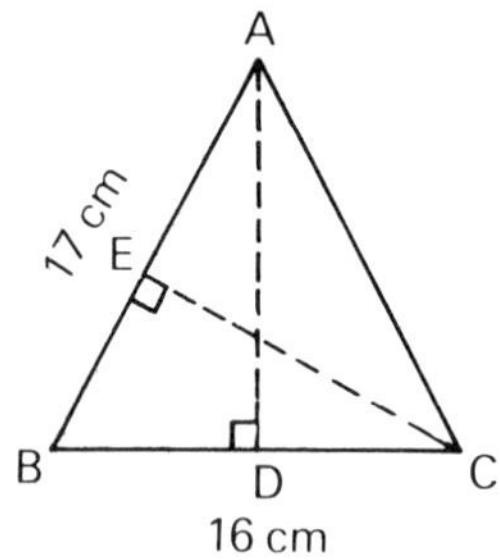

18 Calculate the angles marked with a letter.

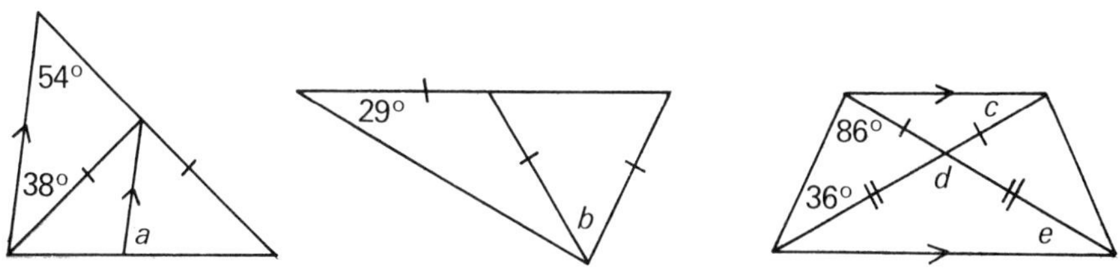

19 The triangular prism is solid wood. The end is a right-angled triangle, base 12 cm, height 9 cm and the prism is 20 cm long.

(a) Find the volume of the solid.

(b) Draw a net for the solid.

(c) Find the total surface area.

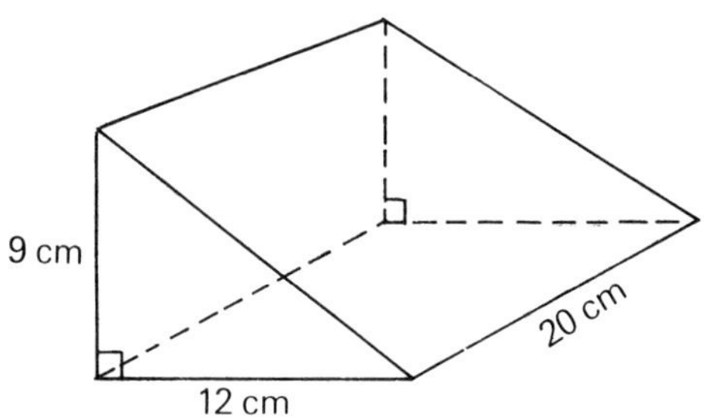

20 Two lines, AB and CD, are drawn cutting the x and y axes. The coordinates of the intersection are A$(-5, 0)$, B$(0, 4)$, C$(2\frac{1}{2}, 0)$ and D$(0, -5)$.

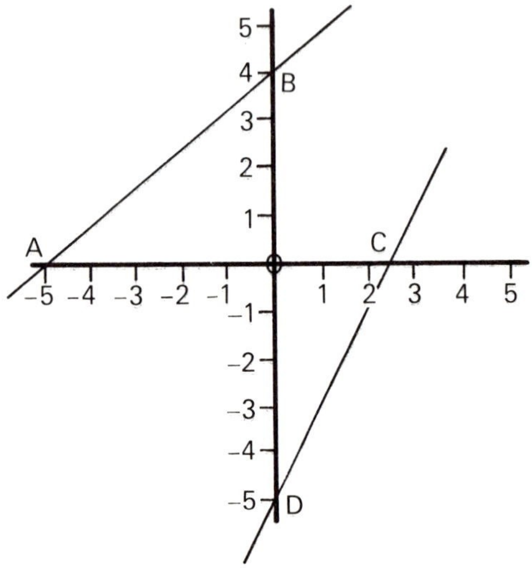

(a) Make a copy of the drawing on squared paper.
(b) Find the coordinates of the midpoints of lengths AB, BC, DC and DA.
(c) Mark those midpoints and join them to form a quadrilateral.
(d) What special name is given to that quadrilateral?

Algebra Revision notes

Notation

$x + y$: x add y.
$x - y$: y subtracted from x.
xy: x multiplied by y.
$\frac{x}{y}$: x divided by y.

Three times a number, subtract a second number: $3a - b$.

The sum of two quantities divided by 5: $\frac{a + b}{5}$.

The product of two different numbers: ab.
A number times itself: $a \times a = a^2$.

Directed Numbers

$+$ and $-$ signs indicate numbers > 0 and < 0 respectively.

$$^{-}3 < 0 \quad ^{+}3 > 0 \quad ^{-}1 < ^{+}2 \quad ^{+}\tfrac{1}{2} > ^{-}1\tfrac{1}{2} \quad ^{-}4 < ^{-}2$$

Adding: $^{-}3 + ^{-}2 = ^{-}5$, $^{+}4 + ^{-}2 = ^{+}2$, $^{-}6 + ^{+}3 = ^{-}3$.
Subtracting: $^{-}3 - ^{-}2 = ^{-}1$, $^{+}4 - ^{-}2 = ^{+}6$, $^{-}6 - ^{+}3 = ^{-}9$.
Multiplying: $^{-}3 \times ^{-}2 = ^{+}6$, $^{+}4 \times ^{-}2 = ^{-}8$, $^{-}6 \times ^{+}3 = ^{-}18$.
Dividing: $\frac{^{-}3}{^{-}2} = ^{+}1\frac{1}{2}$, $\frac{^{+}4}{^{-}2} = ^{-}2$, $\frac{^{-}6}{^{+}3} = ^{-}2$.

When a number is positive, the directive sign is often omitted, i.e. $^{+}7$ is written 7 and $^{+}2\frac{1}{2}$ is written $2\frac{1}{2}$.

Brackets

$5(a + b) = 5a + 5b$
$x(x - y) = x^2 - xy$
$3x - 2(x - y) = 3x - 2x + 2y = x + 2y$.

$(x - 2)(x + 3)$
$= x^2 - 2x + 3x - 6$
$= x^2 + x - 6$.

$(x - 4)^2$
$= (x - 4)(x - 4)$
$= x^2 - 4x - 4x + 16$
$= x^2 - 8x + 16$.

$(2x + 3)(3x - 2)$
$= 6x^2 + 9x - 4x - 6$
$= 6x^2 + 5x - 6$.

Factorisation

$12x - 15y = 3(4x - 5y)$
$9x^2y + 6xy^2 - 3x^3 = 3x(3xy + 2y^2 - x^2)$
$a^2 - b^2 = (a + b)(a - b)$
$3a^2 - 12b^2 = 3(a^2 - 4b^2) = 3(a + 2b)(a - 2b).$

$x^2 - x - 6$
Factors of -6 are -3 and $+2$.
$x^2 - x - 6 = (x - 3)(x + 2).$

$2x^2 - 7x + 6$
Factors of 2 are 2 and 1.
Factors of 6 are -3 and -2.
$2x^2 - 7x + 6 = (2x - 3)(x - 2).$

See later notes in Part 2.

Formulae

When $a = b + c$, then $b = a - c$ and $c = a - b$.
When $a = b - c$, then $b = a + c$ and $c = b - a$.

When $a = bc$, then $b = \dfrac{a}{c}$ and $c = \dfrac{a}{b}$.

When $a = \dfrac{b}{c}$, then $b = ac$ and $c = \dfrac{b}{a}$.

When $x = a + by$, *find* y.

$$by = x - a$$
$$y = \frac{x - a}{b}$$

When $a = \sqrt{b - 2c}$, *find* c.

$$a^2 = b - 2c$$
$$2c = b - a^2$$
$$c = \frac{b - a^2}{2}.$$

Indices

$a^3 = a \times a \times a$ $\quad a^{-1} = \dfrac{1}{a}$ $\quad a^{1/2} = \sqrt{a}$ $\quad a^0 = 1$

$a^{3/2} = \sqrt{a^3}$ $\quad a^{-2} = \dfrac{1}{a^2}$ $\quad a^{-1/2} = \dfrac{1}{\sqrt{a}}$

When terms are multiplied, indices are added.
When terms are divided, indices are subtracted.

$x^2 \times x^3 = x^5.$
$ax^3 \times a^2x = a^3x^4.$
$by^{-1} \times b^{1/2}y^{1/2} = b^{3/2}y^{-1/2}.$

$a^5 \div a^2 = a^3.$
$b^4y^2 \div b^2y = b^2y.$
$ax^{-1} \div a^2x^{-1} = a^{-1}x^0 = a^{-1}.$

See later notes in Part 2.

Equations

$3x = 15$
$x = 5$

$x - 3 = 7$
$x = 10$

$2x + 4 = 6$
$2x = 2$
$x = 1$

$\dfrac{x}{3} = \dfrac{5}{2}$
$2x = 15$
$x = 7\frac{1}{2}$

To find the positive whole number value of x when

$5 < 3x < 7$
$3x = 6$
$x = 2.$

$17 > x^2 > 15$
$x^2 = 16$
$x = 4.$

$4x > 17$ and $3x < 16$
$x > 4\frac{1}{4}$ and $x < 5\frac{1}{3}$
$x = 5.$

When solving equations, remove brackets and fractions first.

Solve the equation $\frac{3x}{2} = 5 - 2(x - 1).$

$$\begin{aligned} 3x &= 10 - 4(x - 1) \\ 3x &= 10 - 4x + 4 \\ 4x + 3x &= 10 + 4 \\ 7x &= 14 \\ x &= 2. \end{aligned}$$

Simultaneous Equations

Numerical coefficients of similar terms must be made equal.

Find values of x and y which satisfy both these equations:

$$\begin{aligned} 2x - 2y &= 10 \\ 3x + 5y &= 7. \end{aligned}$$

Multiply the first equation by 5 and the second by 2.
This will give $-10y$ and $+10y$ in the equations.

$$\begin{aligned} 10x - 10y &= 50 \\ 6x + 10y &= 14 \end{aligned}$$

Add the equations to eliminate the terms in y.

$$\begin{aligned} 16x &= 64 \\ x &= 4. \end{aligned}$$

Substitute $x = 4$ in the first of the original equations.

$$\begin{aligned} 2x - 2y &= 10 \\ 8 - 2y &= 10 \\ 2y &= 8 - 10 \\ 2y &= -2 \\ y &= -1. \end{aligned}$$

The simultaneous values are $x = 4$ and $y = -1$.
Check by substitution in the second equation: $12 - 5 = 7$.

See later notes in Part 2.

Graphs of Equations

When a graph of $y = mx + c$ is drawn,
the gradient of the line is m,
the graph cuts the y-axis where $y = +c$,
the graph cuts the x-axis where $x = \frac{-c}{m}$.

Using the equation $y = mx + c$, in the graph of $2y = 3x - 4$, when the equation is written $y = \frac{3}{2}x - 2$, we can see the gradient is $\frac{3}{2}$.

It cuts the y-axis where $x = 0$.
By substitution in the equation, $y = -2$.
It cuts the x-axis where $y = 0$.
By substitution in the equation, $3x - 4 = 0 \quad x = \frac{4}{3}$

Logarithms (Base 10)

A logarithm is an *index*. Because

$$10^0 = 1, \quad \log 1 = 0.$$
$$10^1 = 10, \quad \log 10 = 1.$$
$$10^2 = 100, \quad \log 100 = 2.$$
$$10^3 = 1000, \quad \log 1000 = 3 \text{ (etc.)}.$$

Logs of numbers between 1 and 10 are between 0 and 1 (commence 0.).
Logs of numbers between 10 and 100 are between 1 and 2 (commence 1.).
That gives the log its *characteristic*.
The log tables give the log its *mantissa*.

For log 8.63: It is between 1 and 10, i.e. characteristic 0.
863 in the tables gives a mantissa of 936.
log 8.63 = 0.936.

Note: The log of a number with one figure preceding the decimal point commences 0., with two figures preceding the decimal point, 1. (etc.).

Logs of numbers between 0.1 and 1 are between −1 and 0. This means the characteristic will be −1 and it is written $\bar{1}$.
Logs of numbers 0.01 to 0.1 have a characteristic of −2, written $\bar{2}$.

Note: For all numbers less than 1, the place value of the first significant figure decides the characteristic of the log.

For log 0.0526: It is between 0.01 and 0.1 and its first significant figure is in the second decimal place. Characteristic $\bar{2}$.
Log 0.0526 = $\bar{2}.721$. Only the characteristic is negative.
For log 0.00743: First significant figure is in the third decimal place giving a characteristic of $\bar{3}$. Log 0.00743 = $\bar{3}.871$

Standard form gives the characteristic, e.g. $0.00743 = 7.43 \times 10^{-3}$. Log characteristic, $\bar{3}$.

Using logs: To multiply numbers, add the logs.
To divide numbers, subtract the logs.
To calculate powers, multiply the log by the index.

You may now attempt **Revisions 9** and **10.**

Revision 9. Algebra

1 $a = 3, b = -2, c = -4, d = -5, e = 8$.

(a) Add a to c. (b) Add c to d. (c) Add d to e.
(d) Take a from e. (e) Take e from a. (f) Take c from b.
(g) Add b to c. (h) Take d from a. (i) Take d from c.

2 Calculate

(a) $18 - {}^{+}13$ (b) $45 + {}^{-}36$ (c) $38 - {}^{-}45$
(d) ${}^{-}30 + {}^{+}56$ (e) $83 - {}^{+}29$ (f) ${}^{-}126 - {}^{+}84$
(g) ${}^{-}75 + {}^{-}39$ (h) $200 - {}^{-}126$ (i) ${}^{-}149 - {}^{-}85$.

3 (a) If L stands for a number of pounds, suggest what $P = 100L$ might mean.
(b) If M is a number of millimetres, what might $M = 10C$ mean?
(c) If C is a length in centimetres, suggest a meaning for $C = 100M$.
(d) If K is a weight in kilograms, suggest what $G = 1000K$ might mean.
(e) If A is area, what could $A = LB$ mean?

4 Find the value of each letter when

(a) $3A = 18$ (b) $15 + x = 50$ (c) $y - 23 = 10$
(d) $\dfrac{B}{3} = 12$ (e) $\dfrac{24}{a} = 3$ (f) $20y = 120$
(g) $\dfrac{50}{c} = 5$ (h) $\dfrac{X}{8} = \dfrac{1}{8}$ (i) $\dfrac{z}{8} = \dfrac{1}{4}$.

5 If A is an integer, find its value when

(a) $A^2 = 64$ (b) $A - 15 = -25$ (c) $A + 18 = -12$
(d) $\dfrac{A}{4} = 0.25$ (e) $A^6 = 1$ (f) $20 - A = -1$
(g) $5 > A > 3$ (h) $18 < A < 20$ (i) $50 > A^2 > 48$
(j) $35 < 3A < 37$ (k) $199 < 4A < 201$ (l) $5 > \dfrac{A}{2} > 3$.

6 Write a shorthand formula in each case:

(a) Twice a number, add a second number, is 15.
(b) A number divided by twice a second number, is 10.
(c) Twelve divided by a number, equals a second number.
(d) A number times itself, equals a second number.
(e) Five times a number, add 8, equals a second number.
(f) One-third of a number add 2, equals 6.

7 Use your own letters for unknowns to make formulae, stating what each letter represents. (See also p. 48.)

(a) A son's age is 25 years less than his mother's age.
(b) The number of millimetres is 1000 times the number of metres.
(c) The amount in pounds equals the amount in pence divided by 100.
(d) The perimeter of a triangle equals the sum of the three sides.

(e) The perimeter of an equilateral triangle is 3 times the side.
(f) Electric power equals Amps multiplied by Volts.
(g) The length of a rectangle is area divided by breadth.

8 Find the value of a, when $b = 3, c = 0, d = 2\frac{1}{2}, e = 5$, if

(a) $a = be$ (b) $a = cd$ (c) $a = \frac{e}{b}$ (d) $a = bde$

(e) $a = bd + e$ (f) $a = \frac{cd}{b}$ (g) $a = e^2 - b^2$ (h) $a = \frac{d+e}{b}$.

9 Find B, when $x = 4.5, y = 2\frac{1}{2}, a = 100, c = 15$.

(a) $B = x - y$ (b) $B = ax$ (c) $B = cy$ (d) $B = \frac{x}{a}$

(e) $B = \frac{x}{c}$ (f) $B = \frac{ax}{c}$ (g) $B = \frac{a}{y}$ (h) $B = \frac{ay - 10c}{a}$.

10 Expand
(a) $5(a - c)$ (b) $3(x - 2y)$ (c) $a(x + y)$
(d) $2(3a - 2c)$ (e) $a(a + c)$ (f) $8(4x - 3y)$
(g) $4(5x + 2a - 3c)$ (h) $c(2x - b + 3a)$ (i) $a(a + 3b - 4c)$.

11 Find the value of A, when $x = 4, y = 2, z = 6$.
(a) $A = 3(2x + 3y)$ (b) $A = 2(x + 3z)$ (c) $A = y(x + z)$
(d) $A = x + 2(x + z - y)$ (e) $A = 4(z - y) + 2z$ (f) $A = 3z - 3(x + y)$.

12 Rewrite each formula to read $a =$, when
(a) $b = a + c$ (b) $c = b + a$ (c) $b = c - a$

(d) $b = ac$ (e) $c = \frac{a}{b}$ (f) $c = a - b$

(g) $b = 2a + c$ (h) $c = a - 3b$ (i) $b = \frac{c}{a}$.

13 In each formula find x when $a = 10$ and $c = 4$, if
(a) $a = x - c$ (b) $a = c + x$ (c) $c = a + x$

(d) $c = \frac{x}{a}$ (e) $a = \frac{c}{x}$ (f) $2c = 3a - x$

(g) $a = x - 5c$ (h) $c = 2x + a$ (i) $4a = 10c + x$.

14 What number is
(a) 3 less than 0 (b) 5 less than 1 (c) 10 less than 5
(d) 4 more than −8 (e) 9 more than −15 (f) 12 more than −4
(g) 16 less than 2 (h) 100 more than −50?

15 Find the value of

(a) -7×8 (b) 4×-25 (c) 9×-9
(d) $-3 \times \frac{1}{2}$ (e) -10×-9 (f) $-10 \times -1\frac{1}{2}$
(g) $-\frac{1}{2} \times -\frac{1}{2}$ (h) $-12 \times \frac{1}{3}$ (i) -6×3.5.

16 If $a = -4, c = -3, x = 2$, find the value of

(a) $3(x + a)$ (b) $4(a + c)$ (c) $6(a - x)$
(d) $5(x - a)$ (e) $3(c - x)$ (f) $10(x - c)$
(g) $x(a + c)$ (h) $x(c - a)$ (i) $a(c - x)$.

17 Find the value of A, when $x = 5, y = -4, z = -3$, if

(a) $A = 2x - y$ (b) $A = z - 2x$ (c) $A = 3y - x$

(d) $A = xy - z$ (e) $A = yz + xy$ (f) $A = \dfrac{x}{y}$

(g) $A = \dfrac{xz}{y}$ (h) $A = \dfrac{x + y}{y - z}$ (i) $A = \dfrac{z - x}{3y}$.

18 Find the value of X, when $a = -2, b = -1, c = -3$, if

(a) $X = a^2$ (b) $X = b^5$ (c) $X = c^2 + a^2$
(d) $X = b^2 - a^2$ (e) $X = a^2 + b^2 + c^2$ (f) $X = a^3 + b^3 + c^3$.

19 Calculate the value of a, when $b = 5, c = -5, d = -2$, if

(a) $b = c + a$ (b) $b = a - d$ (c) $c = 2a + d$

(d) $c = \dfrac{a}{d}$ (e) $d = \dfrac{2a}{b}$ (f) $d = \dfrac{bc}{a}$.

20

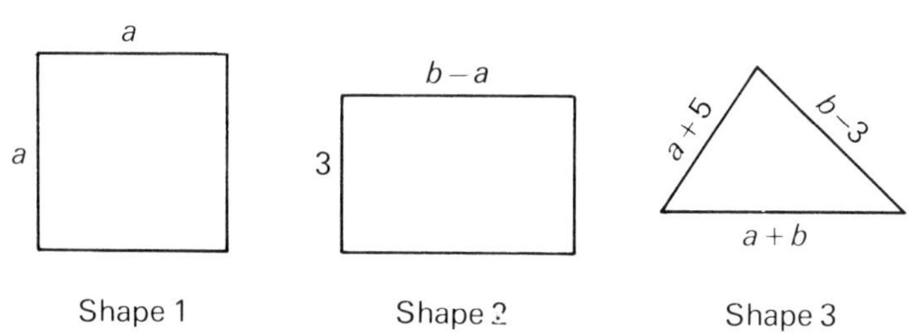

(a) If $a = 11$, what is the area of shape No. 1?
(b) If $a = 7$, what is the perimeter of shape No. 1?
(c) If $b = 9$ and $a = -2$, find the area of shape No. 2.
(d) If $b = -3$ and $a = -10$, find the perimeter of shape No. 2.
(e) If $a = -2$ and $b = 7$, what is the perimeter of shape No. 3?

Revision 10. Algebra

1 Simplify

(a) $3x - 6 + 3 - x - 10$ (b) $5a - 2b - 3a - 2c - 7b$
(c) $6a - 3b + 7 - 2b - 4a - 8$ (d) $5(2a - 3b - 4)$
(e) $2(3x - 2y) + 3(4x - 3y)$ (f) $4(2a - 3b) - (5b - 4a)$.

2 Calculate

(a) $3^2 \times 2^3$ (b) $3 \times 2^2 \times 4^2$ (c) $5^2 \div 2^2$
(d) $2 \times 9^{1/2}$ (e) $16^{1/2} \times 2^{-1}$ (f) $25^{1/2} \div 2^{-2}$
(g) $3^2 \times 81^{-1/2}$ (h) $4^{1/2} \times 2^{-2}$ (i) $36^{-1/2} \div 5^{-2}$.

3 Simplify

(a) $a^2 b^2 \times a^3 b$ (b) $ab^3 c \times a^4 bc^2$
(c) $a^4 bc^2 \div ab^2 c$ (d) $a^5 b^3 c^2 \div ab^4 c^3$
(e) $5a^2 b^2 c^5 \times 3ab^4 c$ (f) $4a^3 bc^4 \div 6ab^5 c^5$
(g) $\dfrac{3a^3 b^2 c^3}{12a^2 b^3 c^5}$ (h) $\dfrac{2a^2 b^3}{5a^3 bc^4} \times \dfrac{10ab^2 c^2}{6ab^2 c}$.

4 Simplify

(a) $a^3 b^{-2} \times a^{-1} b$ (b) $a^{-1} b^3 \times a^2 b^{-2}$
(c) $a^{-2} b \times a^{-3} b$ (d) $a^{1/2} b^{-1} \times a^2 b^2$
(e) $a^{-2} b^{1/2} \times a^{1/2} b^{-1}$ (f) $a^{-1/2} b^{-1/2} \times a^2 b$
(g) $a^2 b^{-1} \div a^{1/2} b^{-1}$ (h) $a^{1/2} b^{-1/2} \div a^{-2} b^{-2}$
(i) $a^{-2} b^{1/2} \div a^{1/2} b^{-1}$ (j) $a^{1/2} b^{-2} \div a^{-1} b^{-2}$.

5 Find the value of x if

(a) $2^x = 64$ (b) $4^x = 256$ (c) $2^x \times 3^x = 216$
(d) $\sqrt{2^x} = 8$ (e) $\sqrt{3^x \times 2^4} = 12$ (f) $10^x \times 10^x = 0.0001$.

6 If $\log 7 = 0.845$, $\log 3 = 0.477$, $\log 4 = 0.602$, find

(a) log 700 (b) log 4000 (c) log 12 (d) log 28
(e) log 63 (f) log 1.75 (g) log 6.75 (h) log 343.

7 If $\log a = x$ and $\log b = y$, what is

(a) $\log a^2$ (b) $\log b^2$ (c) $\log ab$ (d) $\log \dfrac{a}{b}$ (e) $\log a^2 b$?

8

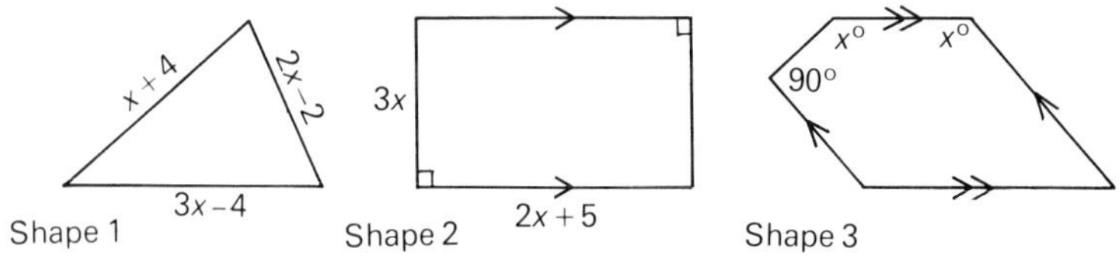

(a) If the perimeter of shape No. 1 is 28, what is the value of x?
(b) Find the smallest possible whole number value for x in shape No. 1.
(c) Give the simplest expanded expression for the area of shape No. 2.
(d) If the perimeter of shape No. 2 is 35, what is the value of x?
(e) Find the value of x in shape No. 3.

9 There are T children in a school and of those children, b are boys.
(a) Give a formula for the number of girls.
(b) Write a formula to show the percentage of boys on roll.
(c) If there are 4 girls for every 5 boys, what is the formula for T in terms of b?

10 Solve the equations
(a) $3x - 2 = x + 6$ (b) $11 + 5(x - 2) = 6x - 10$ (c) $5x - 3 = 2x - 7$
(d) $2x + 3 = x - 5$ (e) $3x + 8 = 4x - 5(x - 1)$ (f) $\frac{3x}{4} = x - 1$
(g) $\frac{x}{5} = \frac{3}{4}$ (h) $5(x+1) - 3x = 5(x+2) - 2$ (i) $\frac{3x-2}{2} = \frac{x+4}{3}$.

11 If $a = 3, b = -3, c = -2$, find D in the formula
(a) $D = 2ab - c$ (b) $D = \frac{ab}{2}$ (c) $D = ab^2c$
(d) $D = 3(b - c)$ (e) $D = \frac{a - b - c}{2}$ (f) $D = b(a - c)$
(g) $D = ab - bc$ (h) $D = c(3a - b)$ (i) $D = \frac{2c - 4b}{4a}$.

12 Four numbers A, B, C and D are connected by the equations
$$A = 2C - D \quad \text{and} \quad B = 3D - 2C.$$
(a) Find the value of $A - B$ in terms of C and D.
(b) If $A = B$, find C in terms of D.
(c) If $C = D$, is it true to say $A = B$?
(d) If $A = D$, is it true to say $B = C$?
(e) If $A = C$, is it true to say $B = D$?
(f) If $A = 1$ and $B = -1$, find the values of C and D.

13 Solve these simultaneous equations
(a) $2x + y = 3$, $2x - 2y = 12$ (b) $x - 3y = 1$, $2x + 3y = 11$ (c) $2x - 3y = -6$, $3x + 2y = 4$
(d) $3x = 2y - 2$, $2x - 5y + 16 = 0$ (e) $5x = 3y$, $2y - x = 7$ (f) $3x = 3y - 6$, $2x - 4 = 3y$.

14 (a) Calculate 3^4.
(b) Express 625 as a power of 5.
(c) If $a^2 = \frac{c^3}{b}$, find a when $c = 4, b = 9$.
(d) Evaluate $9^{3/2} - 8^{2/3}$.
(e) Find the value of $16^{1/4} + 2^{-2} - 3^0$.
(f) Express $\frac{1}{4}$ as a power of 2.

15 Expand

(a) $(a-3)(a+4)$ (b) $(a+5)(2a-2)$ (c) $(2a-3)(2a+3)$
(d) $(3a-1)(2a-3)$ (e) $(3-4a)(2a+5)$ (f) $(3a-4)(3a+4)$
(g) $(2a-7)(2+3a)$ (h) $(5a+3)(5a+1)$ (i) $(4a-5)(5+4a)$.

16 Use logs to find the value of

(a) 36.2×1.08 (b) $73.9 \div 11.6$ (c) $(4.28)^2$

(d) $\sqrt{50.4}$ (d) $\dfrac{8.01 \times 4.26}{10.5}$ (f) $\dfrac{(13.8)^2}{52.9}$

(g) $\dfrac{4.21 \times 13.7}{(1.6)^2}$ (h) $\dfrac{5.2}{\sqrt{2.8}} + \dfrac{(3.71)^2}{4.2}$.

17 Factorise

(a) x^2+3x+2 (b) x^2-x-6 (c) $x^2-7x+10$
(d) $2x^2-x-1$ (e) $2x^2-3x-9$ (f) $3x^2+7x+2$
(g) $6x^2-14x+8$ (h) $4x^2+4x-15$ (i) $12x^2-7x-12$.

18 If $A=3x-1, B=2x-3, C=x-2$, find in terms of x

(a) A^2-B^2 (b) $(A-B)^2$ (c) $C(A-B)$.

19 The length of a rectangle can be represented by $3x$ centimetres and its breadth may be written as $(2x+1)$ centimetres.

(a) Find the value of x which converts the rectangle into a square.
(b) Write an expression in x for the perimeter of the rectangle.
(c) If the area of the rectangle is 30 cm^2, what is the value of x?

20 (a) If $A=3x-5$, what is the smallest whole number value of x for which $A>0$?
(b) If $B=3y-8$, what is the largest whole number value of y for which $B<0$?
(c) Find the smallest whole number value of a for which $a^2>30$.
(d) If $A=x+2$ and $B=2x-3$, find the largest whole number value of x for which $A>B$.

Part 2 Selective Revision

Revision in this part of the book is more concentrated. Presented under topic headings, the basic revision is taken to the problem stage. There are more notes for revision purposes, but it may also be necessary to refer to the earlier notes in Part 1. Worked examples are preceded by the symbol ▶.

Exercises preceded by an asterisk, *, are considered to be more selective and in some cases may cover aspects of mathematics beyond the demands of certain examinations.

Your technical calculator

Some Examining Boards allow the use of an electronic calculator in certain sections of their examinations. The basic operations can be carried out on all calculators, but the technical calculators offer other functions which will work problems involving percentages, mixed operations, logarithms, square roots and trigonometry. Where one set of keys provides two sets of functions, the 'function change' key should be operated before using special function keys.

Different makes of calculator may use different symbols for the same operation (e.g. M+ = SUM, MR = RCL), or may require different key operations for the same result (e.g. for percentage add-ons and discounts, antilogs, etc.). The examples in this chapter follow the system used on a Casio Technical Calculator. **For other calculators you should read the instruction booklet carefully.**

Percentages

Since a percentage is 'per hundred', a percentage part demands division by 100 and conversion to a percentage is worked by a multiplication by 100, but a % key allows you to add or subtract a value from the original amount.

(a) After paying £35 for a cycle, a dealer sold it to make a profit of 15%. How much did he charge for the cycle?

Key operation : [C] 35 [×] 15 [%] [+] [=]

Display : 40.25 Answer: £40.25

(b) On a bill for £29.50, a woman receives a discount of 8%. How much does she actually pay?

Key operation : [C] 29 [•] 50 [×] 8 [%] [−] [=]

Display : 27.14 Answer: £27.14

Memory

The key marked M+ will enter the display into the memory and also add the display to the memory. To subtract display from memory use M−. The key marked MR will recall the memory store to the display panel and MC will clear the memory store. Those keys will be used in some of the next examples.

Logarithms

Some calculators have log keys to the base 10 and some use natural logs to the base e. The ordinary log to the base 10 can be used as a set of common log tables, but both types of logs will work operations. Natural log keys may be marked ln or ln x and the antilog keys e^x or x.

(a) Calculate $\left(\frac{36}{29}\right)^3$ correct to 3 significant figures.

Key operation : [C] 36 [÷] 29 [=] [ln] [×] 3 [=] [x]

Display : 1.9129 Answer: 1.91

Or by using the memory,

Key operation : [C] [MC] 36 [ln] [M+] 29 [ln] [M−] [MR] [×] 3 [=] [x]

Display : 1.9134 Answer: 1.91

(b) Calculate $\sqrt{\frac{4.1 \times 28.5}{34.8}}$ correct to 3 significant figures.

Key operation : [C] 4.1 [×] 28.5 [÷] 34.8 [=] [ln] [÷] 2 [=] [x]

Display :1.8324 Answer: 1.83

Or by using the memory,
Key operation :

[C] [MC] 4.1 [ln] [M+] 28.5 [ln] [M+] 34.8 [ln] [M−] [MR] [÷] 2 [=] [x]

Display : 1.8323 Answer: 1.83

Square Root

If a calculator has a square root key the last example could be worked as follows.

Key operation : [C] 4.1 [×] 28.5 [÷] 34.8 [=] [√]

Display : 1.8324 Answer: 1.83

Use of π (Pi)

The value of π used by a calculator is 3.1415926/7 and that is not suitable for some examination questions where a different value for π may be given.
Using the formula $V = \frac{4}{3}\pi r^3$, find the volume of a sphere, radius 3.5 cm, correct to 1 decimal place.

Key operation : [C] 3.5 [×] [=] [=] [×] 4 [×] [π] [÷] 3 [=]

Display : 179.59437 Answer: 179.6 cm^3

Note the use of = to find the cube of 3.5.

The calculation could be done using π, logs and memory.

Key operation :

[C] [MC] 3.5 [ln] [×] 3 [=] [M+] [π] [ln] [M+] 4 [ln] [M+] 3 [ln] [M−] [MR] [x]

Display : 179.61 Answer: 179.6 cm^3

Trigonometry

All technical calculators are designed to use angles measured in degrees or radians. Since radians are only used in advanced mathematics, it is advisable to keep the calculator switched to degrees.

Keys are marked sin, cos, tan, and the inverse functions to obtain angles when sine, cosine or tangent is known, are marked either $\sin^{-1}$, $\cos^{-1}$, $\tan^{-1}$ or arcsin, arccos, arctan.

(a) Calculate X correct to 3 significant figures when $X = 3.8 \cos 56°$

Key operation : [C] 56 [cos] [×] 3.8 [=]

Display : 2.124922 Answer: 2.12

(b) Calculate angle A correct to the nearest degree when $\tan A = \dfrac{7.4}{6.7}$

Key operation : [C] 7.4 [÷] 6.7 [=] [tan^{-1}]

Display : 47.841 Answer: 48°

Note: Fractional parts of a degree are in decimal form, not minutes.

(c) Calculate Y correct to 3 significant figures when $Y = \dfrac{8.7}{\sin 38°}$

Here we can use the reciprocal key $\dfrac{1}{x}$ by first working $\dfrac{\sin 38°}{8.7}$

Key operation : [C] 38 [sin] [÷] 8.7 [=] [1/x]

Display : 14.131176 Answer: 14.1

Or we may use logs and memory,

Key operation : [C] [MC] 8.7 [ln] [M+] 38 [sin] [ln] [M−] [MR] [x]

Display : 14.13 Answer: 14.1

Further Examples

(a) The hypotenuse and one side of a right-angled triangle are 9.2 cm and 5.5 cm respectively. Third side $= \sqrt{9.2^2 - 5.5^2}$.
Key operation :

[C] [MC] 9.2 [×] 9.2 [=] [M+] 5.5 [×] 5.5 [=] [M−] [MR] [ln] [÷] 2 [=] [x]

Display : 7.3746 Answer: 7.37 cm (3 sig. fig.)

(b) Use the formula $A = P(1 + r)^n$ to calculate the amount A when £500 is invested for 6 years at 8% compound interest. $A = 500(1.08)^6$.

Key operation : [C] [MC] 1.08 [ln] [×] 6 [=] [M+] 500 [ln] [M+] [MR] [x]

Display : 793.42 Answer: £793.42

Other Functions

Some calculators possess functions which reduce the number of operations required for certain calculations.

(a) A power or root, can be obtained more easily with keys marked, y^x and $\sqrt[x]{y}$. To use those functions, enter the number, use the power or root key and then enter the size of the power or root.

(b) Bracket keys, marked (and) may be used without any manipulation of the example, or may allow a certain part of a complicated operation to be isolated.

(c) To enter a negative quantity, some calculators possess a key marked +/−. The key will also alter the sign of the display.

(d) A key marked EXP allows for an entry with more than eight digits. For large and small quantities, within certain limits, the key will display the value in standard form.

(e) Keys marked ME, or $x \leftrightarrow$ M, enable the display and the memory store to change places. A key marked $x \rightarrow$ M will cancel the existing memory and enter the display as a new memory store.

(f) Some calculators allow the operator to view figures after the eighth digit, with a key marked ◄►.

Financial Matters

Revision notes

Taxes Tax = Taxable income × rate of tax.

▸ A woman earns £80 a week and has a non-taxable allowance of £1400.
(a) What is her gross annual income?
(b) What is her taxable income?
(c) If the rate of tax is 33p in the £ (33%), find her annual tax.
(d) If she has a 10% pay rise next year and her allowance remains the same, what tax will she pay in a year when the rate of tax is reduced to 31%?

(a) Gross annual income = £80 × 52 = £4160.
(b) Taxable income = £4160 − £1400 = £2760.
(c) Annual tax = 2760 × £0.33 = £910.80.
(d) New annual income = £4160 × $\frac{110}{100}$ = £4576.
Taxable income = £4576 − £1400 = £3176.
Annual tax = 3176 × £0.31 = £984.56.

Savings and Loans Extended Compound Interest $A = P\left(1 + \frac{r}{100}\right)^n$

▸ Principal P, rate of interest r, number of years n, Amount A.
(a) Calculate the Compound Interest on £500 at 8% for 2 years.
(b) I took a loan of £4000 at an annual interest rate of 9%. My repayments were at the rate of £35.50 a month. What was my outstanding debt at the end of one year?
(c) Use a formula to find the Compound Interest over a period of 12 years, on a loan of £5000 at 11% rate of interest.

(a) First year's interest = £500 × $\frac{8}{100}$ = £40.
Amount second year = £540.

Second year's interest = £540 × $\frac{8}{100}$ = £43.20.
Total interest = £40 + £43.20 = £83.20.

(b) One year's interest $= £4000 \times \frac{9}{100} = £360$.

Total at the end of one year = £4360.
Repayment = £35.50 × 12 = £426.
Outstanding loan = £4360 − £426 = £3934.

(c) $A = 5000 \times (1.11)^{12}$.
Working by logs: Logs

$$\begin{array}{r} 0.0453 \\ \times\ \ 12 \\ \hline 0.5436 \\ +\ 3.6990 \\ \hline 4.2426 \\ \hline \end{array}$$

$A = £17\,480$.
Compound interest = £17 480 − £5000 = £12 480.

Insurance

Life Assurance promises to pay a Capital sum plus bonuses, which are often worked out by Simple Interest.

A Premium is the annual amount paid by the assured. Insurance of property has a premium worked out according to the value of the property.

▶ (a) An assurance policy for £5000 requires a premium of £26 a month. The policy is paid after 20 years plus a bonus at 3% Simple Interest.
  (i) How much was paid in premiums over the 20 years?
  (ii) How much is paid out on the policy after 20 years?

(b) My house, valued at £25 000, is insured on a premium of £1.35 per £1000. Find the annual premium.

(c) I have the contents of my house valued at £8500 and the annual premium is £25.50. What is that per £500 of property?

(a) (i) Total premium = £26 × 12 × 20 = £6240.

(ii) Interest $= £5000 \times \frac{3}{100} \times 20 = £3000$.
Total paid out = £5000 + £3000 = £8000.

(b) Annual premium = £1.35 × 25 = £33.75.

(c) Number of £500's $= \frac{8500}{500} = 17$.
Premium per £500 = £25.50 ÷ 17 = £1.50.

Revision exercises

1 A stereo system priced at £245 can be obtained on hire purchase.
Scheme 1: Deposit £50 and 12 equal instalments of £17.35.
Scheme 2: Deposit £60 and 8 equal instalments of £24.45.
(a) How much more than the cash price would you pay if you accept the terms of Scheme 1?
(b) If you decide on hire purchase, how much would you save by using Scheme 2 instead of Scheme 1?

2 An item of furniture costs £210. On hire purchase a deposit of £60 is required. The store then adds 8% to the remainder of the cash price to be paid in instalments.
(a) What is the total which must be paid in instalments?
(b) When paid in 8 equal parts what is one instalment?

3 A television set costs £250. On hire purchase, one-fifth of the cash price is required as a deposit. To the remainder of the price is added 11% to be paid in 24 equal instalments.
(a) How much is paid in instalments altogether?
(b) What is one instalment?

4 A town has a rateable value of £8 537 500. If the general rate one year was 49p in the £ and in the following year it was increased to 55p in the £, how much extra in rates will that produce?

5 By levying a rate of 50p in the £ one year, a town collected £2 456 450. What was the town's total rateable value?

6 A town has a rateable value of £10 482 650 and it is found necessary to raise £5 241 325 for spending on the town's services next year. What rate should be levied?

7 A man earned £91 a week regularly throughout the year and his non-taxable allowance was £1820. If the rate of tax is fixed at 35p in the £, how much tax did he pay each week?

8 How much is a (a) 10% profit on £6,
(b) 15% loss on £3.60,
(c) 35% discount on £18.20,
(d) $12\frac{1}{2}$% increase on a salary of £3550?

9 Seven savings groups had these amounts at the end of one year:
A. £35 B. £36 C. £27 D. £13.50 E. £18 F. £22.50 G. £28.
(a) Illustrate those figures in a bar-graph or pie-chart.
(b) What percentage of the total was saved by group B?
(c) Which group had saved (i) $7\frac{1}{2}$%, (ii) $12\frac{1}{2}$% of the total?
(d) What percentage of the total was saved by group G, correct to the nearest 1%?

10 (a) The first year's interest on my loan is £642 and I pay back the loan at £62 a month. How much of the capital have I repaid at the end of one year?
(b) I repay a loan at £58 a month and a year's interest is £585. How much of the loan have I repaid after one year?
(c) The interest on my loan last year was £312 and I paid £65 a month. How much of the capital loan did I repay?
(d) In the last year of a man's mortgage repayments, he owed £200 plus £22 interest. If he was paying £53 a month, how did he complete the repayments?

11 Complete this table by working out the annual repayment, the interest and the remainder of the loan after one year in each case.

	Loan	%	Monthly	Annual	Interest	Remainder of Loan
(a)	£5000	10%	£48			
(b)	£4800	11%	£52			
(c)	£7500	9%	£64			
(d)	£10 000	11%	£98			
(e)	£8200	$10\frac{1}{2}$%	£78			

12 Use the formula $A = P\left(1 + \frac{r}{100}\right)^n$

where A is the accrued amount, P is the invested principal, r is the rate of interest and n is the number of years. Find A in each case.
(a) $P =$ £2200, $r = 6\%$, $n = 12$ years. (b) $P =$ £3500, $r = 4\%$, $n = 6$ years.
(c) $P =$ £2000, $r = 3\frac{1}{2}\%$, $n = 5$ years.

13 A man invests £500 for 5 years at 8% compound interest. At the end of the fifth year he adds a further £1000 to his investment and leaves it to accrue interest for a further 10 years at 7% compound interest. What then will be the total amount?

14 A life assurance policy promised to pay £2000 after 25 years or the death of the holder. The premium paid by the holder was £7.50 a month.
(a) If the holder paid the premium for the full 25 years, how much was that altogether?
(b) If the holder was alive at the end of 25 years and bonuses were paid at 3% per year simple interest, how much was actually paid out on the policy?

15 An insurance policy to protect a private building requires a premium of £1.24 per £1000 of the building's value. What would be the annual premium on buildings valued at (a) £24 000 (b) £28 000 (c) £9500 (d) £81 000?

16 If the premium on a fire policy is £1.25 per £1000 of the property value and the owner pays a premium of £17.50, what is the value of the property?

17 A man takes out a policy assuring £3000 at death or after 30 years. He must may a monthly premium of £10.50.

(a) If he is still alive after 30 years, how much will he have paid in premiums?

(b) If the man had died after a period of 12 years, his wife would have received £3000 plus bonuses worked at 4% per annum simple interest. How much would she have received altogether?

18 A man has a life assurance for £8000 payable only at his death, for which he pays a premium of £24.80 a month. His house valued at £25 000 is insured at £1.25 a year per £1000 and the contents valued at £8000 are insured at £1.15 a year per £400 of the value.

(a) How much, in premiums per year, is the man paying altogether for the three policies?

(b) If he dies 15 years after taking out the life policy, how much will he have paid on that one policy alone?

(c) On his death, after paying the life assurance premium for 15 years, his wife received the assured sum plus bonuses at $4\frac{1}{2}$% per year simple interest. What total did she receive?

19 Find the price to the nearest penny when 15% VAT is added to

(a) £8.25 (b) £25.14 (c) £36.38 (d) £216.49 (e) £109.99.

20 A woman earns £5350 a year and her non-taxable allowance is £2650. If the taxable income is taxed at 35%, how much does she pay in one year?

21 A man earns £522 a month and has a non-taxable allowance of £1835. He is taxed at 33p in the £.

(a) How much does he earn in one year? (b) How much is his annual tax?

22 A firm's manager earns £692 a month and has a non-taxable allowance of £2324. The first £5500 of his taxable income is taxed at 35p in the £ and the remainder is subject to 40% tax.

(a) How much does he earn in one year? (b) What is his taxable income?

(c) How much tax does he pay in one year?

23 A man's annual salary is £5500 and his annual free-pay allowance is £2110. He is taxed at 33p in the £.

(a) What is his annual tax?

(b) How much is his tax per week to the nearest penny?

24 A director is paid £3750, four times a year. He has a non-taxable allowance of £2650. The first £6500 of his taxable income is taxed at 33p in the £. The next £1000 is taxed at 38%, the next £1000 at 45%, a further £1000 at 50% and the remainder at 55%.

(a) What was his annual income?

(b) How much tax would be deducted each time he was paid?

25 A rectangular lawn measures 15 metres by 8.4 metres. Weedkiller is applied at 52 grams per square metre and costs 65p per kilogram. Calculate the cost of treating the lawn correct to the nearest penny.

26 If electricity costs 4.5p a unit for the first 80 units and 1.5p a unit for the remainder, find the cost of
(a) 634 units (b) 1100 units (c) 1650 units (d) 2346 units.

27 At the start of a quarter an electricity meter read 13668 and at the end of the quarter it read 17000. There is a fixed charge of £5.15 on every bill and the cost of the electricity is 4.97p a unit. Calculate the total quarterly bill correct to the nearest penny.

28 For a colour television set the rental is £12.45 a month. I pay 12 months' rental in advance and receive a discount of $8\frac{1}{2}$%. How much do I actually pay correct to the nearest penny?

29 A sale offers a reduction on all prices of 12%. A woman buys articles originally priced as follows: Boy's suit £24.50, Girl's dress £12.35, Man's tie £1.90, Woman's shoes £14.34. Work out the total sale price correct to the nearest penny.

30 The cash price of an electric appliance is £180. I may obtain it on hire purchase for a deposit equal to one-sixth of the cash price, plus fifteen equal instalments of £10.80.
(a) If I pay cash, I am allowed a discount of 4%. How much would the appliance cost me?
(b) How much does the equipment cost on hire purchase?
(c) How much of the cash price am I actually borrowing from the shop when I take out the hire purchase agreement?
(d) How much do I pay on HP in excess of the cash price?
(e) What percentage interest is the shop charging?

31 A man works from 08.30 to 12.45 and from 13.45 to 17.45, Monday to Friday, and is paid £2.20 an hour. On Saturday from 09.00 to 12.30 he is paid at $1\frac{1}{2}$ times normal rate per hour. Find his week's wage.

32 (a) A town has a total rateable value of £50 000 000. If the rate is fixed at 63p in the £, how much is collected in rates?
(b) If a penny rate in a district raises £14 800 what is the total rateable value?
(c) A city has a rateable value of £65 500 000 and wishes to collect £34 060 000 in rates. What rate in the pound should be fixed?

33 The exchange rate between Britain and a foreign country is \$1.80 to £1, travelling in both directions.
(a) On holiday, a woman wishes to change £78.50 into foreign money. How much will she receive?
(b) On returning, she has \$13.68 which she changes back into British money. How much was that amount?

34 (a) If a man makes a $5\frac{1}{2}$% loss selling a cycle which originally cost him £136, how much does he receive for it?
(b) A second-hand car is sold for £3660 which is 75% of the price when it was bought. How much did the owner pay for the car in the first place?

Probability

Revision notes

Development of Choice

▶ The choice is from 3 cards each with letter X, 2 cards each with letter Y and 5 cards each lettered Z. (After each single choice, the card is kept.)

(a) What is the probability of choosing letter Y twice?
(b) What are the chances letter X could be chosen three times?
(c) Work out the chances of obtaining XYZ in that order.
(d) What are the chances of obtaining XYZ in any order?

(a) Total possibilities = 10.

Chances of obtaining Y first time $= \frac{2}{10} = \frac{1}{5}$.

There are now only 9 possibilities and only 1 is letter Y.

Chances of obtaining second Y $= \frac{1}{9}$.

Chances of choosing letter Y twice $= \frac{1}{5} \times \frac{1}{9} = \frac{1}{45}$.

(b) Chances of obtaining X once $= \frac{3}{10}$.

Chances of X second time $= \frac{2}{9}$.

Chances of X third time $= \frac{1}{8}$.

Chances of X three times $= \frac{3}{10} \times \frac{2}{9} \times \frac{1}{8} = \frac{1}{120}$.

(c) Probability of obtaining X $= \frac{3}{10}$.

Probability of Y on second choice $= \frac{2}{9}$.

Probability of Z on third choice $= \frac{5}{8}$.

Probability of obtaining XYZ $= \frac{3}{10} \times \frac{2}{9} \times \frac{5}{8} = \frac{1}{24}$.

(d) This involves addition of probabilities for these combinations:

XYZ XZY YXZ YZX ZXY ZYX

Chances of obtaining XYZ $= \frac{1}{24}$ (from last working).

The probability for each combination is $\frac{1}{24}$.

Add the probabilities $\frac{1}{24} + \frac{1}{24} + \frac{1}{24} + \frac{1}{24} + \frac{1}{24} + \frac{1}{24} = \frac{6}{24} = \frac{1}{4}$.

Using a Branch Diagram

When mixed choices are involved or when a choice depends upon a previous choice, a branch diagram is sometimes useful.

▶ In a pack of 5 cards are 2 Red cards and 3 Blue cards. When a card is chosen it is returned to the pack. After two choices what is the probability of getting (a) two Blue cards (b) one of each colour?

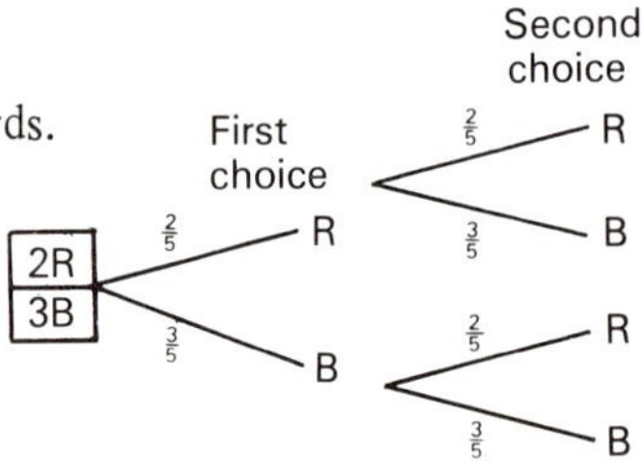

(a) The branch diagram shows each probability. Five cards are involved each time.

Probability of two Blue cards $= \frac{3}{5} \times \frac{3}{5} = \frac{9}{25}$.

(b) Probability of different colours involves Red-Blue, Blue-Red.

Probability of Red-Blue $= \frac{2}{5} \times \frac{3}{5} = \frac{6}{25}$.

Probability of Blue-Red $= \frac{3}{5} \times \frac{2}{5} = \frac{6}{25}$.

Probability of different colours $= \frac{6}{25} + \frac{6}{25} = \frac{12}{25}$.

If a card is kept after a random choice instead of being returned to the pack, the diagram shows the difference in probabilities.

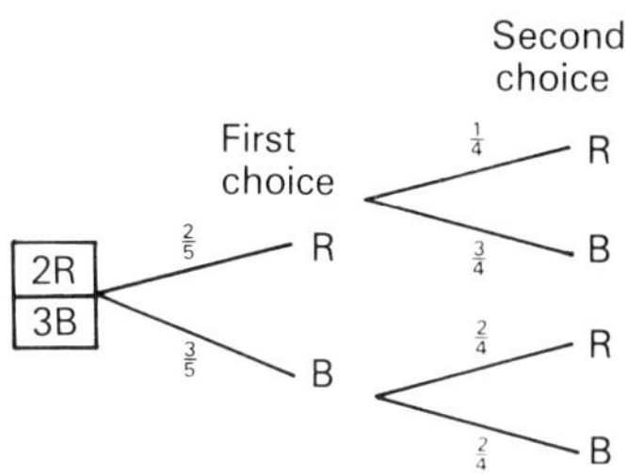

Notice that there are only four cards in the second choice.

The probability of two blue cards $= \frac{3}{5} \times \frac{2}{4} = \frac{3}{10}$.

The probability of different colours $= \left(\frac{2}{5} \times \frac{3}{4}\right) + \left(\frac{3}{5} \times \frac{2}{4}\right)$

$= \frac{3}{10} + \frac{3}{10} = \frac{6}{10} = \frac{3}{5}$.

Revision exercises

1 In a drawer are two white socks and two black socks. If you had to make a choice in the dark
   (a) what are your chances of choosing one black sock,
   (b) and you take out two socks, what are your chances of bringing out a pair, black or white,
   (c) how many would you have to take out of the drawer to make sure you had a pair?

2 In a drawer are 3 black ties, two blue ties and a red one. If you had to make a choice without looking at the ties
   (a) what are your chances of choosing a blue tie,
   (b) what are your chances of missing a blue tie,
   (c) what are the chances you would get a red or blue tie?

3 There are 2 pairs of white gloves and two pairs of black gloves in a drawer. You are not allowed to feel the gloves to decide on a left or a right.
   (a) What are your chances of obtaining one glove of the colour you name?
   (b) What are the chances you can choose a pair, black or white?
   (c) How many gloves must you remove from the drawer to make sure you had a pair?

4 Draw a branch diagram to show all the chances for the tossing of (a) three coins, (b) four coins.

5 A spinner has three numbers, 1, 2, and 3 on it and it may stop at any number. Draw a branch diagram to obtain all the possible chances if we spin it (a) twice, (b) three times.

6 A box contains four coloured cards from which you can choose one card. After replacing the card, you may then choose again. The four colours are Red, Blue, Yellow and Green. Using the first letters of the colours, draw the branch diagram to show all the possible sequences if you make two choices; then, without a diagram, say how many possibilities there are for four choices.

7 Use your branch diagram for tossing three coins, to say what the chances are of obtaining
(a) three heads,
(b) two tails, one head,
(c) three coins the same,
(d) only one head,
(e) at least one tail,
(f) at least two heads.

8 Look back to your branch diagram for tossing four coins. What are the chances of obtaining
(a) two heads, two tails,
(b) all coins the same,
(c) three tails, one head,
(d) at least two heads,
(e) one coin different from the others,
(f) three coins the same,
(g) at least three tails,
(h) at least one head?

9 Refer to the branch diagram you made for the spinner (Q.5) with three numbers 1, 2, and 3. If we make three spins what are the chances of getting
(a) three numbers the same,
(b) one of each number in any order,
(c) only two numbers the same,
(d) at least two numbers the same,
(e) at least one number 2,
(f) at least two number 3's?

10 Look at the branch diagram for choosing twice from the box of coloured cards, Red, Blue, Yellow and Green (Q.6). The first card is replaced before the second is chosen. How many possibilities are there? What are the chances of
(a) choosing two colours the same,
(b) taking out at least one blue card,
(c) obtaining blue and red in any order,
(d) getting a red or yellow followed by green,
(e) choosing a yellow followed by blue or green,
(f) getting a red, yellow or green followed by blue,
(g) taking out any two different colours?

11 The names of 8 boys and 12 girls are placed in a hat. Four boys and two girls wear spectacles. If you choose a name from the hat what are the chances it will be
(a) a boy's name,
(b) a girl's name,
(c) a girl without spectacles,
(d) a boy with spectacles?

12 In a race are three Americans, two Russians, three UK runners and four Germans. What are the chances that
(a) the winner will be a Russian,
(b) a UK runner will be last,
(c) the winner will not be an American,
(d) the last man will not be a German?

13 On sale are 10 red ties, 15 blue ties, 12 brown ties and 11 green ties. My wife may choose any colour tie for my birthday. What are the chances I shall receive
(a) a blue tie, (b) a brown tie, (c) a red tie, (d) a tie which is not blue, (e) a tie which is not blue or green?

14 In each suit in a pack of cards there is one Ace, one King, one Queen, one Knave and one of each of the numbers two to ten, so in the pack there are 4 Aces, 4 Kings, 4 Queens and so on. If I choose one card from the whole pack, what are the chances I shall pick
(a) an Ace, (b) a King or Queen, (c) a red Knave, (d) a card which is any number from 2 to 10?

15 A particular game uses only 4 Aces, 4 Kings, 4 Queens, 4 Jacks and 4 Tens. If I choose one from that pack, what is the probability I shall obtain
(a) a Queen,
(b) an Ace or a Ten,
(c) a card other than an Ace or a Jack,
(d) a red Ace or red King,
(e) a card which is not black and is not a Queen?

* **16** In a bag are four Red balls and six Blue balls. Use a branch diagram to work out the chances of choosing
(a) Red, Blue, (b) Blue, Red, (c) Blue, Blue.
With which combination is there the best chance?

* **17** In a box are twelve ribbons. Three of them are Blue, four are Red and five are Green. What are the chances of choosing
(a) two Red ones, (b) two Green ones,
(c) two Blue ribbons,
(d) Blue, Red, Green in that order?
In the last instance would the probability be better for choosing them in reverse order?

* **18** In a box are nine cards, three with figure 0, five with figure 1 and one with a 2 on it. Cards are taken, kept and placed in the order of being chosen to form a number. Find the chances of making
(a) 21 (b) 12 (c) 10 (d) 120 (e) 100 (f) 111 (g) 1200 (h) 2000.

* **19** A box contains 6 red discs, 4 blue discs and 2 yellow discs.
(a) What are the chances of choosing (i) two red discs, (ii) two blue discs, (iii) two yellow discs?
(b) Add your three answers to find the probability of choosing two discs of the same colour.

* **20** Using 4 Kings, 4 Queens, 4 Knaves, what are the chances of choosing
(a) two cards of the same kind,
(b) King, Queen, Knave in that order,
(c) King, Queen, Knave in any order?

* **21** Three teams A, B and C each enter three runners in a race. What are the chances that
(a) team A will come first and second,
(b) team C will come first and second,
(c) any team will occupy the first two places,
(d) team B will take the first three places,
(e) The result will be A, B, C, in that order?

* **22** In a group of sixteen children, four are born in January and the other twelve in other months of the year. I do not know in which month any child is born when I am choosing a team. What is the probability I shall choose
(a) a team of two born in January,
(b) a team of two, neither born in January,
(c) a team of two, only one of whom has a birthday in January,
(d) a team of three, only two of whom were born in January,
(e) a team of four, all born in January?

* **23** In a group of 21 people, 7 are British, 9 are American and 5 are Australian. They are applying to join me on an expedition and I do not know their nationalities. If I only require two people from that group, what are the chances I shall choose
(a) two Americans,
(b) two British people,
(c) two Australians,
(d) an American and a British person,
(e) a British member and an Australian?

If I decide to take three from that group, what are the chances I shall choose
(f) three Australians,
(g) one of each nationality?

Algebra

Revision notes

Indices When terms are multiplied, indices are added.
When terms are divided, indices are subtracted.

▶ Simplify (a) $a^3b^2c \times 2ab^3c^2$ (b) $6x^4yz^3 \div 2xy^2z$ (c) $\dfrac{4x^2y^4z}{2xyz^3}$

(d) $\dfrac{9ab^2c}{3a^4bc^3}$ (e) $\dfrac{2a^2b}{6ac^2} \times \dfrac{3ab^3c}{2bc^3}$ (f) $\dfrac{4x^2y^3}{x^5y} \div \dfrac{8xy^2}{3xy^3}$

(a) $a^3b^2c \times 2ab^3c^2$

$= 2a^4b^5c^3$.

(b) $6x^4yz^3 \div 2xy^2z$

$= 3x^3y^{-1}z^2$ or $\dfrac{3x^3z^2}{y}$.

(c) $\dfrac{4x^2y^4z}{2xyz^3}$

$= 2xy^3z^{-2}$ or $\dfrac{2xy^3}{z^2}$.

(d) $\dfrac{9ab^2c}{3a^4bc^3}$

$= 3a^{-3}bc^{-2}$

or $\dfrac{3b}{a^3c^2}$.

(e) $\dfrac{2a^2b}{6ac^2} \times \dfrac{3ab^3c}{2bc^3}$

$= \dfrac{6a^3b^4c}{12abc^5}$

$= \frac{1}{2}a^2b^3c^{-4}$ or $\dfrac{a^2b^3}{2c^4}$

(f) $\dfrac{4x^2y^3}{x^5y} \div \dfrac{8xy^2}{3xy^3}$

$= \dfrac{4x^2y^3}{x^5y} \times \dfrac{3xy^3}{8xy^2}$

$= \dfrac{12x^3y^6}{8x^6y^3}$

$= \dfrac{3}{2}x^{-3}y^3$ or $\dfrac{3y^3}{2x^3}$.

Fractional indices indicate roots.
Negative indices indicate reciprocals.

$x^{-1} = \dfrac{1}{x}$ $y^{-3} = \dfrac{1}{y^3}$ $3^{-1} = \dfrac{1}{3}$ $2^{-2} = \dfrac{1}{2^2} = \dfrac{1}{4}$

$x^{1/2} = \sqrt{x}$ $y^{1/3} = \sqrt[3]{y}$ $4^{1/2} = \sqrt{4} = 2$ $8^{-1/3} = \dfrac{1}{\sqrt[3]{8}} = \dfrac{1}{2}$.

Simultaneous Equations

Eliminate one of the unknowns.
Substitute to find the second unknown.

▶ Solve these simultaneous equations:

$$2x - 3y = 12$$
$$5x + 2y = 11.$$

To eliminate y, multiply the first equation by 2 and the second by 3.
This produces these new equations:

$$4x - 6y = 24$$
$$15x + 6y = 33$$

Add the terms of the equations: $19x = 57$

$$x = 3$$

Substitute $x = 3$ in the first original equation:

$$6 - 3y = 12$$
$$-3y = 6$$
$$y = -2.$$

The simultaneous solution is $x = 3$ and $y = -2$.

Factorisation

Just as 12 resolved into factor form is $2 \times 2 \times 3$,
so $4x^2 - 8x - 12$ in factor form is $4(x-3)(x+1)$.

$4(x-3)(x+1)$ expanded is $4(x^2 - 2x - 3) = 4x^2 - 8x - 12$.

▶ Factorise (a) $4xy - 8x^2y$ (b) $x^2 - 4y^2$ (c) $x^2 - x - 6$ (d) $12x^2 + 12x - 9$.

(a) $4xy - 8x^2y$
$= 4xy(1 - 2x)$.

(b) $x^2 - 4y^2$
$= (x + 2y)(x - 2y)$.

(c) $x^2 - x - 6$
$= (x - 3)(x + 2)$.

(d) $12x^2 + 12x - 9$
$= 3(4x^2 + 4x - 3)$
$= 3(2x - 1)(2x + 3)$.

Quadratic Equations

Obtain the factors when the expression is equated to 0. Each factor may then be equal to 0.

▶ Solve (a) $x^2 - 2x - 15 = 0$ (b) $6x^2 = 3 - 7x$.

(a) $x^2 - 2x - 15 = 0$
$(x + 3)(x - 5) = 0$
Either $x + 3 = 0$ or $x - 5 = 0$
$x = -3$ or 5.

(b) $6x^2 = 3 - 7x$
or
$6x^2 + 7x - 3 = 0$
$(2x + 3)(3x - 1) = 0$
Either $2x + 3 = 0$ or $3x - 1 = 0$
$x = -1\frac{1}{2}$ or $\frac{1}{3}$.

By formula, when a graph is drawn, the solution of a quadratic equation is shown where the graph cuts the x-axis (where $y = 0$). If that does not happen, it has no real roots (no solution).

In the form $ax^2 + bx + c = 0$ the solution can be found using the formula

$$x = \frac{-b \pm \sqrt{b^2 - 4ac}}{2a}$$

by substituting the values for a, b and c from the equation.

▶ Use the formula to solve $3x^2 + 4x = 3$.

The equation may be written $3x^2 + 4x - 3 = 0$.
In this case $a = 3, b = 4, c = -3$.

$$x = \frac{-4 \pm \sqrt{16 + 36}}{6}$$

$$= \frac{-4 \pm \sqrt{52}}{6} = \frac{-4 \pm 7.21}{6}$$

$$= \frac{3.21}{6} \quad \text{or} \quad \frac{-11.21}{6}$$

$$= 0.54 \quad \text{or} \quad -1.87 \text{ (2 decimal places).}$$

If $b^2 < 4ac$ the equation has no real solution.

Revision exercises

1 Solve each equation by finding the value of x.

(a) $3x - 2 = x + 6$ (b) $4x + 4 = 2x + 10$
(c) $2x + 6 = 7x - 4$ (d) $10x - 4 = 4x + 11$
(e) $3x + 2(x + 3) = 4$ (f) $2x - 3(2x - 3) = 2(x - 1)$
(g) $4(2 - x) - (x - 3) = 2$ (h) $4(2 - x) = 5 - 3(2x + 1)$.

2 Solve these equations

(a) $\dfrac{2x - 3}{3} = 5$ (b) $\dfrac{3x + 2}{2} = \dfrac{1}{3}$

(c) $\dfrac{2x - 1}{3} = 2x$ (d) $\dfrac{x - 4}{2} = \dfrac{2x + 1}{3}$

(e) $\dfrac{4x - 1}{2} = 3x - 2$ (f) $5 - \dfrac{(x + 1)}{3} = \dfrac{2x - 1}{5}$.

3 Draw graphs of these equations, using axes labelled from -5 to 5. State the gradient of each graph.

(a) $y = 3x + 2$ (b) $y = 2x - 1$ (c) $y = 3x - 2$
(d) $y = 4x - 3$ (e) $y = -2x + 2$ (f) $y = -3x - 1$
(g) $2y = x - 2$ (h) $3y = -x + 2$ (i) $2y = 3x - 6$.

4 Where do these graphs cut the y-axis ($x = 0$)?
(a) $y = x$ (b) $y = 5x$ (c) $y = 2x - 1$ (d) $y = 2x + 1$
(e) $y = 3x - 4$ (f) $y = \frac{x}{3} + 2$ (g) $3y = x - 12$ (h) $y + x = 2$
(i) $y + 2x + 3 = 0$ (j) $y = 3 - 2x$ (k) $\frac{y}{2} = 4 - 2x$ (l) $y + 3 = -2x$.

5 Where do these graphs cut the x-axis ($y = 0$)?
(a) $y = -x$ (b) $y = 3x$ (c) $y = x - 1$ (d) $y = 2x + 1$
(e) $y = -x + 4$ (f) $y = 3x - 1$ (g) $y = 5x - 2$ (h) $\frac{y}{2} = -x - 2$
(i) $y = \frac{x}{2} - 3$ (j) $y = \frac{x}{3} + 4$ (k) $y = -\frac{x}{2} + 3$ (l) $y = -4x - 1$.

6 Simplify
(a) $a^2b \times a^3b$ (b) $b^4c^2 \times bc$ (c) $b^5y^2 \times b^3y$
(d) $a^5c^4 \div c^2a$ (e) $y^5d^3 \div d^2y^4$ (f) $a^7d^5 \div da^5$
(g) $2b^4y^3c \times 5b^2yc^2$ (h) $\frac{10b^2a^3c}{2ba^2c^4}$ (i) $\frac{8by^2c^4}{6yc}$.

7 Simplify (a) $\frac{adc^2e}{c^3d^2} \times \frac{2d^4}{5da^2}$ (b) $\frac{2b}{3e^2} \times \frac{9d^4e}{8d^2b^3}$
(c) $\frac{2a^2bc^4}{a^2c^2} \div \frac{3ab^5c}{2b^3c}$ (d) $\frac{3b^3de^2}{4d^2e^2} \div \frac{b^2d^2e}{2be^3}$.

8 Find the value of
(a) 2^{-1} (b) $4^{1/2}$ (c) $25^{1/2}$ (d) 3^{-1} (e) 2^{-2} (f) $100^{1/2}$ (g) 3^0
(h) 4^{-2} (i) 1^{-1} (j) 1^0 (k) $4^{-1/2}$ (l) $16^{-1/2}$.

9 Simplify
(a) $a^2b \times a^{-1}b^2$ (b) $a^{-2}b \times a^2b^2$ (c) $a^3b^2 \div a^{-1}b^{-1}$
(d) $ab^{-2} \div a^2b^{-1}$ (e) $a^{-1}b^{-2} \times a^3b^{-1}$ (f) $a^{1/2}b^{-1/2} \div ab$.

10 Find the value of
(a) $4^{3/2}$ (b) $8^{2/3}$ (c) $1^{5/2}$ (d) $27^{-1/3}$ (e) $100^{-3/2}$ (f) $(-1)^0$
(g) $(\frac{1}{4})^{1/2}$ (h) $(\frac{9}{16})^{1/2}$.

11 Solve these simultaneous equations
(a) $y + 2x = 6$, $5x + y = 12$ (b) $3x + y = 12$, $7x = y + 8$ (c) $y - x = 15$, $y = 29 + 3x$
(d) $4y = 2x + 2$, $3y + 3 = 3x$ (e) $5x = 2y - 5$, $3x = 23 - 4y$ (f) $2x + 5y = 3$, $3x + 5 = 2y$
(g) $3y - 5x = 35$, $2x = 2y - 18$ (h) $4y - 12x = 25$, $2x = 10 - 5y$ (i) $8x = 10y - 27$, $10x = 8y - 27$.

12 (a) By drawing graphs on the same axes, solve the simultaneous equations $5x = y - 13$ and $2x - 3y = 0$.
(b) Check your results with a calculation.

13 $A = 4x + 2y$ and $B = 3x - 3y$.
(a) Find $A + B$ in terms of x and y.
(b) Find $A - B$ in terms of x if $x = y$.
(c) Find x and y if $A = -14$ and $B = 3$.

14 Using the equations $2A = 3C - 2D$ and $B = 2C + 3D$
(a) find $2A - B$ when $C = -1$ and $D = 2$,
(b) when $C = D$ find $2A - 2B$ in terms of C,
(c) find $\frac{A}{B}$ when $C = -2$ and $D = 1$,
(d) find C and D when $A = -\frac{1}{2}$ and $B = -18$.

15 Write the factors of the expressions
(a) $6x^2 + 5x$ (b) $3y - y^2$ (c) $4y^2 - 10y$
(d) $8x^2y + 2xy - 6xy^2$ (e) $9xy^2 - 12y^2x^2$ (f) $5x^2y - 10xy^2 - 5y^2$
(g) $x^2y^2 + 3x^2y - 4xy^2$ (h) $5xy^2 - 10x^2y^2 - 5y^3$ (i) $12x^3 - 6yx^2 + 9y^2x^2$.

16 Factorise
(a) $x^2 - 9$ (b) $x^2 - 36$ (c) $9x^2 - 49$ (d) $25y^2 - 64$
(e) $18x^2 - 8y^2$ (f) $12x^2 - 75y^2$ (g) $27a^2 - 48b^2$ (h) $54x^2 - 24y^2$.

17 Factorise
(a) $x^2 + x - 12$ (b) $x^2 - 3x - 10$ (c) $x^2 - 9x + 20$
(d) $2x^2 + x - 1$ (e) $2x^2 - x - 1$ (f) $2x^2 - 3x + 1$.

18 Factorise
(a) $2x^2 - 4x + 2$ (b) $2x^2 + x - 3$ (c) $6x^2 - 3x - 3$
(d) $6x^2 + 8x - 8$ (e) $6x^2 + 14x + 4$ (f) $3x^2 - 2x - 8$
(g) $5x^2 - 27x + 10$ (h) $6x^2 + 22x - 8$ (i) $10x^2 + 14x - 12$.

19 (a) Use the equation $y = 2x^2$. After working out a set of values, draw a graph. What difference does the coefficient 2 make to the shape of a graph? What are the coordinates of the turning point? Is it a maximum or a minimum value of the function?

(b) Without drawing a graph, say whether $y = -2x^2$ will have a maximum or minimum turning point.

(c) Draw the graph of $y = \frac{x^2}{2}$. Note the effect of the coefficient $\frac{1}{2}$.

(d) Without drawing a graph, describe what you would expect using $y = -\frac{x^2}{2}$.

20 Here is a table of values for $y = x^2 - 2$:

x	-5	-4	-3	-2	-1	0	1	2	3	4	5
y	23	14	7	2	-1	-2	-1	2	7	14	23

Plotting those points produces this graph:

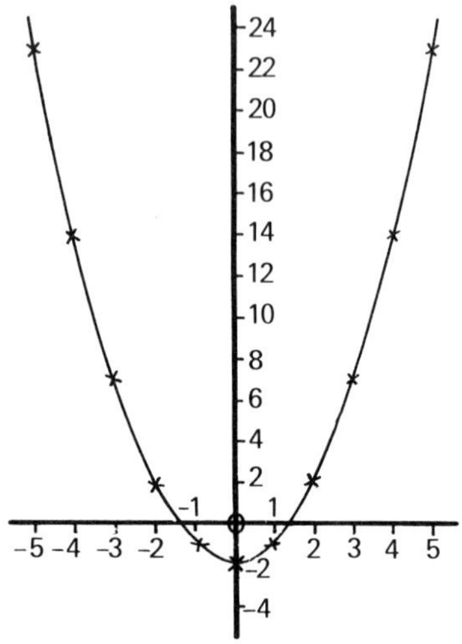

Notice what has happened to the graph. On your own piece of graph paper draw that graph of $y = x^2 - 2$.

Without any drawing, describe the graph of $y = -x^2 - 2$.

21 Describe the graph of $y = x^2 + 2$. Calculate a table of values and draw the graph to check your description.

* **22** This is the graph of $y = 2x^2 - x - 3$:

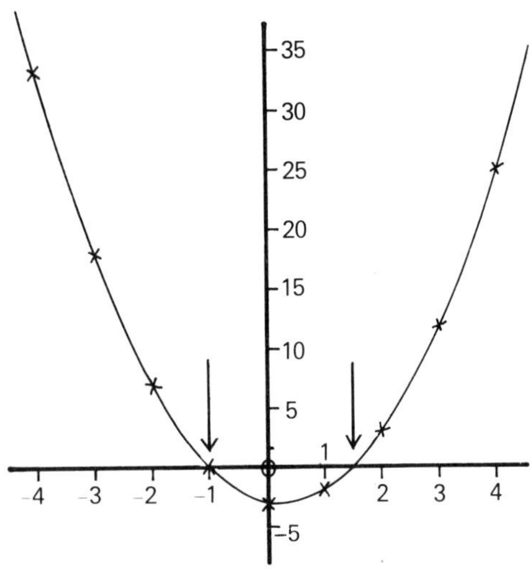

Work out some values and plot the graph yourself. The minimum value is a turning point at $(\frac{1}{4}, -3\frac{1}{8})$.

If we give y the value of 0 in the equation, we can write

$$2x^2 - x - 3 = 0.$$

That is called a quadratic equation and its solution is given on the graph where $y = 0$. The graph cuts the x-axis at $1\frac{1}{2}$ and -1.
The solution of $2x^2 - x - 3 = 0$ is $x = 1\frac{1}{2}$ or $x = -1$.

* **23** (a) Make a table of values for the function $y = 2x^2 + 5x - 3$ from $x = -6$ to $x = 3$. Plot the parabola.
(b) From your graph find the solution of the equation $2x^2 + 5x - 3 = 0$.

* **24** By plotting a graph of $y = 2x^2 + 3x - 9$ using values of x from -4 to 3, solve the equation $2x^2 + 3x - 9 = 0$.

* **25** (a) Use factors to solve the equation $x^2 + 2x - 8 = 0$.
(b) Draw a graph of $y = x^2 + 2x - 8$ and use it to check the solution you obtained by factors.

* **26** Use factors to solve the equations

(a) $x^2 - 16 = 0$	(b) $9x^2 - 4 = 0$	(c) $6x^2 - 5x + 1 = 0$
(d) $3x^2 - 14x + 8 = 0$	(e) $x^2 - 5x = 36$	(f) $6x^2 - 6x - 12 = 0$
(g) $2x^2 + 3x - 9 = 0$	(h) $4x^2 = 1$	(i) $2x^2 + x - 15 = 0$
(j) $4x^2 + 12x = 7$	(k) $9x^2 - 6x + 1 = 0$	(l) $4x^2 - 12x + 9 = 0$.

* **27** In the form $ax^2 + bx + c = 0$, what are the values of a, b and c in each of these equations?

(a) $3x^2 + 2x - 2 = 0$	(b) $5x^2 - 6x + 3 = 0$	(c) $5x - 2 - 2x^2 = 0$
(d) $8 - 3x - x^2 = 0$	(e) $6x + 3 - x^2 = 0$	(f) $x^2 - 6 = 0$
(g) $3x^2 - 8x = 0$	(h) $15 - 3x^2 = 0$	(i) $5x - 2x^2 = 0$.

* **28** Use a formula to solve the equations

(a) $x^2 - 5x - 36 = 0$	(b) $6x^2 - 5x + 1 = 0$	(c) $3x^2 + 4x - 15 = 0$
(d) $6x^2 - 6x - 12 = 0$	(e) $3x^2 - 14x + 8 = 0$	(f) $15x^2 + 24x - 12 = 0$
(g) $16x^2 - 25 = 0$	(h) $x^2 - x - 20 = 0$	(i) $10x^2 - x - 2 = 0$.

* **29** Find the roots of the equations

(a) $3x^2 - 9x + 2 = 0$	(b) $3x^2 + 6x - 2 = 0$	(c) $2x^2 - 13x + 15 = 0$
(d) $7 - 26x - 8x^2 = 0$	(e) $3x^2 = 3 - 4x$	(f) $4x^2 + 2 = 8x$
(g) $5x^2 - 8x = 1$	(h) $7x^2 + 9x - 2 = 0$	(i) $4 + 3x - 6x^2 = 0$.

* **30** An equation has no real roots if $b^2 < 4ac$. Which of these equations have real roots?

(a) $2x^2 + 3x + 6 = 0$	(b) $3x^2 - 5x + 5 = 0$	(c) $6x - 2x^2 - 1 = 0$
(d) $9 + x^2 - 6x = 0$	(e) $3x - 4x^2 = 1$	(f) $7x - 3 = 2x^2$
(g) $5x^2 + 4x - 3 = 0$	(h) $4x^2 = 7x - 1$	(i) $6x^2 - 8x = 0$.

Pythagoras

Revision notes

▶ (a) XY is the diameter of a circle centre O. Z is a point on the circumference, such that XZ = YZ = 8 cm.

Calculate the radius of the circle.

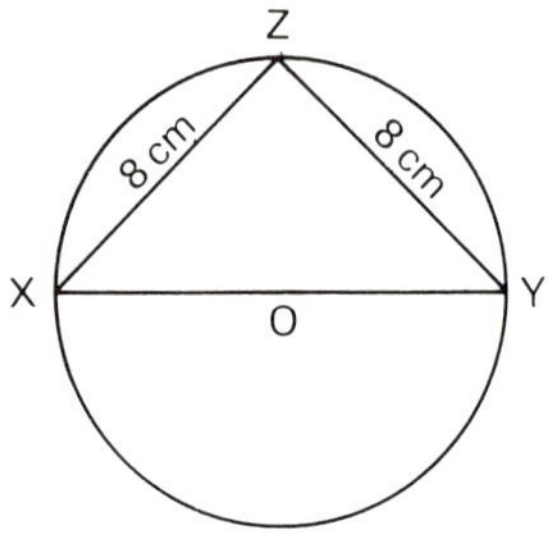

(b) Two ships left the same port A. When they were 12.5 km apart, one gave its position from A as 7 km, bearing 180°, and the second said it was 10.2 km due East of A. If the distances are correct, prove that there had been a slight error in navigation.

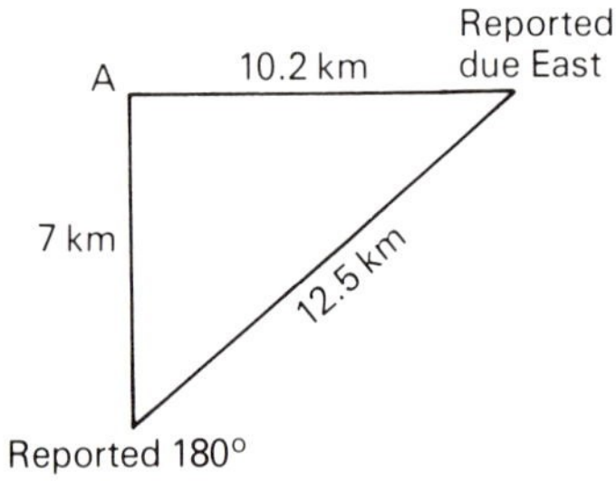

(a) Since XY is a diameter, $\angle XZY = 90°$.

$$\begin{aligned} XY^2 &= XZ^2 + ZY^2 \\ &= 64 + 64 \\ &= 128 \\ XY &= 11.3 \text{ cm.} \end{aligned}$$

The radius of the circle is 5.65 cm.

(b) $(12.5)^2 = 156.25$

$7^2 = 49 \quad (10.2)^2 = 104.04.$

$7^2 + (10.2)^2 = 153.04.$

Since $156.25 > 153.04$, one or both of the bearings 180° and 090° must be incorrect.

(It is worth noting that certain right-angled triangles can be formed with sides which are whole numbers. The better known sets of numbers are 3, 4, 5 and 5, 12, 13.)

Revision exercises

1 Construct each triangle ABC and in each case measure the largest angle. Prove by calculation that your answer is correct.

(a) AB = 2.4 cm, BC = 4.5 cm, AC = 5.1 cm.
(b) BC = 2.1 cm, AB = 7.2 cm, AC = 7.5 cm.
(c) AC = 4 cm, BC = 4.2 cm, AB = 5.8 cm.
(d) AB = 1.2 cm, BC = 3.5 cm, AC = 3.7 cm.
(e) AC = 4 cm, AB = 7.5 cm, BC = 8.5 cm.

2 In each triangle, decide whether the largest angle is right, acute or obtuse.

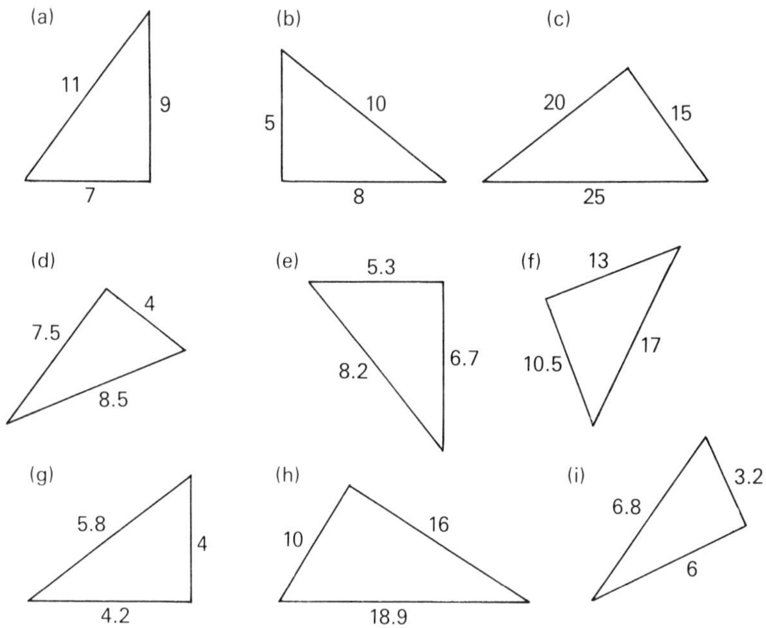

3 In this right-angled triangle, the lengths of the three sides are represented by letters *a*, *b* and *c* with letter *a* as the hypotenuse. We know from the Pythagoras rule that $a^2 = b^2 + c^2$. Rewrite the formula (a) to read $b^2 =$, (b) to read $c^2 =$

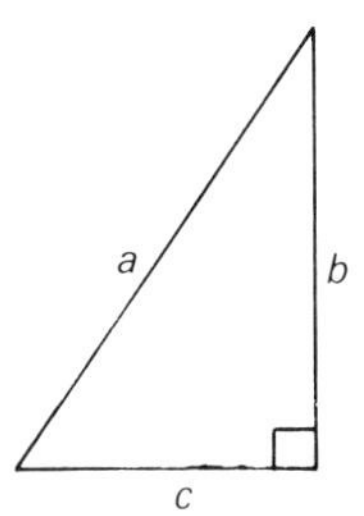

4 In each triangle calculate the side marked with a letter. You may use tables. Give answers correct to three significant figures.

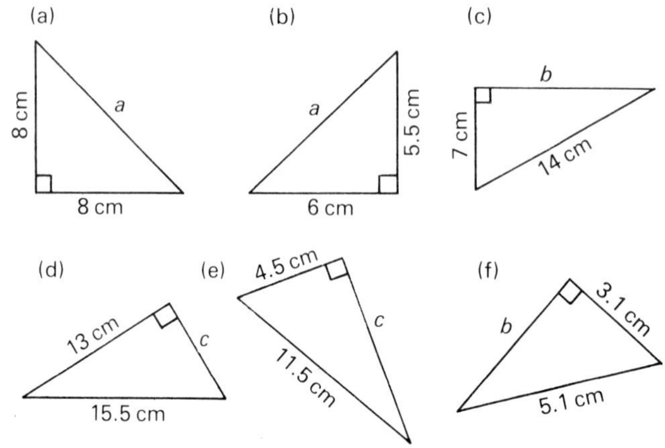

5 In the formula $a^2 = b^2 + c^2$, find correct to 3 significant figures

(a) a when $b = 10, c = 9$
(b) b when $a = 21, c = 12$
(c) c when $a = 2, b = 1$
(d) b when $c = 1\frac{1}{2}, a = 2\frac{1}{2}$
(e) a when $b = 15.2, c = 2.4$
(f) c when $a = 10.4, b = 4.5$.

In all the remaining exercises, correct answers to 3 significant figures.

6 A square has a side of 3.8 cm. Use the Pythagoras rule to find the length of the diagonal.

7 In this triangle
(a) find the vertical height x in metres,
(b) calculate the side y.

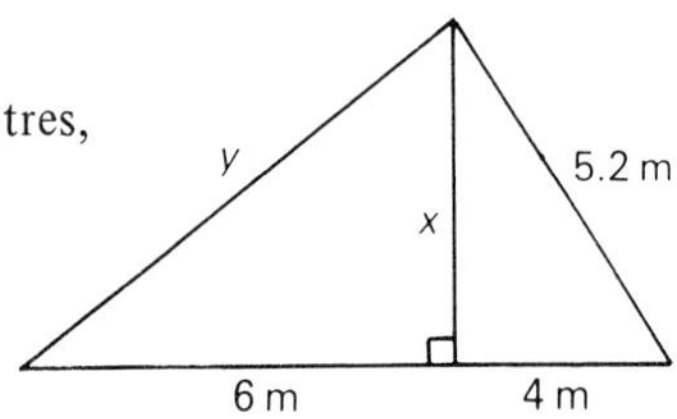

8 In this triangle ABC, AB = 3.2 cm, AC = 4.6 cm and the vertical height BD = 2.4 cm.
Calculate the length of the third side BC.

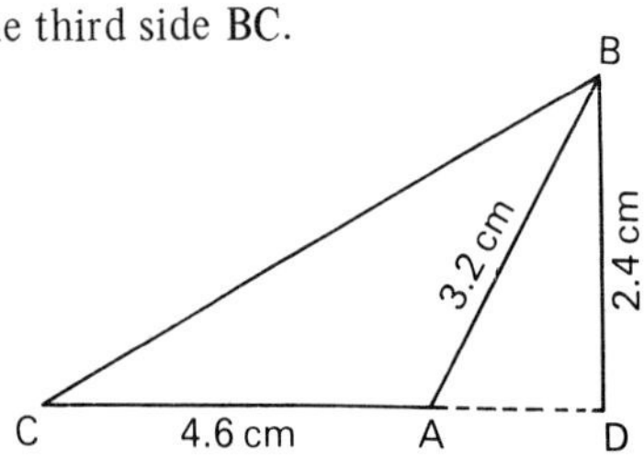

9 In the rhombus ABCD, the length of a side is 8 cm and the longer diagonal BD is 13 cm.
Calculate the length of the shorter diagonal AC.

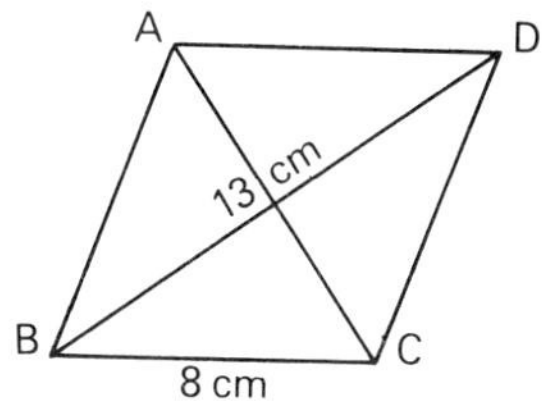

10 In the kite ABCD, side AD = 3 cm, side CD = 5 cm and the diagonal BD = 3.2 cm.
Calculate the length of diagonal AC.

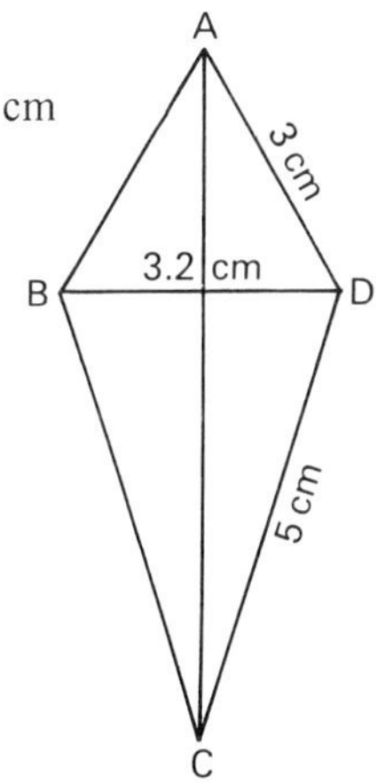

11 A rectangular floor has a length of 6.2 metres and a width of 5.2 metres. How long is the diagonal?

12 A ladder, $4\frac{1}{2}$ metres long, is resting against a vertical wall with its foot on horizontal ground $1\frac{1}{2}$ metres from the bottom of the wall. How far up the wall is the top of the ladder?

13 From the same port, one ship travels North a distance of 23 kilometres and a second ship travels East for a distance of 15 kilometres. How far are the ships apart at that time?

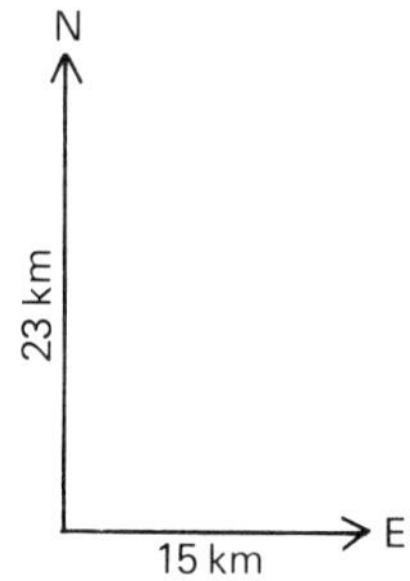

14 Town A is 35 km from town B on a bearing of 045°. Town C is 55 km from town B on a bearing of 135°. Calculate the straight line distance between town C and town A.

15 A plane flies 48 km from A, due East to B, then 48 km due North to C and finally 28 km on a bearing 315° to D.

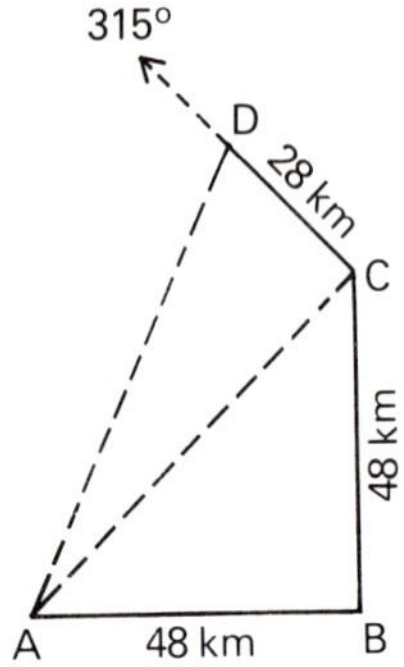

(a) What is ∠BCA? (b) What is ∠ACD?
(c) Calculate distance AC. (d) Calculate distance AD.

16 This is a regular arrowhead with measurements as shown in the diagram.
Calculate (a) AB (b) BC.

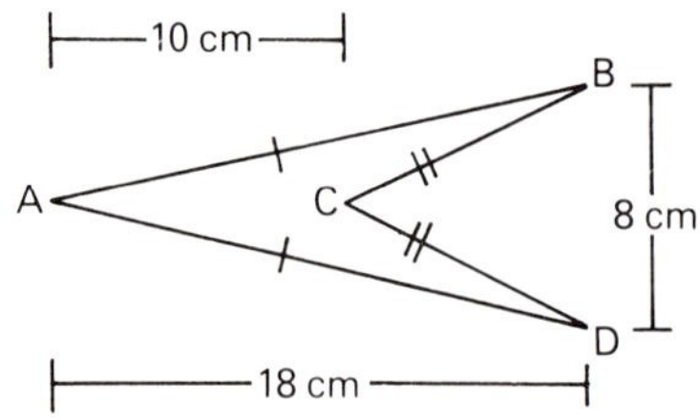

17 (a) An equilateral triangle ABC has a side of 8.4 cm. Find the vertical height of C above AB.

(b) An isosceles triangle ABC stands on base AB which is 15 cm long. Angle A equals angle B and the length of BC is 9.5 cm. Calculate the distance of C from the midpoint of AB.

18 AB is the diameter of a circle centre O. AC is a chord 6 cm long and CB is a chord 5 cm long. D is the centre point of BC.
Calculate (a) the radius AO (b) length OD.

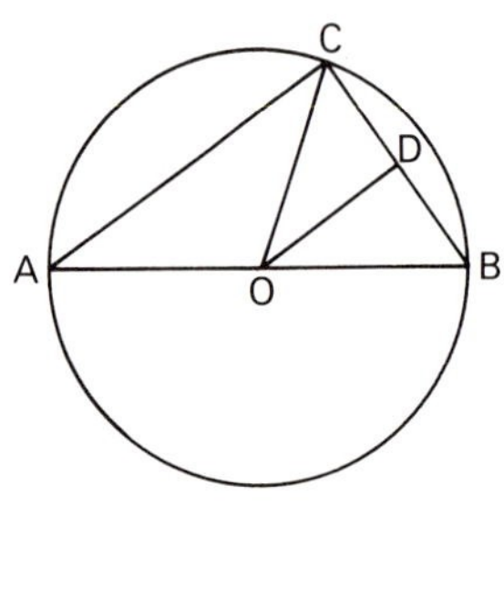

19 Two guy ropes are attached to a pole XY. AB = 8 metres and CD = 7 metres. B is attached 1.5 metres from the top X. AY = 3 metres and CY = 2.5 metres. Calculate (a) XY (b) BD.

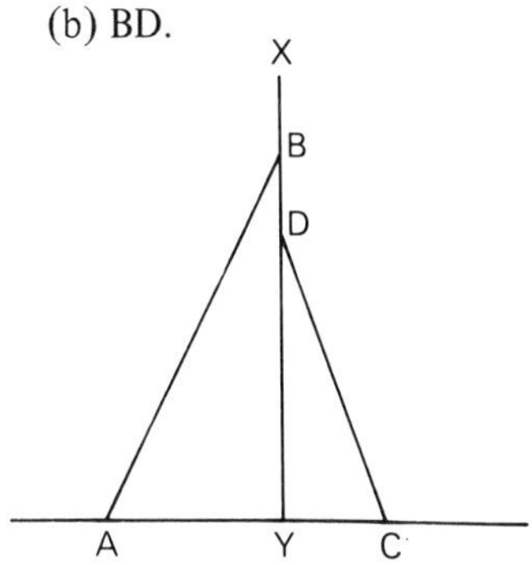

20 Two circles of radii 25 cm and 39 cm respectively, intersect so that the length of the common chord is 30 cm. Calculate the straight-line distance between the two centres.

Statistics

Revision notes

The *frequency* is the number of times a particular item appears. A frequency curve is obtained by plotting a graph of the frequencies (vertical axis) against the items (horizontal axis). When items in a frequency table are added successively, a cumulative frequency table is obtained and those figures can be used to obtain a cumulative frequency curve (ogive).

▶ Use this table of weights to answer the questions which follow:

64	33	55	66	72	50	37	46
80	38	71	61	89	49	43	58
86	77	69	55	91	86	75	87
53	62	71	47	33	50	85	65

(a) Calculate the arithmetic mean of the weights.
(b) Find the median of those statistics.
(c) Make a frequency table to obtain the modal weight.
(d) Use intervals of 0 to 5, 6 to 10 and so on, up to 96 to 100, to obtain a frequency table of those intervals.
(e) Convert those figures into a cumulative frequency table from which an ogive could be drawn.
(f) Use an assumed mean to obtain a mean value.

(a) Total of the weights = 2004.
Number of weights = 32.
Arithmetic mean = 2004 ÷ 32 = 62.625.

(b) Arranged in ascending order:

33	43	50	55	64	71	77	86
33	46	50	58	65	71	80	87
37	47	53	61	66	72	85	89
38	49	55	62	69	75	86	91

From that list, the median is 63.

(c) From the list, the weights 33, 50, 55, 71 and 86 are modes.

(d) and (e)

Interval	Frequency	Cum. Freq.	Interval	Frequency	Cum. Freq.
0 to 5	0	0	51 to 55	3	13
6 to 10	0	0	56 to 60	1	14
11 to 15	0	0	61 to 65	4	18
16 to 20	0	0	66 to 70	2	20
21 to 25	0	0	71 to 75	4	24
26 to 30	0	0	76 to 80	2	26
31 to 35	2	2	81 to 85	1	27
36 to 40	2	4	86 to 90	4	31
41 to 45	1	5	91 to 95	1	32
46 to 50	5	10	96 to 100	0	32

The figures in the cumulative frequency column are used for the graph.

(f) The first six items can be ignored since the frequency is 0.
Obtain the centre value of each interval. Assume a mean of 64.
Find the differences between the centre values and assumed mean.
Multiply that value by the frequency to obtain this table:

Interval	Centre	Difference	Frequency	D × F
31 to 35	33	−31	2	−62
36 to 40	38	−26	2	−52
41 to 45	43	−21	1	−21
46 to 50	48	−16	5	−80
51 to 55	53	−11	3	−33
56 to 60	58	−6	1	−6
61 to 65	63	−1	4	−4
66 to 70	68	+4	2	+8
71 to 75	73	+9	4	+36
76 to 80	78	+14	2	+28
81 to 85	83	+19	1	+19
86 to 90	88	+24	4	+96
91 to 95	93	+29	1	+29
96 to 100	98	+34	0	0
			Total	−42

Divide by the number of items: $-42 \div 32 = -1.3125$.
Correct the assumed mean (64) by that amount: $64 - 1.3125 = 62.6875$.
(Compare with the arithmetic mean worked out earlier.)

Revision exercises

1 A group of children made a list to show how many were in each of their families. Here are some from the list, in which the children are identified by initials only.

J.A. 4	A.C. 6	D.E. 3	C.L. 7	W.T. 5
T.B. 4	J.C. 5	L.F. 6	E.M. 5	S.W. 3
L.B. 6	B.D. 8	A.H. 6	S.S. 5	A.W. 4

(a) Draw a bar-graph using fifteen columns.
(b) Make a frequency list and find the mode.

2 A class had tests in English and Mathematics with these results. The maximum possible was 20 marks.

	Eng.	Maths.		Eng.	Maths.		Eng.	Maths.
A.A.	12	7	D.E.	9	11	W.S.	8	11
L.A.	15	14	W.E.	8	5	A.T.	9	6
J.A.	9	8	L.F.	9	12	F.T.	12	11
L.B.	10	16	A.G.	16	11	H.T.	11	15
T.B.	8	11	A.H.	16	12	B.W.	10	5
A.C.	7	15	S.H.	14	15	C.W.	9	11
J.C.	9	14	C.L.	9	4	G.W.	8	10
V.C.	14	8	E.M.	15	10	J.W.	13	7
B.D.	13	6	S.S.	10	8	S.W.	14	7

Make frequency tables to find the mode for each list of marks.

3 Rearrange each list to find the median value.
(a) 4, 9, 8, 2, 6, 3, 4.
(b) 21, 15, 1, 3, 20, 4, 10, 8, 7, 4, 21.
(c) 9, 14, 12, 10, 8, 9, 8, 13, 8, 11, 18, 13.
(d) 18, 10, 6, 3, 11, 13, 11, 3, 4, 1, 6, 14, 5.
(e) 20, 12, 16, 9, 12, 24, 20, 16, 12, 20, 19, 10, 13, 10.

4 In one term, a group of twenty children had these attendances out of a total of 120:

120	96	106	96
101	98	93	95
120	120	111	102
103	102	120	111
93	109	102	120

(a) Find the modal number from that list of attendances.
(b) Find the median value.

5 Use the English and Mathematics marks in Question 2 to find the average mark or mean for that list.

6 In Question 4 there is a list of attendances in one term. Find the arithmetic mean of those numbers.

7 One number shown by a question mark (?) is not given in this list:

8, 9, 9, 12, 12, (?), 13, 13, 15, 15, 16.

We do know that the total of all eleven numbers is 134. Complete the list and find (a) the mean (b) the mode (c) the median.

8 Find the mean value of each set of numbers.

(a) $1, -2, 3, -4, 2, 5, -3, 6.$
(b) $-6, 3, -4, -1, 5, 7, -8, 12, -2, -1.$
(c) $-4, -2, 8, -1, 4, 2, -6, -5.$
(d) $-10, 4, -6, 5, -8, -3, 2, -4.$
(e) $-18, 12, 3, -25, 14, -14, -12, 22, -10, -7.$
(f) $2.3, 3.4, 5.6, 3.8, 3.5, 5.1, 8.8, 0.3.$
(g) $\frac{1}{2}, 2, 1\frac{1}{2}, 3\frac{1}{2}, -2, -2\frac{1}{2}, 1\frac{1}{2}, -\frac{1}{2}, 4\frac{1}{2}, -3\frac{1}{2}.$

9 A group of boys each made a guess at the number of marbles in a jar. These were their guesses:

116, 156, 170, 108, 138, 185, 105, 109, 177, 190, 136, 126.

The actual number in the jar was 142.

(a) Find the mean value from the list of guesses.
(b) List the differences between the actual value and the guesses, showing those which were less than 142 as negative values.
(c) Find the mean difference value.
(d) Find the median value among the list of differences and hence the median value in the guesses.

10 These marks were obtained by forty candidates in an examination:

84	45	52	35	67	52	42	51
65	73	34	62	59	71	40	10
67	43	46	34	51	95	64	24
82	31	15	68	42	46	80	52
61	18	82	47	79	77	52	38

Find (a) the mean (b) the mode (c) the median.

11 (a) If you were a candidate in the examination mentioned in the last question, why would the mean mark be important?
(b) If you had the median mark would you be average in that group, above average or below average?

* **12** See the marks in Question 10 again. The next table shows how many candidates occurred in each interval of five marks. You can see there was no candidate with a mark between 0 and 5, 1 candidate between 6 and 10 and so on.

Interval	Frequency	Interval	Frequency
0 to 5	0	51 to 55	6
6 to 10	1	56 to 60	1
11 to 15	1	61 to 65	4
16 to 20	1	66 to 70	3
21 to 25	1	71 to 75	2
26 to 30	0	76 to 80	3
31 to 35	4	81 to 85	3
36 to 40	2	86 to 90	0
41 to 45	4	91 to 95	1
46 to 50	3	96 to 100	0

(a) Make a column graph of those frequencies, making sure that each column is the same width.

(b) Put a cross at the centre of the top of each column.

(c) Draw a smooth curve taking in all those crosses. It is called a frequency curve. It will look like this:

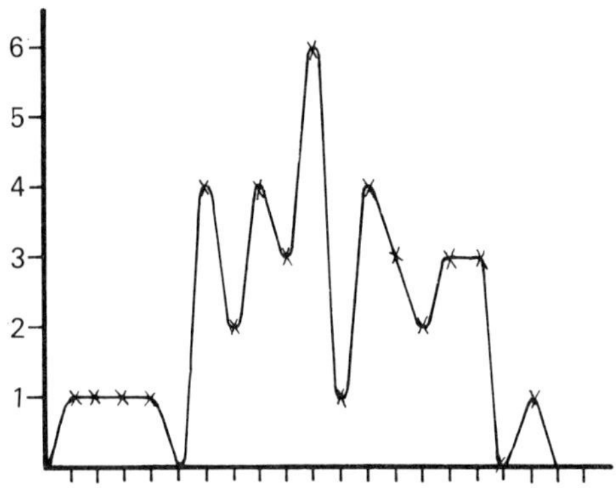

Those points can be obtained of course without drawing columns.

(d) Make a frequency table of the same marks using an interval of ten. Your list will show the frequency of marks from 0 to 10, 11 to 20, 21 to 30 and so on.

(e) Draw a frequency curve using that new list. Compare its shape with the first curve. Which graph gives the better picture of what happened in the examination?

* **13** Thirty darts players threw three darts each and scored as follows:

33	29	64	89	109	83
59	64	93	102	63	35
42	68	51	42	41	56
86	75	30	64	59	64
100	48	76	89	76	66

(a) Find the mean, median and mode of those scores.

(b) Make a frequency table using intervals of ten up to 120.

(c) Draw a frequency curve.

* **14** The teams in the English Association Football League Division 1, scored the following number of goals:

62	49	75	49	53	77	59	49	51	53	62
59	49	65	34	55	52	56	52	64	44	61

(a) Calculate the average mean value from that list.
(b) Make a frequency table in intervals of five, beginning with 31 to 35 and ending with 76 to 80.
(c) Draw a frequency graph.
(d) Use an assumed mean to find the mean value. Compare that answer with the one you worked earlier in the exercise.

* **15** The hours of sunshine recorded during the month of July last year are shown here in daily figures:

3.8	1.7	8.6	2.2	10.2	9.4	1.3	6.6
5.4	6.3	9.2	3.8	9.8	3.8	0.8	5.6
6.5	7.2	4.7	8.9	8.1	2.7	1.2	3.6
3.6	7.5	5.8	10.4	8.9	2.4	5.5	

(a) Make a frequency table and find the mode and median of the list of hours.
(b) Calculate the mean value correct to one decimal place.
(c) Use intervals of 1 hour to make a table of frequencies and then draw a frequency curve.
(d) Obtain a value for the mean by the assumed mean method.

* **16** A coach party of 36 people had these weights in kilograms:

34	46	38	51	73	65	55	66	45
73	59	43	49	89	60	72	78	87
70	88	75	86	90	54	78	35	82
65	65	84	50	32	48	73	34	63

(a) Make a frequency table using intervals of 5 kilograms commencing 31 to 35. Draw a frequency curve.
(b) Make another frequency table using intervals of 10 kg and construct another frequency curve.
(c) Find the mean value by finding the total weight and dividing it by 36.
(d) Use an assumed mean to obtain a mean value from the first frequency table.
(e) Construct an ogive from a cumulative frequency table. On the graph mark the median and two quartiles.

Trigonometry

Revision notes

In a triangle ABC right-angled at B, the longest side AC (opposite the right angle) is the *hypotenuse.*
Choosing one of the angles:

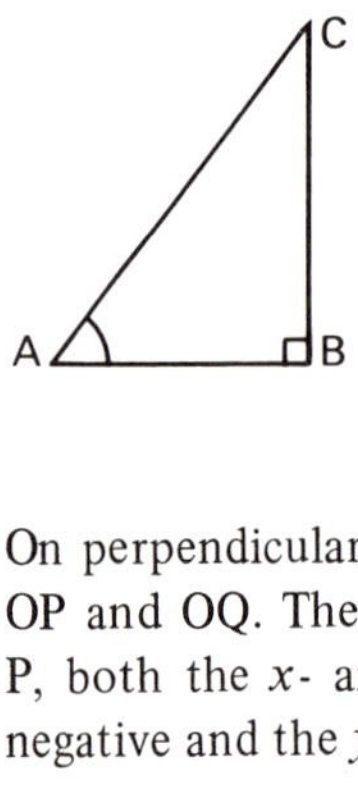

$$\text{Sine } \angle A = \frac{\text{Side opposite}}{\text{Hypotenuse}} \text{ or } \frac{\text{Perpendicular}}{\text{Hypotenuse}} = \frac{BC}{AC}$$

$$\text{Cosine } \angle A = \frac{\text{Side adjacent}}{\text{Hypotenuse}} \text{ or } \frac{\text{Base}}{\text{Hypotenuse}} = \frac{AB}{AC}$$

$$\text{Tangent } \angle A = \frac{\text{Side opposite}}{\text{Side adjacent}} \text{ or } \frac{\text{Perpendicular}}{\text{Base}} = \frac{BC}{AB}.$$

On perpendicular axes OX and OY, a rotating radius length r, is shown in positions OP and OQ. The angles of rotation are $\angle$XOP and $\angle$XOQ respectively. In position P, both the x- and y-coordinates are positive. In position Q, the x-coordinate is negative and the y-coordinate is positive.

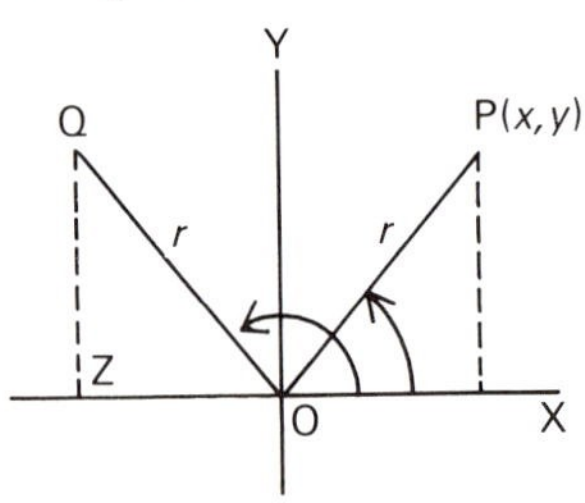

$\text{Sin } \angle XOP = \frac{y}{r}$, $\text{Cos } \angle XOP = \frac{x}{r}$, $\text{Tan } \angle XOP = \frac{y}{x}$.

For position OQ, the rotated angle XOQ $= 180^\circ - \angle$ZOQ.
Since the x-coordinate of Q is negative,
Sin $\angle$XOQ = Sin $\angle$ZOQ, Cos $\angle$XOQ = $-$Cos $\angle$ZOQ, Tan $\angle$XOQ = $-$Tan $\angle$ZOQ.

$\text{Sin } \angle XOQ = \frac{y}{r}$, $\text{Cos } \angle XOQ = -\frac{x}{r}$, $\text{Tan } \angle XOQ = -\frac{y}{x}$.

▶ In a right-angled triangle ABC, AB = 5 cm and BC = 13 cm. The angle A = 90°. Write in fraction form (a) Sine ∠B (b) Sine ∠C (c) Tangent ∠C.

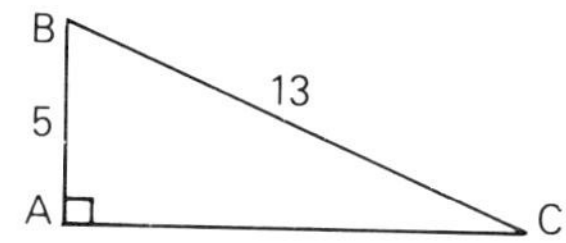

Since ∠A = 90°, then AC = 12 cm (Pythagoras 5, 12, 13).

(a) Sine $\angle B = \frac{AC}{BC} = \frac{12}{13}$. (b) Sine $\angle C = \frac{AB}{BC} = \frac{5}{13}$. (c) Tangent $\angle C = \frac{AB}{AC} = \frac{5}{12}$.

▶ A ship X sails due West from port Y, a distance of 15 km. Another ship Z sails due South from Y so that the two ships X and Z are 21 km apart.

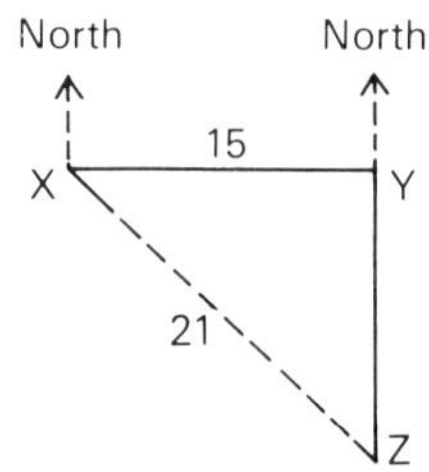

(a) How far has ship Z sailed?
(b) What is the bearing of Z from X?

(a) This can be solved using the Pythagoras relationship. Due West and due South gives ∠Y = 90°.

$$\begin{aligned} YZ^2 &= 21^2 - 15^2 \\ &= 441 - 225 \\ YZ &= \sqrt{216} = 14.7\,\text{km}. \end{aligned}$$

(b) To find ∠X,

$$\begin{aligned} \text{Cosine } \angle X &= \frac{15}{21} = 0.714. \\ \angle X &= 44^\circ\,26'. \\ \text{Bearing} &= 90^\circ + 44^\circ\,26' = 134^\circ\,26'. \end{aligned}$$

Sine and Cosine Rules

In any triangle ABC with sides *a, b, c,* opposite ∠A, ∠B, ∠C respectively, these formulae may be used to solve the triangle:

Sine Rule: $\frac{a}{\text{Sin } \angle A} = \frac{b}{\text{Sin } \angle B} = \frac{c}{\text{Sin } \angle C}$.

Cosine Rule: $a^2 = b^2 + c^2 - (2bc \text{ Cos } \angle A)$.

or $\text{Cos } \angle A = \frac{b^2 + c^2 - a^2}{2bc}$

For obtuse angles: Sine ∠A = Sine (180 − A),
Cosine ∠A = −Cosine (180 − A).

i.e. If Sine 54° = 0.809 then Sine 126° = 0.809.
If Cosine 54° = 0.588 then Cosine 126° = −0.588.

▶ Two planes take off from the same airfield X. Plane Alpha travels a distance of 85 km due North. Plane Beta flies on a bearing of 122°, a distance of 76 km.

(a) How far are the planes apart at that time?

(b) What is the bearing of Beta from Alpha?

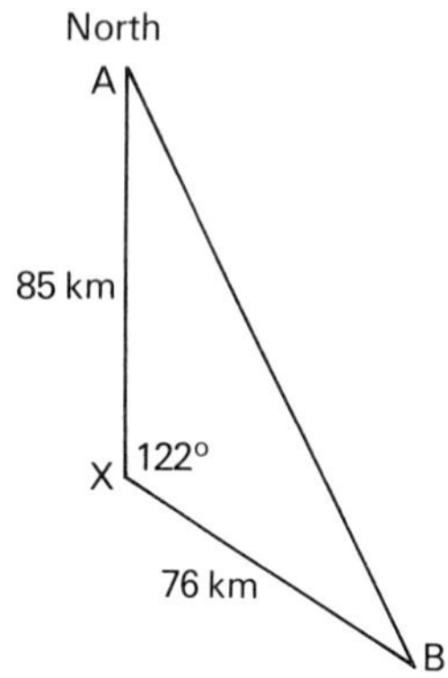

(a) Using the Cosine Rule (*Note* Cos 122° = −Cos 58°)

$$\begin{aligned} AB^2 &= 76^2 + 85^2 - 2(85 \times 76 \times \text{Cos } 122) \\ &= 5776 + 7225 + (12\,920 \text{ Cos } 58°) \\ &= 19\,847.6 \\ AB &= 140.9 \text{ km.} \end{aligned}$$

(b) Using the Sine Rule (*Note* Sine 122° = Sine 58°)

$$\text{Sine } \angle A = \frac{76 \times \text{Sin } 122°}{140.9} = \frac{76 \times 0.848}{140.9} = 0.4574$$

$$\begin{aligned} A &= 27°\ 13'. \\ \text{Bearing} &= 180° - 27°\ 13' = 152°\ 47'. \end{aligned}$$

▶ Angle of elevation:

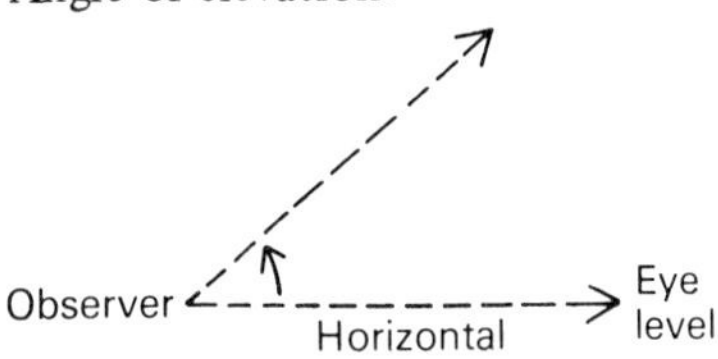

Angle of depression:

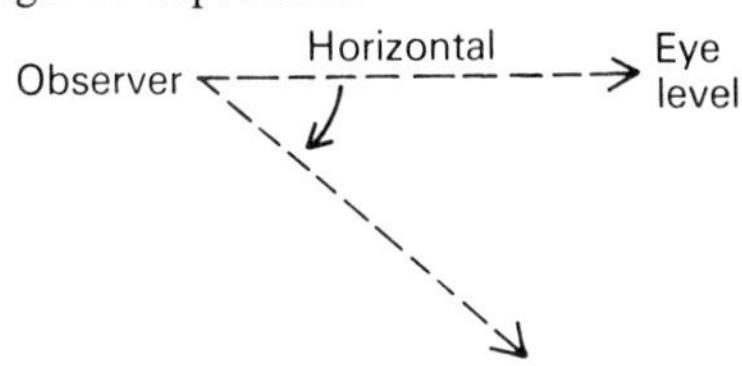

A tree is 15.4 metres high. Viewed from point P, the angle of elevation to the top is 27° and from point Q is is 59°. P and Q are in line with the bottom of the tree. Find PQ.

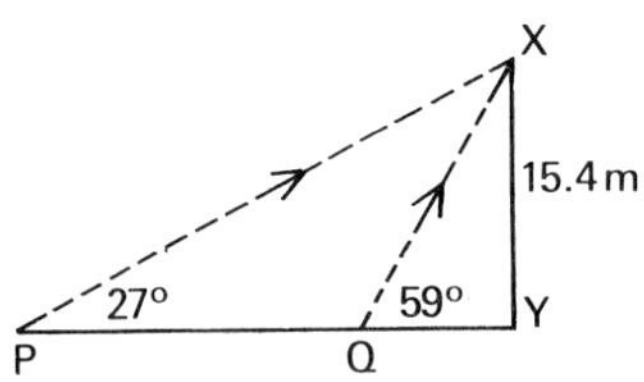

$$\frac{15.4}{QY} = \text{Tan } 59°.$$

$$QY = \frac{15.4}{1.664}$$

$$QY = 9.26 \text{ metres.}$$

$$PY = \frac{15.4}{0.510}$$

$$PY = 30.2 \text{ metres.}$$

$$PQ = 30.2 - 9.26 = 20.94 \text{ m.}$$

A dog stood 30.5 metres from a block of flats, 48.6 metres high. What was the angle of depression which allowed me to see the dog from the roof of the flats?

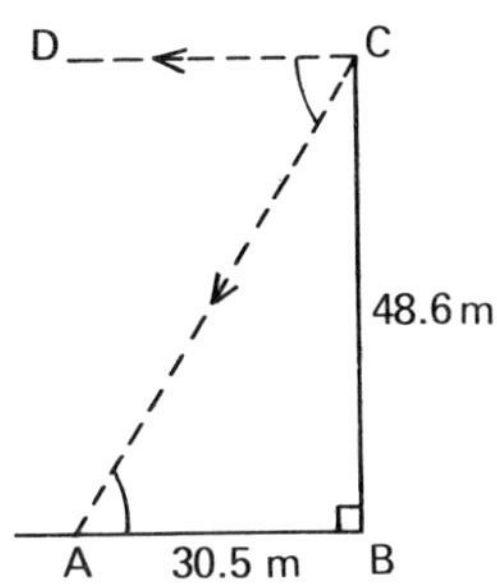

CD and AB are parallel.

$$\angle DCA = \angle BAC.$$

$$\text{Tan } \angle BAC = \frac{48.6}{30.5} = 1.593$$

$$\angle BAC = 57°\ 53'.$$

Angle of depression 57° 53′.

Revision exercises

1 Calculate the angle A in each diagram.

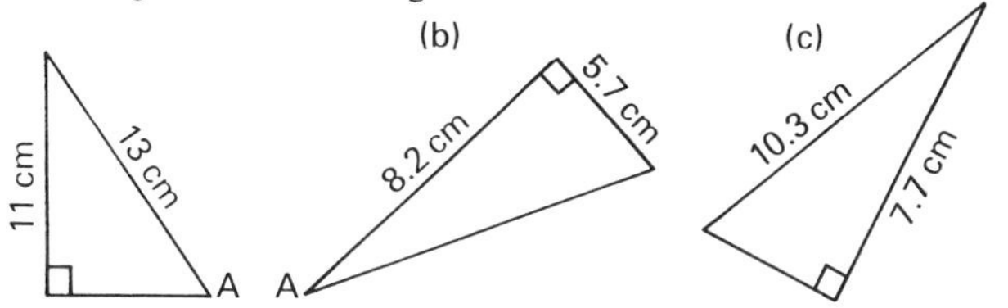

2 Calculate sides AB and BC in each triangle.

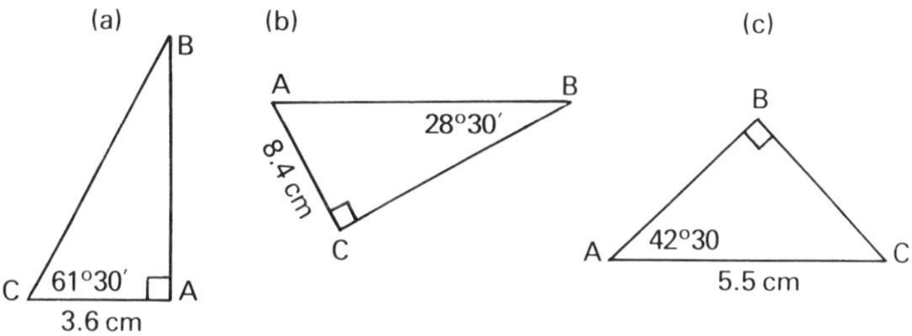

3 The drive leading to a garage is inclined at an angle of 9° to the horizontal. If the drive is 12.6 metres long, what vertical height is the garage floor above the lower end of the drive?

4 The frame of a roof truss has ∠ABC = 90° and ∠ADB = 90°. AB which is 5.3 m long, is inclined to AC at an angle of 40°. Calculate lengths BC, AC and BD.

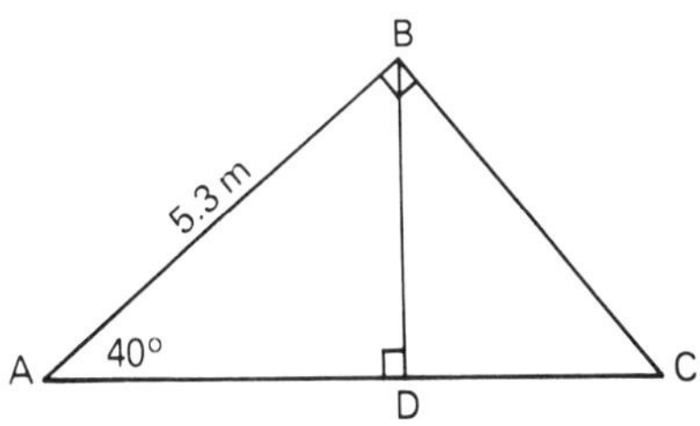

5 The end of a prism is a trapezium ABCD. The angles at A and B are each 90° and the angle at D is 78°. BC = 10.9 cm and AD = 15.7 cm. Find the length AB correct to three significant figures.

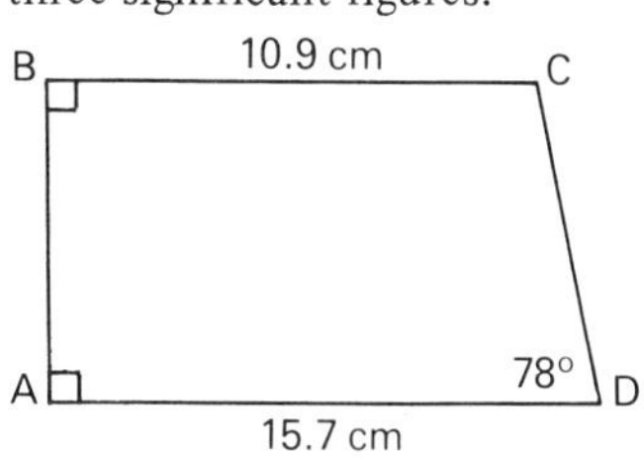

6 An equilateral triangle has a side of 10.6 cm. Calculate the perpendicular distance from any vertex to the opposite side correct to three significant figures.

7 A regular hexagon has a side of 4.1 cm. Calculate the perpendicular distance between X, the centre of side AB, and Y, the centre of the opposite side DE, correct to three significant figures.

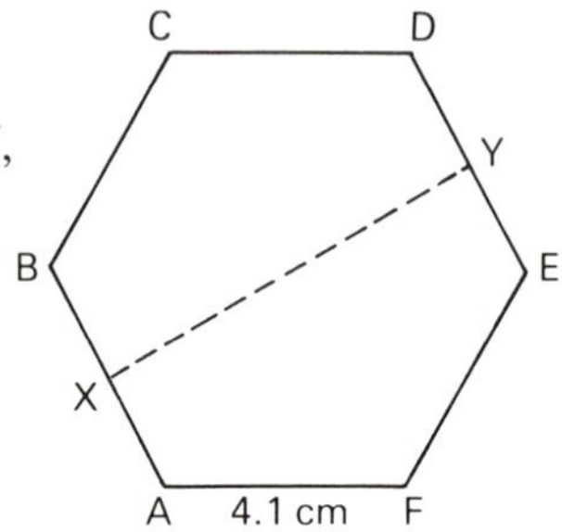

8 Triangle ABC has AB = 8.4 cm, ∠BAC = 50° and ∠BCA = 45°. BD is the perpendicular from B to side AC. Giving answers correct to three significant figures, calculate
(a) BD (b) BC (c) AC.

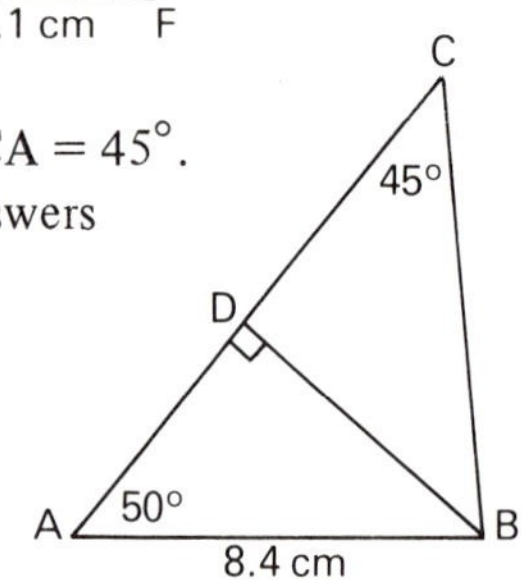

9 A triangular prism has an end ABC which is an isosceles triangle in which ∠ABC = 30° and AC = 6.8 cm. The length of the prism BD is 15.4 cm. Calculate the volume of the prism, correcting your answer to the nearest cm^3.

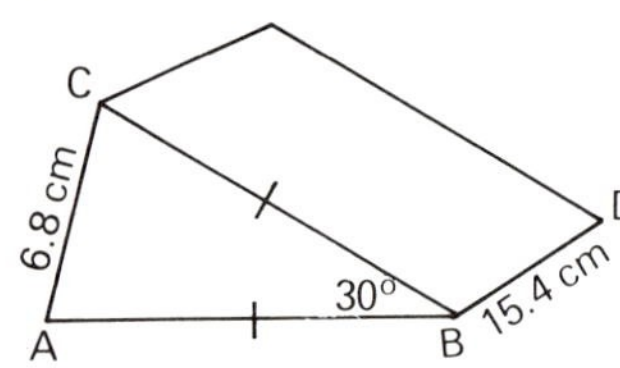

10 The angle between adjacent sides of a rhombus is 39° and its longest diagonal is 15.6 cm. Find the length of the other diagonal.

11 In triangle ABC, ∠BAC = 45° and ∠BCA = 105°. BD is the vertical height. Length AD = 4.5 cm.
(a) Calculate the height BD.
(b) Find length CD.
(c) Calculate the area of the triangle.

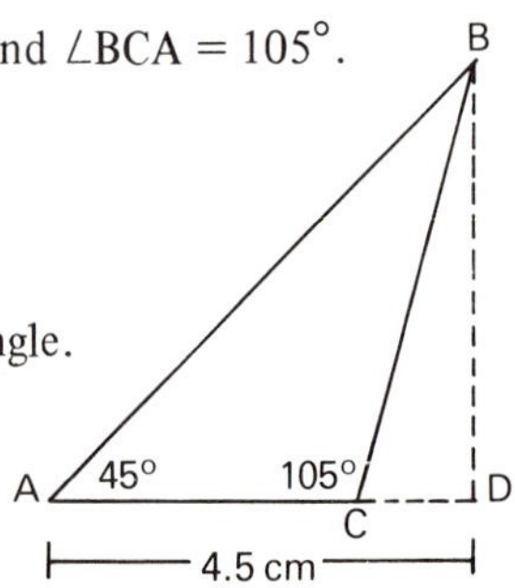

12 A flag pole FB 22 metres high, is held vertically by two guy ropes AD and CE. The point E is 3 metres from F and point D is 8 metres below F. $\angle DAB = 62°$, $\angle ECB = 70°$.

(a) Find the length of EC.
(b) Find the length of AD.
(c) What is the distance between the points A and C?

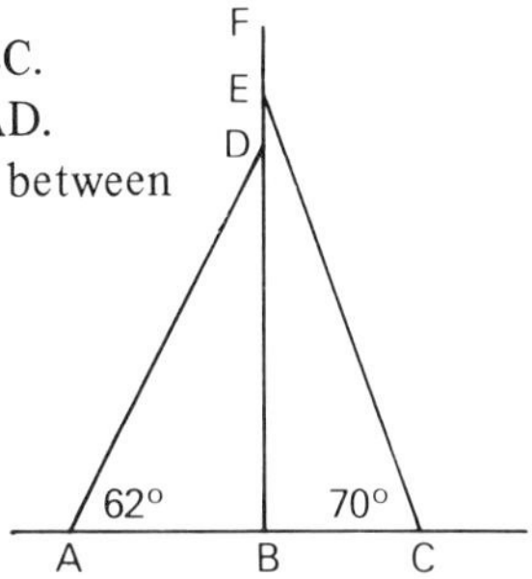

13 Kite ABCD has AB = AD = 15 cm. Diagonals AC and BD intersect at E. $\angle ABD = 26°$ and $\angle CBD = 68°$.

(a) Calculate length BD.
(b) Find the length of diagonal AC.
(c) Find side BC.

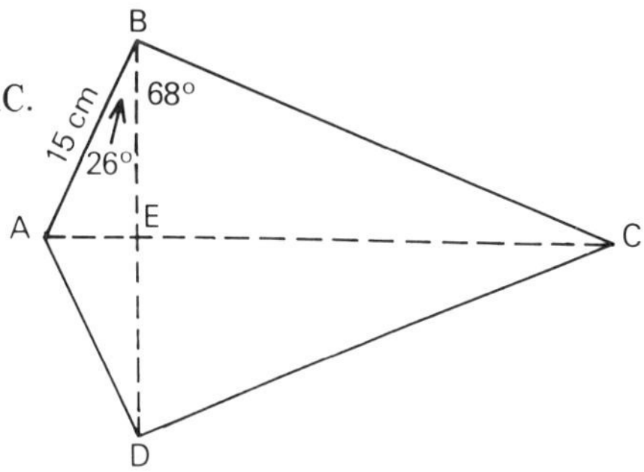

14 The elevation of the sun was 35°. At that time, what was the length of the shadow of a pole 12.3 metres high?

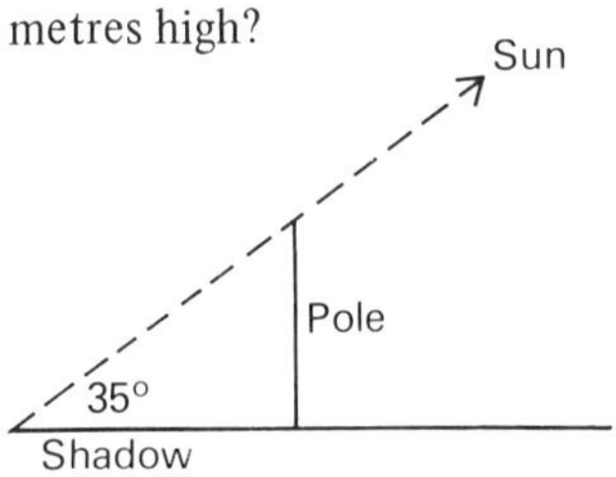

15 Looking at the top of a tree, a man found the angle of elevation was 28°. The man was 1.8 metres in height and he was standing a distance of 22.5 metres from the tree. Calculate the height of the tree.

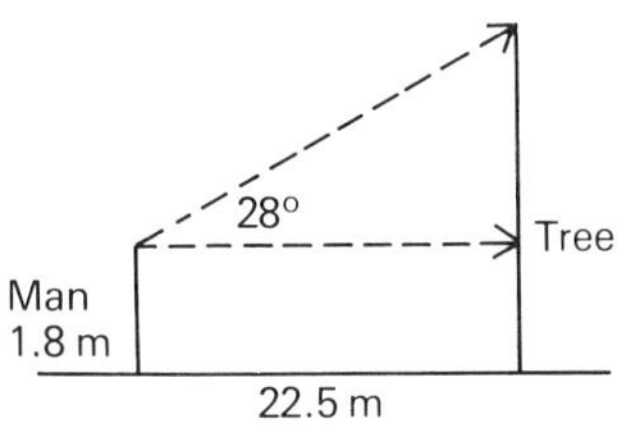

16 From a lighthouse, which was 76.3 metres above sea-level, the keeper viewed a boat at sea on an angle of depression of 63°. How far was the boat from the lighthouse?

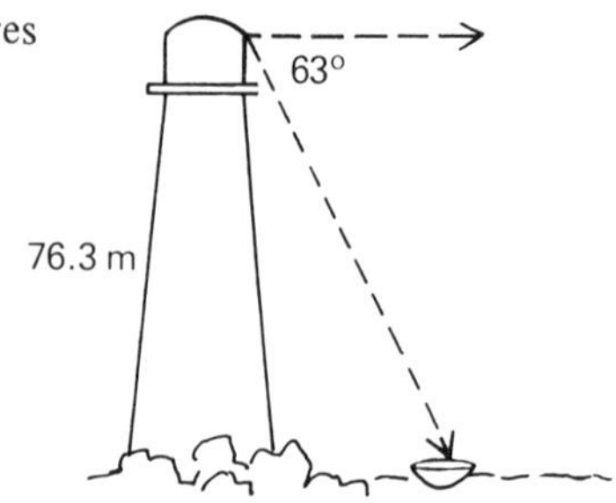

17 If I am 1.75 metres in height and my shadow is 2.8 metres in length, what is the angle of elevation of the sun?

18 From point A, the angle of elevation to the top of a building B was 42°. From the same point A, to the top of an aerial on the building C, the angle of elevation was 52°. If A is 25.8 metres from the building, what length is the aerial BC?

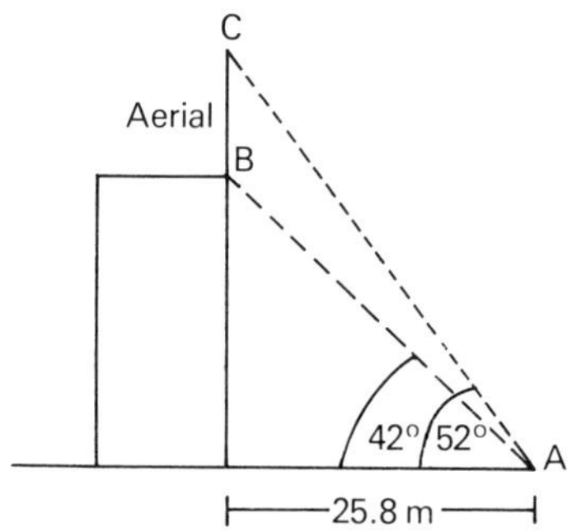

19 A helicopter H is 175 metres above X on the ground, which is on the line joining two points A and B. The pilot finds his angle of depression to observe B is 68° and to see A is 51°. Find the distance between A and B.

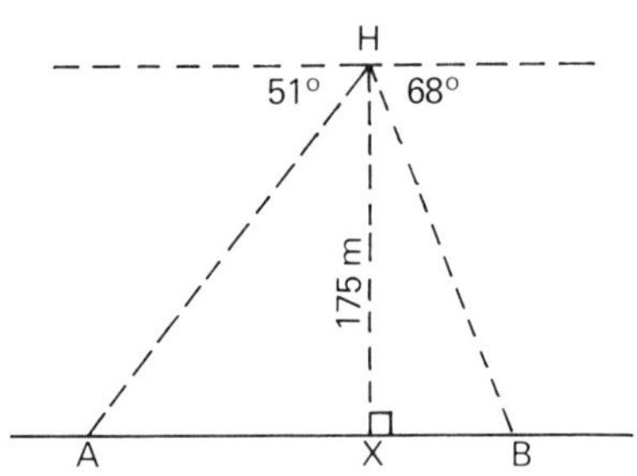

20 If the diagonal of the base of a square pyramid is 13.6 cm, what is the length of a side of the base?

21 The square base of a pyramid was lettered ABCD in that order. Length BC was 9.2 cm. The vertical height of the pyramid OX to the apex O was 6.5 cm. The centre of side AB was lettered E. Draw a diagram and calculate ∠XEO.

22 In the rectangular prism, length AB = 18 cm, breadth BC = 5 cm and height CG = 4.5 cm. Calculate (a) DB (b) ∠DBA (c) ∠HBD (d) HB.

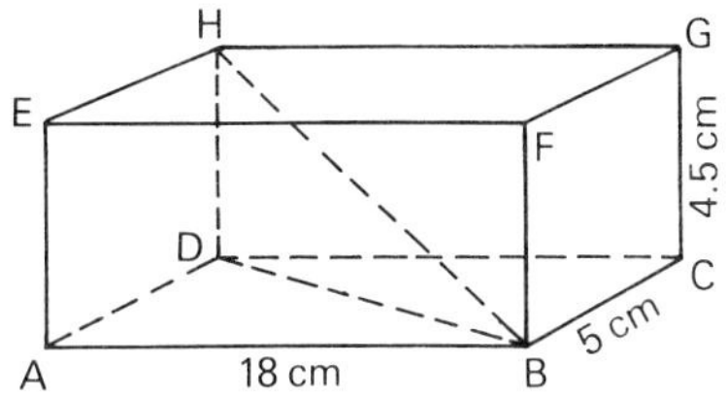

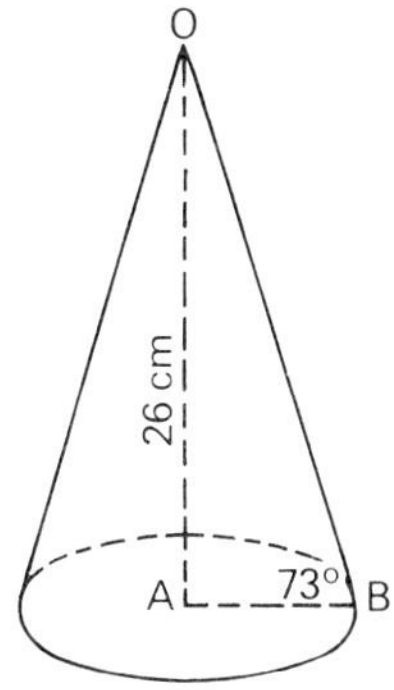

23 In a cone, the length OB makes an angle of 73° with the radius AB of the base. If the vertical height AO is 26 cm, calculate the radius of the base.

* **24** (a) Construct a triangle in which $a = 7$ cm, $b = 6$ cm, $c = 5$ cm.

(b) Measure the angles and calculate $\frac{a}{\text{Sin A}}$, $\frac{b}{\text{Sin B}}$ and $\frac{c}{\text{Sin C}}$.

* **25** In a triangle ABC, $b = 7.3$ cm, $c = 6.4$ cm, ∠ACB = 56°. Giving the angles correct to the nearest half degree, calculate
(a) ∠ABC (b) ∠BAC (c) side a.

* **26** In a triangle ABC, AB = 4.3 cm, BC = 5.2 cm, ∠BAC = 72°. Calculate
(a) ∠ACB (b) ∠ABC (c) side AC.

* **27** In a triangle ABC, $a = 8.4$ cm, ∠A = 82°, ∠B = 64°. Calculate
(a) ∠C (b) side b (c) side c.

* **28** Calculate side x in each triangle.

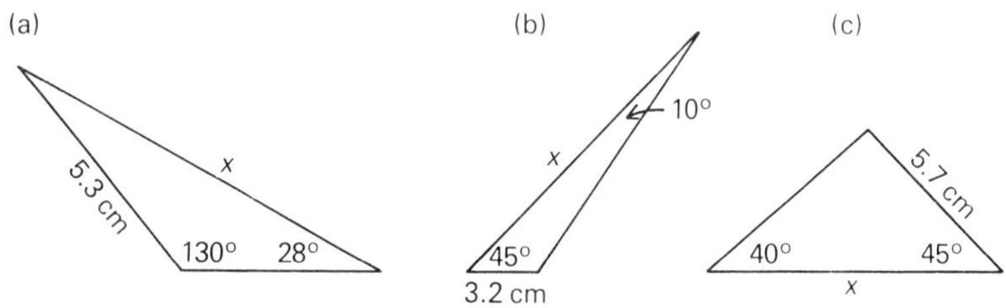

* **29** Calculate the remaining angles in each triangle, correcting each one to the nearest half degree.

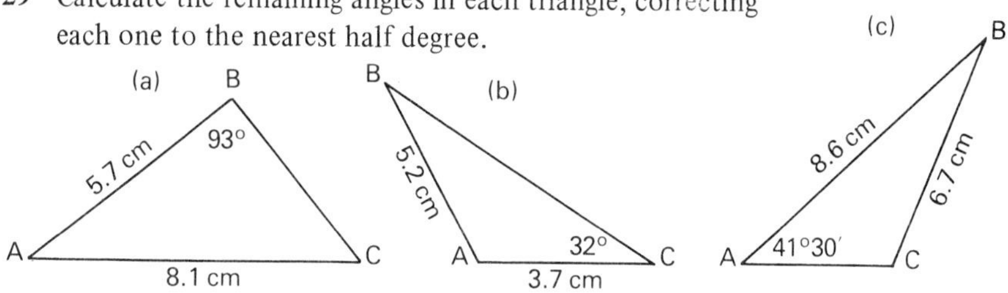

* **30** In each triangle, sides a, b and c are given. Use the Cosine Rule to calculate the three angles of each triangle, correct to the nearest half degree.
(a) $a = 8.4$ cm, $b = 6.9$ cm, $c = 7.1$ cm.
(b) $a = 5.7$ cm, $b = 5.9$ cm, $c = 4.9$ cm.
(c) $a = 3.2$ cm, $b = 3.5$ cm, $c = 4.2$ cm.
(d) $a = 6.6$ cm, $b = 5.6$ cm, $c = 6.8$ cm.

* **31** Use the Cosine Rule to find the third side in each triangle.
(a) $a = 6.5$ cm, $b = 8$ cm, $\angle C = 48°$.
(b) $b = 9.2$ cm, $c = 5.8$ cm, $\angle A = 51° 30'$.
(c) $a = 8.9$ cm, $c = 6.1$ cm, $\angle B = 146°$.
(d) $b = 10.1$ cm, $a = 9.9$ cm, $\angle C = 155° 30'$.

* **32** Give these answers correct to the nearest half degree.
(a) $a = 9.8$ cm, $b = 6.1$ cm, $c = 4.8$ cm. Find $\angle A$.
(b) $a = 4.5$ cm, $b = 10$ cm, $c = 6$ cm. Find $\angle B$.
(c) $a = 14.1$ cm, $b = 9.3$ cm, $c = 7.6$ cm. Find $\angle A$.
(d) $a = 7.3$ cm, $b = 8.5$ cm, $c = 13.9$ cm. Find $\angle C$.

* **33** Calculate all unknown sides and angles in each triangle ABC. Correct each angle to the nearest half degree.

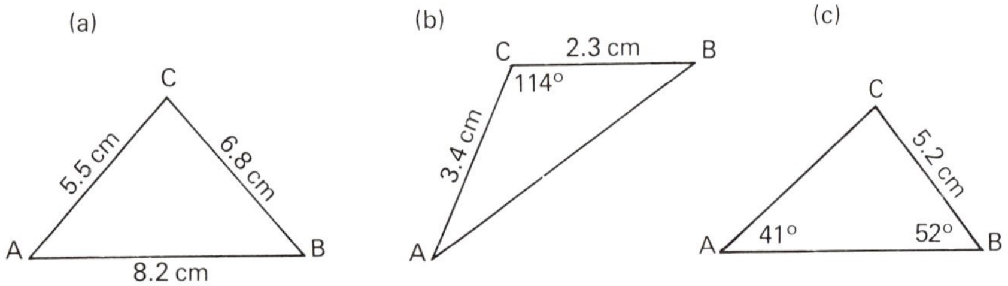

* **34** Two ships start from port A. One travels 35 kilometres on a bearing 042° and the other travels 48 kilometres on bearing 165°.
(a) Use a scale drawing to find how far apart the ships were.
(b) Use a calculation to check that distance.

* **35** Two planes take off from the same airfield A. One plane travels to its destination X a distance of 75 km on bearing 320°. The second plane flies to its destination Y on bearing 035°. The two destinations are 98 km apart.
(a) Construct a scale drawing of the flights.
(b) Calculate $\angle AYX$ and hence the bearing of X from Y correct to the nearest half degree.
(c) Calculate the distance from A to Y.
(d) Verify your answers from the drawing.

Area and Volume

Revision notes

Formulae

Area

Rectangle $= LB.$
Parallelogram $= BH.$
Triangle $= \frac{1}{2}BH.$
Trapezium $= \frac{1}{2}H(A + B).$
Circle $= \pi r^2.$

Circumference

Circle $= 2\pi r.$

Volume

Prisms $=$ End area $\times$ Length.
Pyramids $= \frac{1}{3}$ Base area $\times$ Vertical height.
Sphere $= \frac{4}{3}\pi r^3.$

Curved surface

Cylinder $= 2\pi rl.$
Cone $= \pi rl$ (slant height).

Surface

Sphere $= 4\pi r^2.$

Arcs and Sectors

The arc of a circle can be calculated from the circumference by using the angle subtended at the centre. The area of a sector may also be calculated from the area of the circle in the same way. A sector is that area contained by two radii and an arc of a circle.

▸ (a) In a circle radius 7 cm, an arc subtends an angle at the centre of 80°. Calculate the length of the arc. ($\pi = \frac{22}{7}$)

(b) A circle has a diameter of 6.4 cm. Calculate the area of a sector formed by two radii and an arc which subtends an angle of 60° at the centre. ($\pi = 3.14$)

(a) Circumference $= 2 \times \dfrac{22}{7} \times 7 = 44$ cm.

Arc $= 44 \times \dfrac{80}{360} = 9.78$ cm.

(b) Area of circle $= 3.14 \times 3.2 \times 3.2 = 32.15\ \text{cm}^2.$

Area of sector $= 32.15 \times \dfrac{60}{360} = 5.36\ \text{cm}^2.$

Triangle Other useful formulae for the triangle:

s is the semi-perimeter, i.e. $s = \dfrac{a+b+c}{2}$.

Using s, Area of the Triangle $= \sqrt{s(s-a)(s-b)(s-c)}$.
Using two sides and the included angle, Area of the Triangle $= \frac{1}{2}ab$ Sin C.

Contents of Vessels 1 litre is 1000 millilitres.
1 litre takes up a volume of 1000 cm^3.
1000 cm^3 is 1 cubic decimetre (10 × 10 × 10).
1 litre of water weighs 1 kilogram.

▶ A cylindrical container, radius 2.6 metres, height 2.8 metres, is full of a liquid, 900 kg of which take up the same volume as 1000 kg of water. ($\pi = 3.14$)
(a) Calculate the weight of liquid in the tank.
(b) It is intended to transfer the liquid to a rectangular tank with a base measuring 6.2 metres by 4.8 metres. What will be the depth of liquid in the new tank?

(a) Volume of cylinder $= 3.14 \times 2.6 \times 2.6 \times 2.8 = 59.43\ m^3$.

$$\text{Capacity} = \frac{59\,430\,000}{1000} = 59\,430 \text{ litres.}$$

$$\text{Weight of liquid} = 59\,430 \times \frac{9}{10} = 53\,487 \text{ kilograms.}$$

(b) Base area of the new tank $= 6.2 \times 4.8 = 29.76\ m^2$.

Depth of liquid $= 59.43 \div 29.76 = 2$ metres. (3 significant figures)

Revision exercises

1 Fill in the missing items in this table:

	Base	Height	Area
(a) Rectangle	$2\frac{2}{5}$ cm	$1\frac{1}{4}$ cm	
(b) Parallelogram	16 cm		128 cm^2
(c) Parallelogram		10 m	175 m^2
(d) Rectangle	$4\frac{1}{2}$ m		36 m^2
(e) Rectangle	24 cm	$3\frac{1}{2}$ cm	
(f) Parallelogram		7 m	238 m^2
(g) Rectangle	$4\frac{1}{2}$ cm	$2\frac{1}{3}$ cm	
(h) Parallelogram	8 m		60 m^2

2 Calculate the area of the triangle with

(a) base 6 cm, height $\frac{1}{2}$ cm
(b) base 10 mm, height $1\frac{1}{2}$ mm
(c) base 8 mm, height $2\frac{1}{2}$ mm
(d) base 9 m, height $2\frac{1}{2}$ m
(e) base 12 m, height $1\frac{1}{3}$ m
(f) base 20 cm, height $2\frac{2}{5}$ cm.

3 Find the area of each shape.

(a)

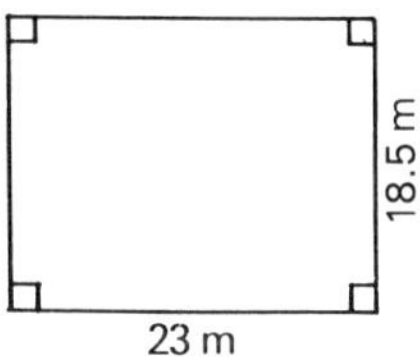

(b)

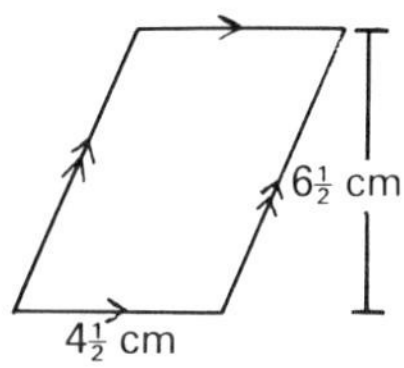

(c)

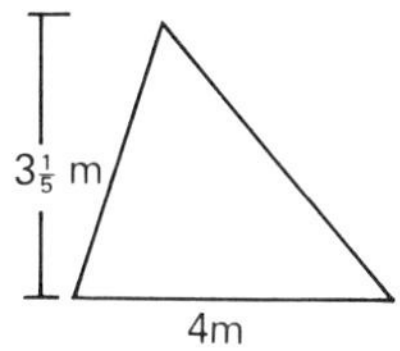

(d)

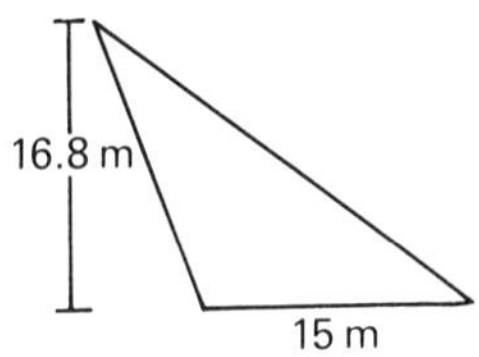

(e)

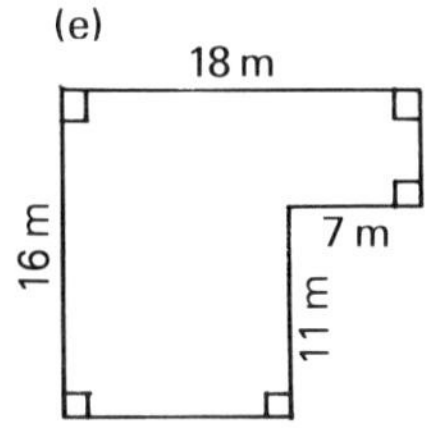

(f)

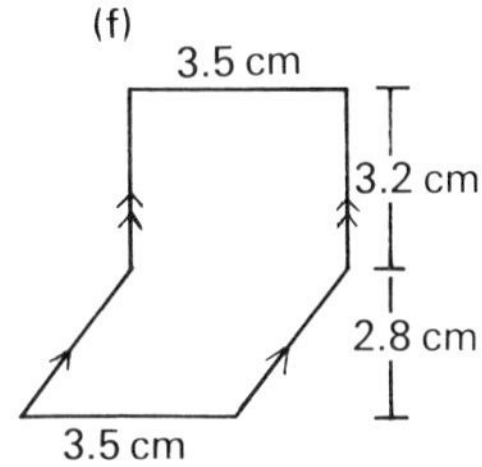

(g)

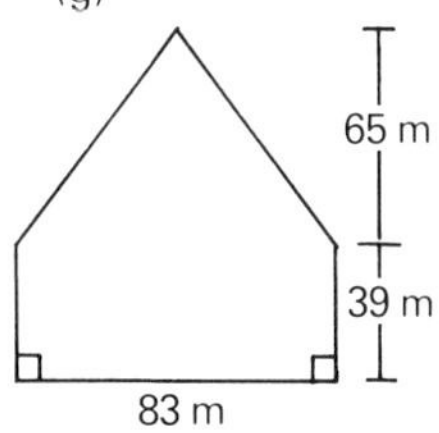

(h)

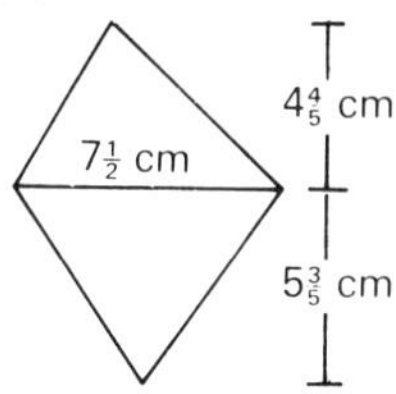

4 Find the height of each triangle.

(a)

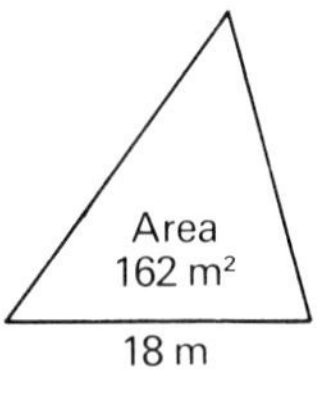

(b)

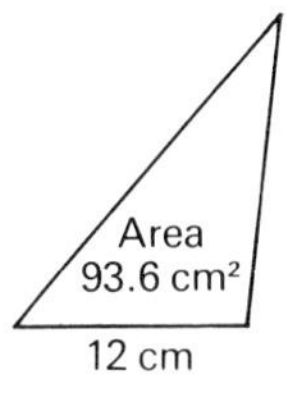

(c)

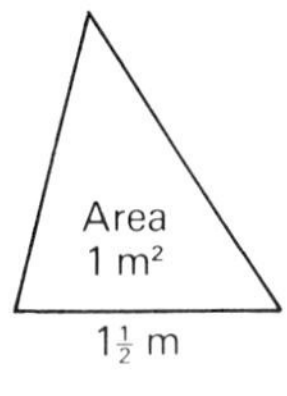

(d)

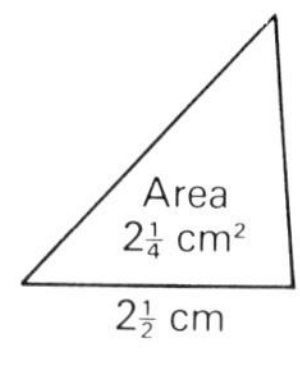

5 Calculate the base of each triangle.

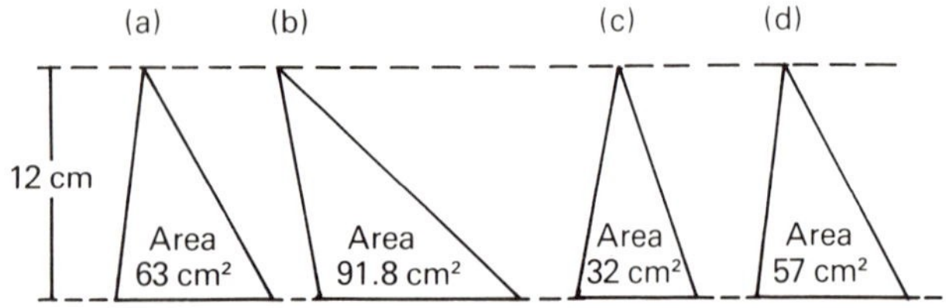

6 Find the approximate value of π correct to 2 decimal places, where C is the circumference, D the diameter and

(a) $C = 12.48$ cm, $D = 4$ cm (b) $C = 47.1$ m, $D = 15$ m
(c) $C = 37.5$ mm, $D = 12$ mm (d) $C = 5$ cm, $D = 1.6$ cm
(e) $C = 16.33$ m, $D = 5.2$ m (f) $C = 28.3$ cm, $D = 9$ cm.

7 Using $\pi = 3\frac{1}{7}$, find the circumference of a circle with a radius of
(a) 7 cm (b) $3\frac{1}{2}$ cm (c) $2\frac{1}{2}$ cm (d) 21 mm (e) $1\frac{2}{5}$ cm.

8 Use $\pi = 3.14$ to calculate the circumference of each circle.

(a) Diameter 12 m (b) Radius 18 mm (c) Radius 50 cm
(d) Radius 1.7 cm (e) Diameter $1\frac{1}{2}$ m (f) Radius 3.8 cm
(g) Diameter 10.5 m (h) Radius $3\frac{1}{4}$ cm (i) Diameter 7.4 cm.

9 This is the plan of a running track:

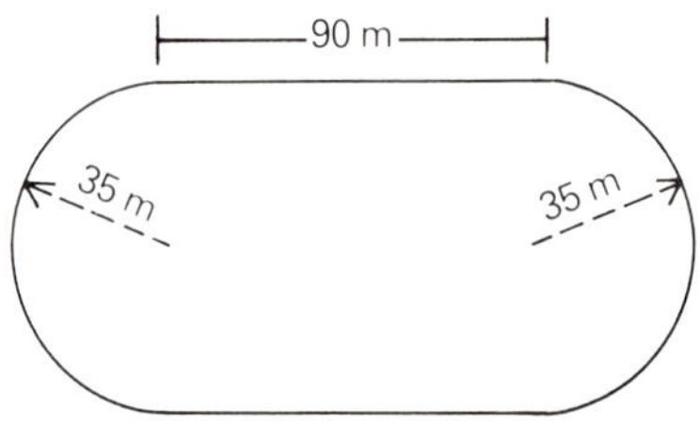

The two straight lengths, 90 m each, are joined by two semicircular ends each with a radius of 35 m. What is the distance round the track to the nearest metre? ($\pi = 3.14$)

10 According to the rules of the game, when a free kick is taken in a soccer game, the ball must move horizontally a distance equal to its circumference. If a soccer ball is 22.5 cm in diameter, approximately what distance must the ball travel at the free kick, correct to the nearest centimetre? ($\pi = 3.14$)

11 Find the area of these circles using $\pi = \frac{22}{7}$.

(a) Radius 7 cm (b) Radius 14 m (c) Radius $3\frac{1}{2}$ cm
(d) Diameter 42 m (e) Diameter $3\frac{1}{2}$ m (f) Diameter 21 cm.

12 Use $\pi = 3.14$ to obtain the area of circles with these radii, giving each answer correct to one decimal place.

(a) 1 cm (b) 3 cm (c) 5 cm (d) 9 m (e) 2.1 cm
(f) 5.3 m (g) 4.6 cm (h) 7.5 m (i) 6.4 cm (j) 10.3 m.

13 Find the area of each shaded portion. Take $\pi = \frac{22}{7}$.

(a)

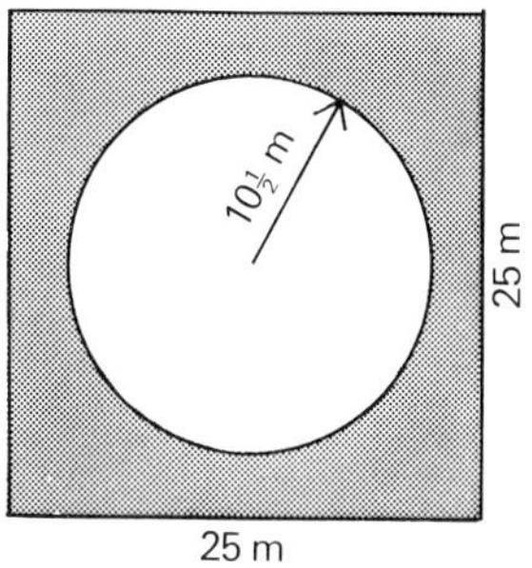

(b)

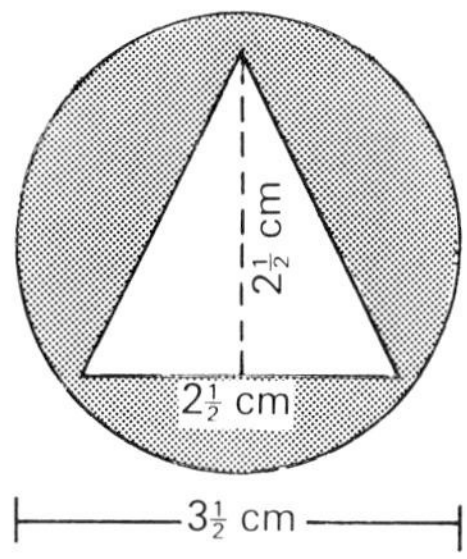

(c)

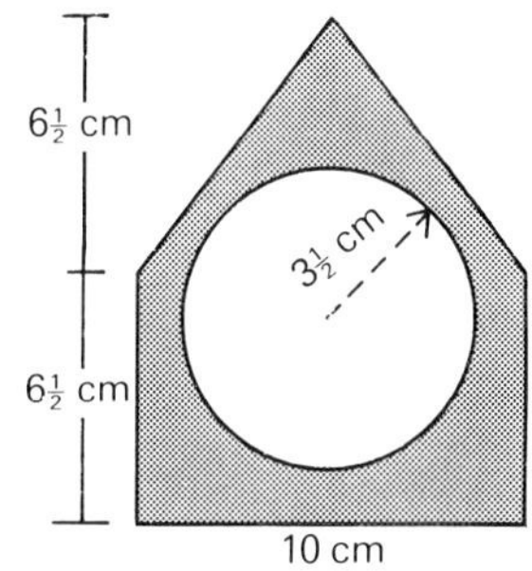

14 Calculate the volumes of cylinders with these measurements. ($\pi = 3\frac{1}{7}$)

(a) Radius $3\frac{1}{2}$ mm, Length 2 mm
(b) Radius $2\frac{1}{3}$ cm, Length 9 cm
(c) Radius $1\frac{3}{4}$ cm, Length 8 cm
(d) Radius $1\frac{1}{2}$ cm, Length 7 cm
(e) Radius $1\frac{2}{5}$ m, Length 10 m
(f) Radius $3\frac{1}{5}$ cm, Length $17\frac{1}{2}$ cm.

15 Use $\pi = 3.14$ to calculate the volumes of these cylinders, giving each answer correct to four significant figures.

(a) Radius 6 m, Length 5 m
(b) Radius 7 cm, Length 3.2 cm
(c) Radius 2.6 m, Length 1.3 m
(d) Radius 0.3 cm, Length 0.9 cm
(e) Radius 8 cm, Length 0.7 cm
(f) Radius 3.5 m, Length 1.7 m.

16 Calculate the volume of each prism, correct to the nearest cubic centimetre. Where necessary take $\pi = 3\frac{1}{7}$.

(a)

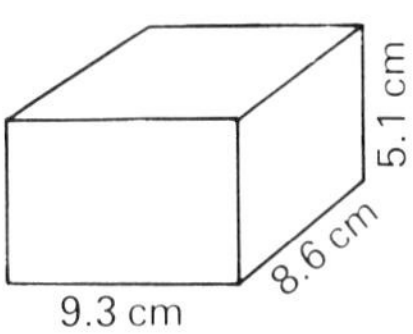

(b)

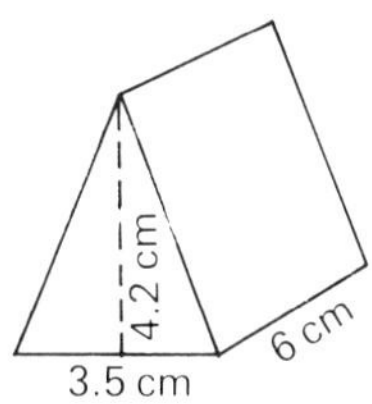

(c)

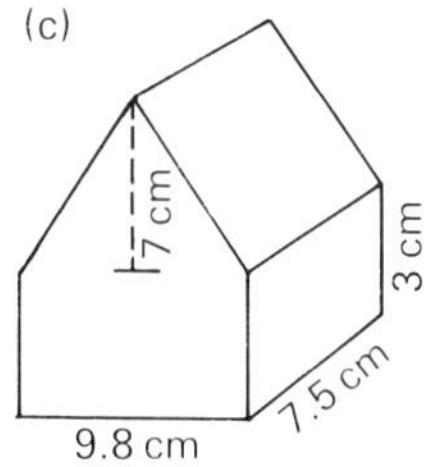

(d)

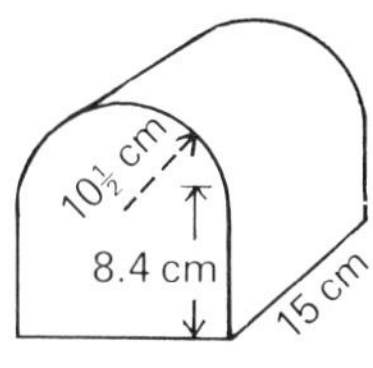

17 Find the volume of each solid correct to one decimal place ($\pi = 3.14$).

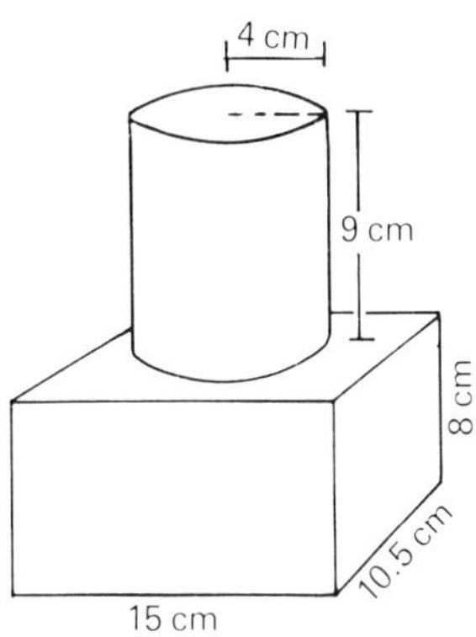

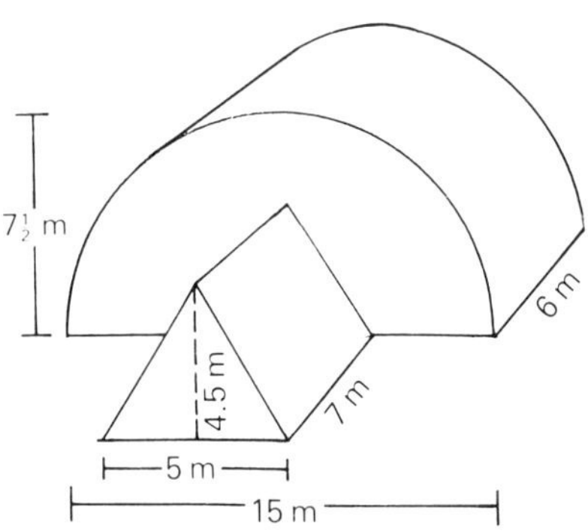

18 Calculate the area of each triangle ABC using the formula:

$$A = \sqrt{s(s-a)(s-b)(s-c)} \quad \text{where} \quad s = \frac{a+b+c}{2}.$$

(a) $a = 5$ cm, $b = 4$ cm, $c = 3$ cm
(b) $a = 12$ cm, $b = 13$ cm, $c = 5$ cm
(c) $a = 3$ cm, $b = 2.5$ cm, $c = 2.5$ cm
(d) $a = 1.3$ cm, $b = 1.2$ cm, $c = 1.1$ cm
(e) $a = 6.5$ cm, $b = 4.5$ cm, $c = 5$ cm.

* **19** (a) In a triangle ABC, $2s = 88$ cm, $a = 25$ cm and $b = 35$ cm. Find the area of the triangle.
(b) When $s = 6.5$ cm, $a = 5$ cm, $b = 4.5$ cm, find the area of the triangle.
(c) When $s = 1.19$ cm, $a = 0.88$ cm, $b = 0.75$ cm, find the area of the triangle.

* **20** (a) Construct the triangle ABC in which $a = 5.5$ cm, $b = 7$ cm, $\angle C = 43°$, using side AC as base.
(b) Construct and measure perpendicular BD from B to AC. Use the base and height to calculate the area of the triangle.
(c) Measure side AB and use the formula:
$A = \sqrt{s(s-a)(s-b)(s-c)}$, to calculate the area of the triangle.

* **21** Find the area of each triangle ABC using a formula of the form Area $= \frac{1}{2}ab$ Sin $\angle C$, where a and b are two sides and $\angle C$ is the included angle.
(a) $a = 3.6$ cm, $b = 4.5$ cm, $\angle C = 55°$
(b) $b = 7.3$ cm, $c = 6.1$ cm, $\angle A = 72°$
(c) $a = 3.1$ cm, $c = 4.9$ cm, $\angle B = 34°\ 30'$
(d) $a = 2.8$ cm, $b = 4.7$ cm, $\angle C = 130°$
(e) $b = 8.8$ cm, $c = 5.2$ cm, $\angle A = 110°$
(f) $a = 10.3$ cm, $c = 8.4$ cm, $\angle B = 145°$.

* **22** Use the given information to find the area of each triangle.

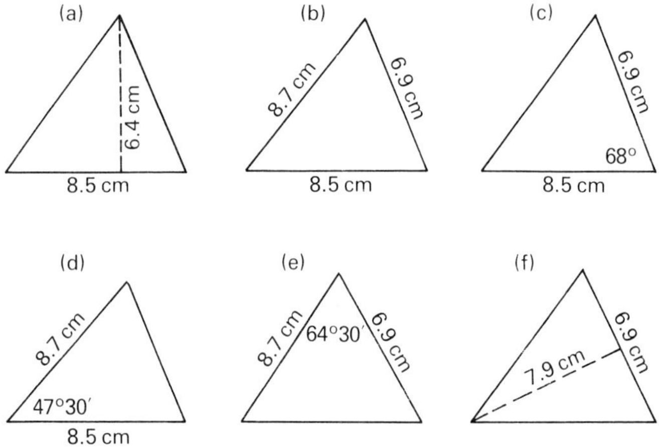

* **23** Find the lengths of arcs which subtend these angles at the centre of circles, with the given radius in each case. ($\pi = 3\frac{1}{7}$)

(a) $60^\circ, r = 7$ cm (b) $30^\circ, r = 3\frac{1}{2}$ cm (c) $20^\circ, r = 14$ cm
(d) $135^\circ, r = 21$ cm (e) $40^\circ, r = 10\frac{1}{2}$ cm (f) $240^\circ, r = 1\frac{3}{4}$ cm.

* **24** In a circle radius 2 cm, find the lengths of arcs which subtend the following angles at the centre ($\pi = 3.14$).

(a) 60° (b) 90° (c) 80° (d) 315° (e) 200° (f) 270°.

* **25** An arc of a circle is $3\frac{2}{3}$ cm and it subtends an angle of 75° at the centre of the circle. Find the radius of the circle. ($\pi = \frac{22}{7}$)

* **26** An arc of a circle is $1\frac{1}{10}$ metres in length and the radius of the circle is $\frac{7}{8}$ metres. What is the angle subtended by the arc at the centre of the circle? ($\pi = \frac{22}{7}$)

* **27** A satellite's orbit is a circle whose centre is the centre of the earth. Subtending an angle of 63°, it travelled a distance of 7315 km. If the earth's radius is 6300 km, how far above the earth's surface was the satellite orbiting? ($\pi = \frac{22}{7}$)

Complete this table using $\pi = 3\frac{1}{7}$:

	Radius	Subtended angle	Length of arc	Area of sector
* **28**	63 m	48°		
* **29**	$4\frac{1}{2}$ cm	70°		
* **30**	18 cm	112°		
* **31**	$40\frac{1}{2}$ m	140°		
* **32**	$17\frac{1}{2}$ cm	54°		

* **33** In a circle radius 5 cm, calculate the lengths of chords which subtend angles

(a) 48° (b) 35° (c) 108° (d) 75° (e) 165°.

* **34** Calculate lengths of chords which subtend an angle of 85° at the centre of circles of radii

(a) 8 cm (b) 2.3 cm (c) 4.9 cm (d) 3.7 cm.

* **35** AB is a common chord to two circles of radii 3.5 cm and 5.4 cm. The chord subtends an angle of 98° at the centre of the smaller circle and an angle of 59° at the centre of the larger circle. Use the smaller circle to find the length of the chord and then verify the answer using the information from the larger circle.

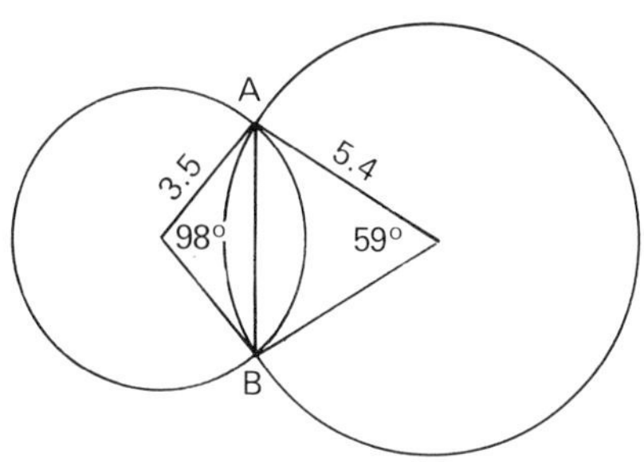

36 A rectangular prism length 7 cm, breadth $2\frac{3}{4}$ cm and height 2 cm, was full of water. The contents, when poured, just filled another container in the shape of a cylinder 4 cm high. Calculate the radius of the top of the cylinder. ($\pi = 3\frac{1}{7}$)

37 Each of these containers has the same volume.

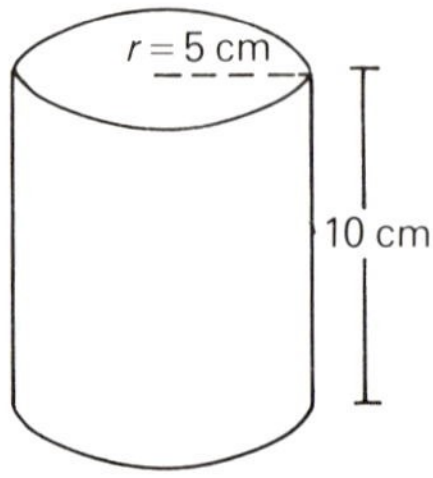

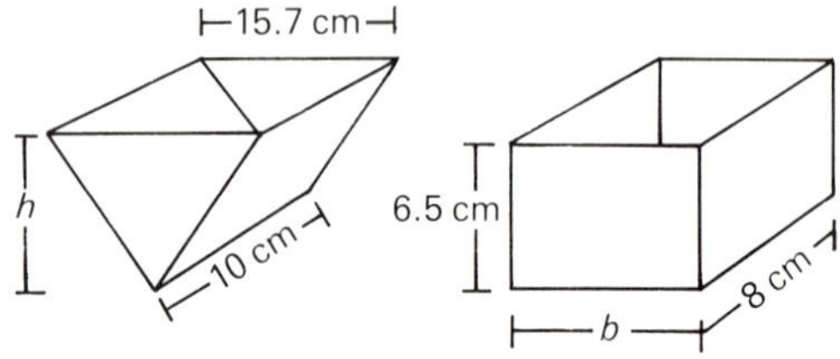

(a) Find the volume of the cylinder. ($\pi = 3.14$)
(b) Calculate the depth (h) of the triangular prism.
(c) Find the breadth (b) of the rectangular container correct to two decimal places.

38 How many litres will each container hold when full?
(a) A cube with an edge of 15 cm as an inside measurement.
(b) A cube with an inside edge of 5 cm.
(c) A rectangular prism with inside measurements of 6 cm, 5 cm and 7.8 cm.
(d) A cylinder with an inside base diameter of 12 cm and a depth of 10 cm. Give the answer correct to the nearest millilitre. Take the value of π to be 3.14.

39 Find the weight of water in kilograms in each container when full, if 1 litre of water weighs 1 kilogram.

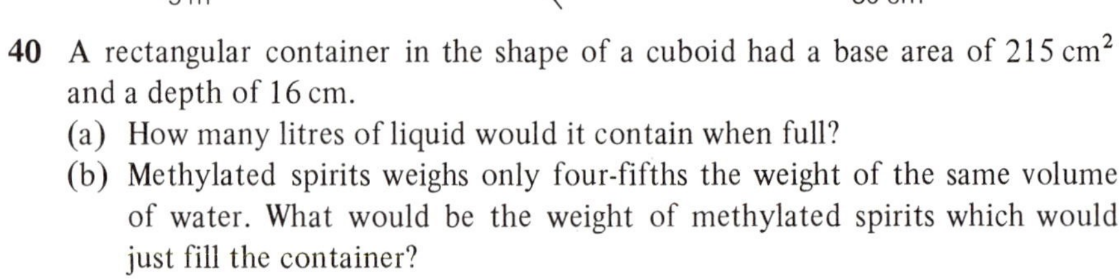

40 A rectangular container in the shape of a cuboid had a base area of 215 cm^2 and a depth of 16 cm.
(a) How many litres of liquid would it contain when full?
(b) Methylated spirits weighs only four-fifths the weight of the same volume of water. What would be the weight of methylated spirits which would just fill the container?

41 A cylindrical tank, base radius 10 cm and depth 20 cm, was used to hold white spirit. Take $\pi = 3.14$.
(a) How many litres of the spirit would it hold?
(b) What would be the weight of white spirit which would half fill the tank? (1000 kg of water takes up the same space as 850 kg of white spirit.)

42 Find the volume of each prism.

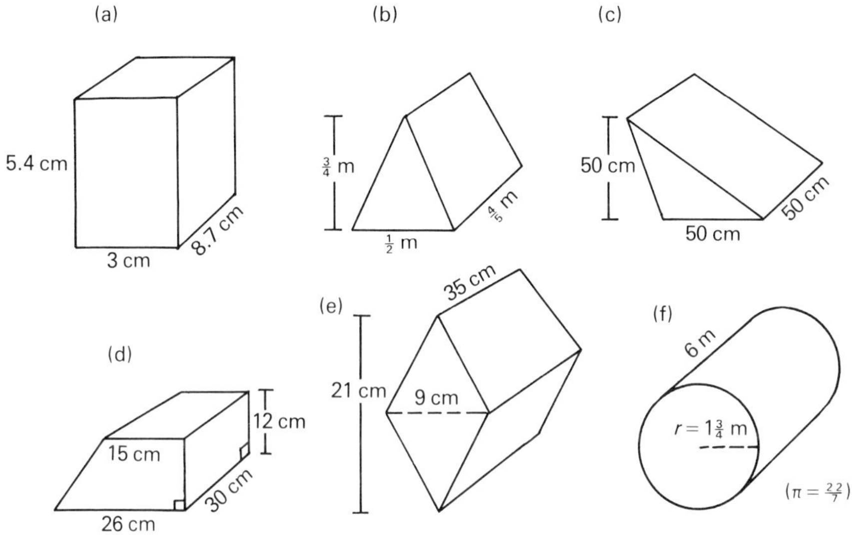

43 Find the surface area of these solids. It will be necessary to calculate some measurements first.

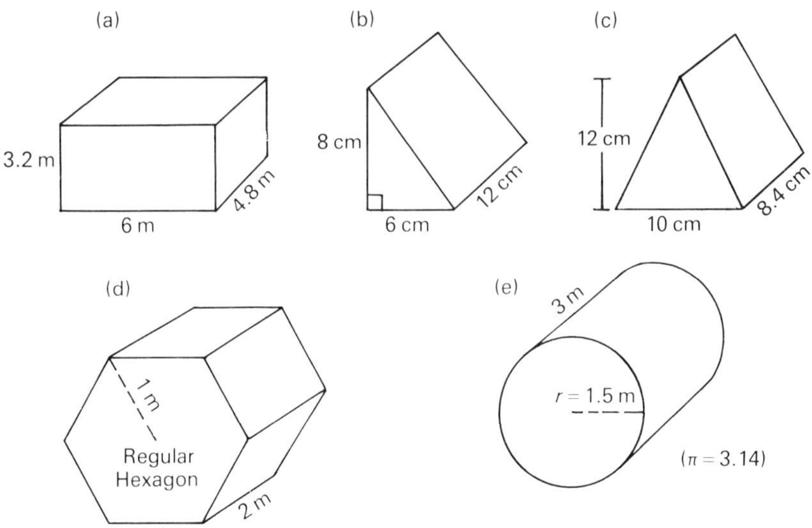

* **44** Find the volumes of pyramids with these measurements:

(a) Base, rectangle 8.3 cm by 4.5 cm, height 6.2 cm.

(b) Base, triangle area 16.4 cm^2, height 7.5 cm.

(c) Base, circle radius $3\frac{1}{2}$ cm, height 15 cm. ($\pi = 3\frac{1}{7}$)

(d) Base, square with a side 7.8 cm, height 8.5 cm.

* **45** The apex O of a pyramid, is vertically over X, the centre of the square base. E is the centre of BC. $\angle OEX = 70°$. The base edge is 16 cm.

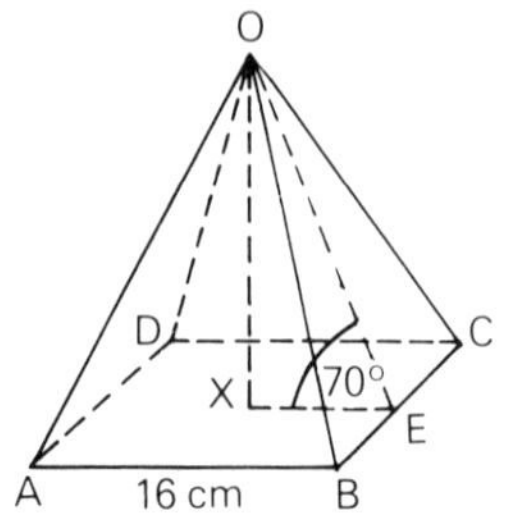

(a) Calculate the vertical height OX correct to 3 significant figures.
(b) Find the volume of the pyramid to the nearest cubic centimetre.

* **46** PQ is the vertical height of a cone and QR the base radius. QR = 28 cm. The slant edge PR = 35 cm.

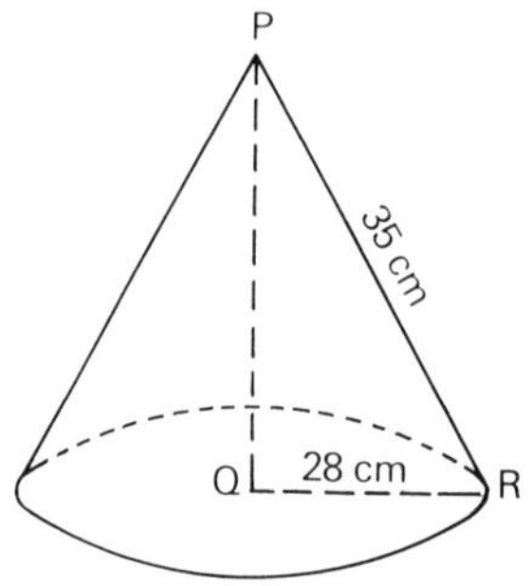

Calculate (a) the vertical height PQ,
(b) the volume of the cone. ($\pi = 3\frac{1}{7}$)

* **47** A ladle is in the shape of an inverted cone. The radius of the top is 15 cm and the depth is 28 cm. The ladle is filled with water which is then poured into a rectangular container whose base measures 60 cm by 25 cm. Take the value of π as $\frac{22}{7}$.
(a) How many litres of water will the ladle hold when full?
(b) What is the depth of water in the rectangular container when one ladle has been emptied into it?

* **48** Find the volumes of spheres with the following radii, correct to three significant figures.
(a) $r = 0.2$ m, $\pi = 3.14$ (b) $r = 7$ cm, $\pi = 3\frac{1}{7}$
(c) $r = 1$ cm, $\pi = \frac{22}{7}$ (d) $r = 1.5$ cm, $\pi = 3.14$.

* **49** A brass paperweight is a hemisphere of radius 5 cm. If 1 cm^3 of brass weighs 8 grams, how heavy is the paperweight in kilograms correct to three significant figures? ($\pi = 3.14$)

* **50** Seven hundred lead spheres each with a radius of 3 cm, are melted down and cast into a rectangular prism length 99 cm, breadth 99 cm, thickness 8 cm. What percentage of the original lead in the spheres was lost in casting? ($\pi = \frac{22}{7}$)

* **51** The diameter of an iron ball used for demolition work is 0.84 metres. If one cubic metre of iron weighs 7800 kilograms, what is the weight of the ball correct to three significant figures? ($\pi = 3.14$)

* **52** Find the curved surface area, correct to 3 significant figures, of a
(a) cone, radius 3 cm, slant height 7 cm, $\pi = 3\frac{1}{7}$,
(b) cone, radius $3\frac{1}{2}$ cm, slant height 6 cm, $\pi = 3\frac{1}{7}$,
(c) sphere, radius 7 cm, $\pi = 3\frac{1}{7}$,
(d) sphere, radius 10 cm, $\pi = 3.14$,
(e) sphere, radius 2.6 cm, $\pi = 3.14$,
(f) cone, radius 3 cm, vertical height 4 cm, $\pi = 3.14$,
(g) cone, radius 35 cm, vertical height 84 cm, $\pi = 3\frac{1}{7}$,
(h) cone, radius 8 cm, vertical height 10 cm, $\pi = 3.14$.

* **53** A building at an exhibition was in the shape of a hemisphere radius 25 metres. Find the outer surface area of the building taking the value of π as 3.14.

* **54** A football has a diameter of 28 cm. Calculate the surface area and then add 15% for seams to find the total surface of leather used to make one ball. ($\pi = 3\frac{1}{7}$)

Latitude and Longitude

Revision notes

The Equator is the earth's circumference.
Circles of longitude pass through the North and South poles.
A circle of longitude is also the earth's circumference.
The earth's circumference is a Great circle.
Circles of latitude (except the Equator) are Small circles.
Distances on the earth are arcs (see earlier notes, p. 99).
Radius of a small circle = Earth radius × Cosine latitude angle.

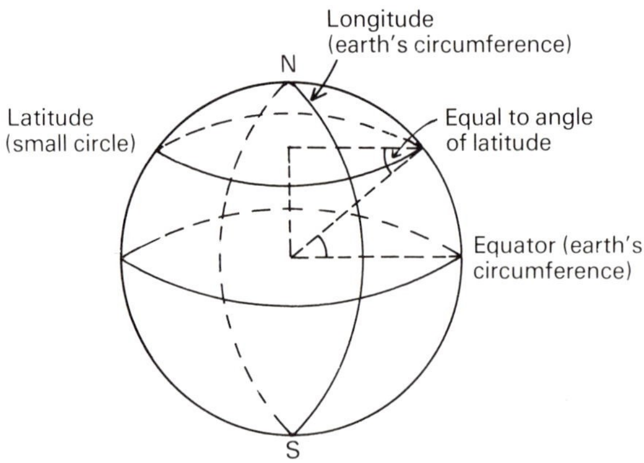

▶ Assume the earth's radius is 6300 km and $\pi = \frac{22}{7}$.

(a) Find the circumference of the earth.

(b) Calculate the distance between two towns on the equator, one at longitude 58° W and the other at longitude 10° W.

(c) Calculate the distance between two towns on the equator, one at longitude 15° W and the other at longitude 65° E.

(d) One town is at latitude 40° N longitude 18° E and another is at latitude 20° S longitude 18° E. Find the distance between them.

(e) Calculate the circumference of the circle of latitude 25° N.

(f) Find the distance between Philadelphia 40° N 75° W and Madrid 40° N 3° W.

(a) Circumference $= 2 \times \frac{22}{7} \times 6300 = 39\,600$ km.

(b) Angle subtended by the arc $= 58 - 10 = 48°$.
Earth circumference $= 39\,600$ km.

$$\text{Distance} = \frac{39\,600}{360} \times 48 = 5280 \text{ km.}$$

(c) Angle subtended by the arc $= 65 + 15 = 80°$.
Circumference $= 39\,600$ km.

$$\text{Distance} = \frac{39\,600}{360} \times 80 = 8800 \text{ km.}$$

(d) Both towns are on longitude 18° E.
Circumference $= 39\,600$ km.
Angle subtended by the arc $= 40 + 20 = 60°$.

$$\text{Distance} = \frac{39\,600}{360} \times 60 = 6600 \text{ km.}$$

(e) Radius of small circle $= 6300 \text{ Cosine } 25° = 6300 \times 0.9063 = 5710$ km.

$$\text{Circumference} = 2 \times \frac{22}{7} \times 5710 = 35\,891 \text{ km.}$$

(f) Both are on latitude 40° N.
Radius of circle $= 6300 \text{ Cosine } 40° = 6300 \times 0.766 = 4826$ km.

$$\text{Circumference} = 2 \times \frac{22}{7} \times 4826 = 30\,335 \text{ km.}$$

Angle subtended $= 75 - 3 = 72°$.

$$\text{Distance} = \frac{30\,335}{360} \times 72 = 6067 \text{ km.}$$

Revision exercises

1 Take the radius of the earth to be 6300 km and π to be $3\frac{1}{7}$. Find the distance between these points on the equator:

(a) long. 25° E and long. 100° E
(b) long. 15° W and long. 140° W
(c) long. 35° E and long. 35° W
(d) long. 18° W and long. 25° E
(e) long. 24° E and long. 94° W
(f) long. 116° W and long. 97° W
(g) long. 110° E and long. 162° E
(h) long. 83° W and long. 76° E.

2 All these places are on the equator.
Bangkinang, Indonesia, long. 100° E
Basoko, Africa, long. 23° E
Curuca, Brazil, long. 48° W
Garissa, Kenya, long. 40° E
Kalkaska, USA, long. 85° W
Uaupes, Brazil, long. 67° W.
Assuming the diameter of the earth to be 12 670 km and $\pi = 3\frac{1}{7}$, calculate the distance between
(a) Bangkinang and Basoko
(b) Caruca and Uaupes
(c) Garissa and Kalkaska
(d) Basoko and Kalkaska
(e) Curuca and Garissa
(f) Bangkinang and Uaupes.

3 Assume the radius of the earth is 6300 km and $\pi = 3\frac{1}{7}$. Find the distance between these positions on the same circle of longitude:
(a) lat. 30° N and lat. 80° N
(b) lat. 15° S and lat. 40° S
(c) lat. 24° N and lat. 38° S
(d) lat. 52° N and lat. 22° S
(e) lat. 36° S and lat. 80° S
(f) lat. 08° N and lat. 63° S.

4 These towns are all on longitude 40° E.
Mozambique lat. 15° S
Mecca lat. 21° N
Medina lat. 25° N
Rostov lat. 57° N
Arkhangelsk lat. 65° N
Zanzibar lat. 06° S.
The earth's radius is 6440 km and $\pi = 3\frac{1}{7}$. Find the distance between
(a) Mozambique and Mecca
(b) Medina and Rostov
(c) Arkhangelsk and Zanzibar
(d) Mozambique and Rostov
(e) Medina and Zanzibar
(f) Arkhangelsk and Mecca.

* **5** Copy and complete this table using $\pi = 3.14$:

	Earth radius	Angle of latitude	Radius of small circle	Circumference
(a)	6370 km	42° 30′ S		
(b)	6300 km	38° N		
(c)	6440 km	59° S		
(d)	6335 km	73° 30′ S		
(e)	6314 km	64° N		
(f)	6328 km	16° S		

* **6** Assume an earth radius of 6370 km and $\pi = 3\frac{1}{7}$, to find the distance between towns at
(a) 60° N 100° E and 60° N 25° E
(b) 12° S 80° W and 12° S 43° W
(c) 18° S 21° E and 18° S 42° W
(d) 33° N 5° W and 33° N 108° E
(e) 24° N 123° W and 24° N 45° E
(f) 71° N 60° W and 71° N 38° E.

* **7** This list gives the positions of six towns.

New York 41° N 74° W — Salt Lake City 41° N 112° W
Durban 30° S 31° E — Istanbul 41° N 29° E
Cordoba 30° S 64° W — Perth 30° S 116° E.

If the earth's radius is taken as 6300 km and $\pi = 3.14$, find the distance between

(a) New York and Istanbul
(b) Perth and Durban
(c) Cordoba and Perth
(d) Salt Lake City and New York
(e) Istanbul and Salt Lake City
(f) Durban and Cordoba.

* **8** A plane flies from Naples 43° N 14° E to Istanbul 43° N 28° E and then on to Minsk 54° N 28° E. Calculate the total journey. (earth radius 6300 km, $\pi = 3.14$)

* **9** A plane's journey commences at Cairo 30° N 31° E and, via Odessa 46° N 31° E, it ends at Berne 46° N 7° E. If the earth's radius is 6300 km and $\pi = 3.14$, how far did the plane travel?

* **10** Find the complete journey from Madrid 40° N 3° W to Birmingham 52° N 3° W and then to Warsaw 52° N 21° E, using an earth radius of 6314 km and $\pi = 3\frac{1}{7}$.

* **11** (a) Calculate the distance between position 25° W and position 35° E, both on the equator. (earth radius 6370 km, $\pi = 3.14$)

(b) Calculate the distance between town A 45° N 30° E and town B 45° N 70° E. (earth radius 6370 km, $\pi = 3\frac{1}{7}$)

* **12** (a) If the distance round a circle of latitude is 31 400 km, what is its radius? ($\pi = 3.14$)

(b) A circle of latitude is of the form $x°$ South. If its circumference is 35 000 km, what is the value of x? Assume an earth radius of 6370 km and $\pi = 3\frac{1}{7}$.

* **13** This list gives the latitude and longitude of four towns.

Lima 12° S 75° W — Philadelphia 40° N 75° W
Madrid 40° N 3° W — Edinburgh 56° N 3° W.

Assume an earth radius of 6370 km and take π to be 3.14. Find the total journey from Lima to Edinburgh calling at Philadelphia and Madrid in that order.

* **14** Around the equator, every degree of longitude is equivalent to a distance of 110 kilometres.

(a) What is the distance between points at longitude 25° W and longitude 60° E, both on the equator?

(b) Find the distance between points at longitude 28° E and longitude 100° E, both on the equator.

(c) Calculate the radius of the earth. ($\pi = \frac{22}{7}$)

Transformations

Revision notes

A *reflection* is a mirror image in a line of given equation.

A *translation* is a movement by a given vector.

A *rotation* is a movement by fixed radius about a given point.

Reflections

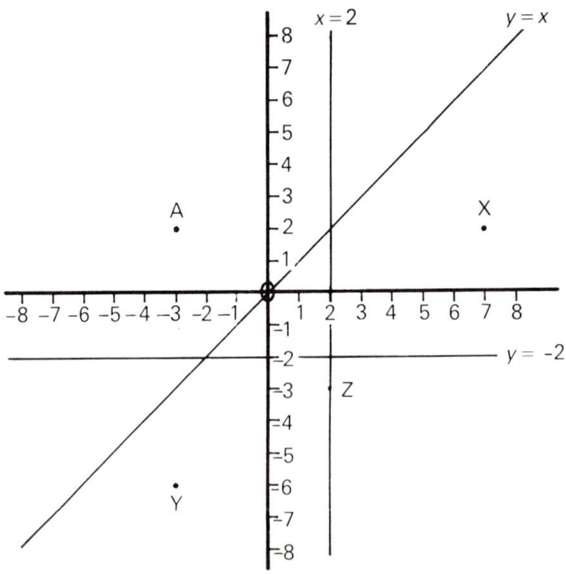

A(−3, 2) is reflected in line $x = 2$, to point X(7, 2).
A(−3, 2) is reflected in line $y = -2$, to point Y(−3, −6).
A(−3, 2) is reflected in line $y = x$, to point Z(2, −3).

Translations

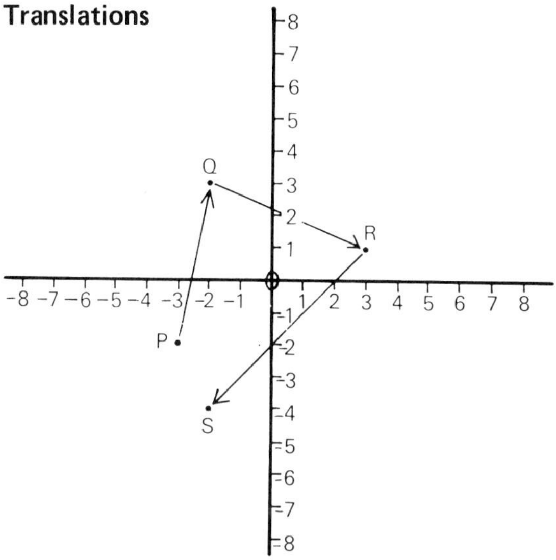

P(−3, −2) is translated by vector $\begin{pmatrix}1\\5\end{pmatrix}$, to Q(−2, 3).

Q(−2, 3) is translated by vector $\begin{pmatrix}5\\-2\end{pmatrix}$, to R(3, 1).

R(3, 1) is translated by vector $\begin{pmatrix}-5\\-5\end{pmatrix}$, to S(−2, −4).

Note. Vector movements can be added: $\begin{pmatrix}1\\5\end{pmatrix}+\begin{pmatrix}5\\-2\end{pmatrix}+\begin{pmatrix}-5\\-5\end{pmatrix}=\begin{pmatrix}1\\-2\end{pmatrix}$.

The total vector movement $\begin{pmatrix}1\\-2\end{pmatrix}$ takes P(−3, −2) to S(−2, −4).

Vectors may also be subtracted.

▶ Vector $\mathbf{a}=\begin{pmatrix}1\\-2\end{pmatrix}$, vector $\mathbf{b}=\begin{pmatrix}3\\4\end{pmatrix}$, vector $\mathbf{c}=\begin{pmatrix}-3\\-1\end{pmatrix}$.

Work out the vector operations
(a) $2\mathbf{a}+\mathbf{b}$
(b) $3\mathbf{b}-\mathbf{c}$
(c) $\mathbf{a}+\mathbf{b}-\mathbf{c}$.

(a) $2\begin{pmatrix}1\\-2\end{pmatrix}+\begin{pmatrix}3\\4\end{pmatrix}=\begin{pmatrix}2\\-4\end{pmatrix}+\begin{pmatrix}3\\4\end{pmatrix}=\begin{pmatrix}5\\0\end{pmatrix}$.

(b) $3\begin{pmatrix}3\\4\end{pmatrix}-\begin{pmatrix}-3\\-1\end{pmatrix}=\begin{pmatrix}9\\12\end{pmatrix}-\begin{pmatrix}-3\\-1\end{pmatrix}=\begin{pmatrix}12\\13\end{pmatrix}$.

(c) $\begin{pmatrix}1\\-2\end{pmatrix}+\begin{pmatrix}3\\4\end{pmatrix}-\begin{pmatrix}-3\\-1\end{pmatrix}=\begin{pmatrix}7\\3\end{pmatrix}$.

Rotations

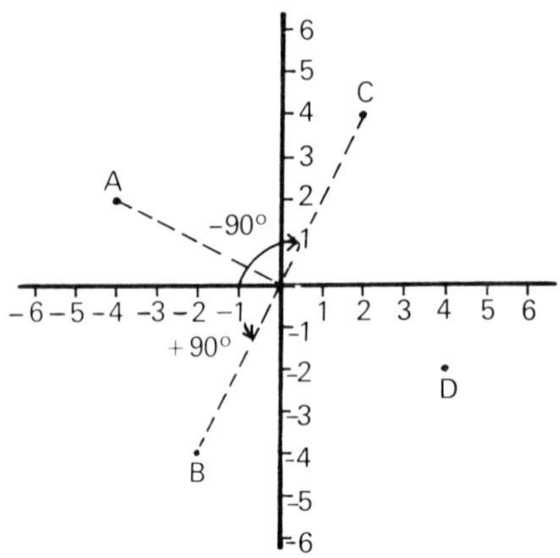

Anticlockwise rotation, positive (+) sign. Clockwise rotation, negative (−) sign.
A(−4, 2) rotated +90° about (0, 0), moves to B(−2, −4).
A(−4, 2) rotated −90° about (0, 0), moves to C(2, 4).
A(−4, 2) rotated 180° about (0, 0), moves to D(4, −2).

Revision exercises

1 (a) Plot the points A(2, 4), B(3, 6), C(4, 4), D(3, 5). Join the points to form the arrowhead ABCD.

(b) Transform the shape ABCD by reflection in line $y = 2$. Give the new coordinates of each point.

2 (a) Plot the points A(−4, 3), B(−2, 3), C(−4, 2), D(−3, 2), E(−4, 1) and F(−2, 1). Join AE, AB, CD and EF to form a large letter E.

(b) Translate the shape by vector $\begin{pmatrix} 2 \\ -3 \end{pmatrix}$. Give the coordinates of the translation.

(c) Without referring to graph paper give the coordinates of the original points after translation by vector $\begin{pmatrix} -2 \\ -4 \end{pmatrix}$.

3 (a) Using the points A to F in the last question, reflect the shape in line $y = -1$.

(b) Translate the points obtained by reflecting A to F, using vector $\begin{pmatrix} 2 \\ 0 \end{pmatrix}$.

4 On these axes are four shapes F1, F2, F3 and F4.
(a) What transformation has taken F1 to F2?
(b) Name the transformations which takes F1 to F3.
(c) What transformations will return F4 to F1?
(d) How would you transform F4 to F2?
(e) How could F3 be transformed to F4?

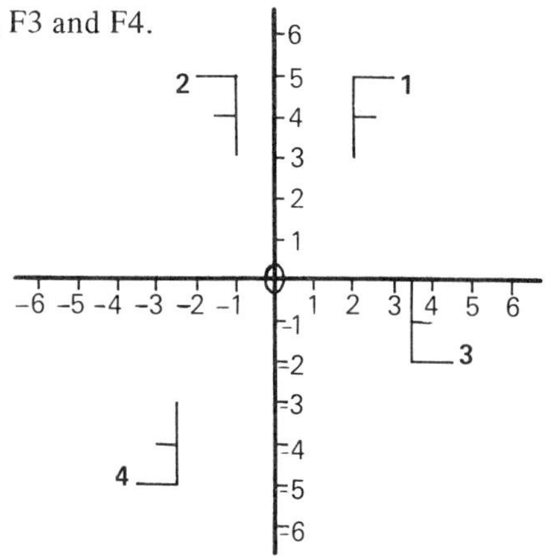

5 (a) Start with three points (1, 2), (2, 3) and (2, 2).
(b) Perform three consecutive reflections using lines $y = 0$, $x = 1$ and $x = -1\frac{1}{2}$.
(c) Start again with the same three points and perform consecutive reflections in $x = -\frac{1}{2}$, $y = 0$ and $x = -3$.
(d) Suggest three reflections which will give the same result.
(e) What can you say about one of the reflections used each time?

6 (a) Plot points $(-3, 4)$, $(-1, 4)$ and $(-2, 4\frac{1}{2})$. Join the points to form an isosceles triangle.
(b) Carry out three successive reflections on the points in lines $y = 1$, $x = 0$ and $x = -1\frac{1}{2}$.
(c) Using a horizontal line as a mirror, give the glide reflection which would produce the same transformation.

7 Use the shapes on these axes to answer the questions which follow.

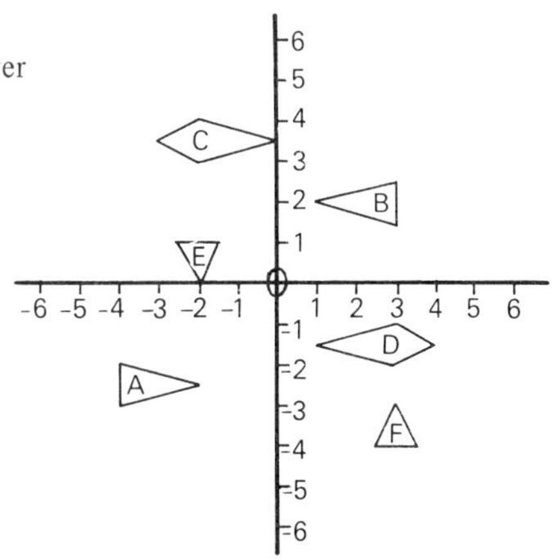

(a) Give the glide reflection which will transform shape A to the position of shape B.
(b) What glide reflection transforms shape C to shape D?
(c) Give the glide reflection which transforms shape E to shape F.
(d) What glide reflection transforms shape F back to shape E?

8 (a) Plot points $(1, -3)$, $(2, -2)$, $(2, -4)$, $(1, -4)$.

Reflect the points in line $y = x$ and then translate with vector $\begin{pmatrix} 2 \\ 2 \end{pmatrix}$.

(b) Plot points $(-4, 1)$, $(-3, -1)$, $(-4, -1)$.

Translate with vector $\begin{pmatrix} 3 \\ -3 \end{pmatrix}$ and then reflect in line $y = -x$.

(c) Draw the line $y = x + 2$.

Use that line to reflect point $(2, -1)$ and then translate with vector $\begin{pmatrix} -3 \\ -3 \end{pmatrix}$.

(d) Plot the parallelogram ABCD using points A$(-4, -1)$, B$(-3, -2)$, C$(-4, -2)$, D$(-5, -1)$.

Reflect the shape in line $y = x - 1$ and then translate with vector $\begin{pmatrix} 4 \\ 4 \end{pmatrix}$.

(e) Plot the triangle PQR with points P$(-3, -3)$, Q$(-2, -5)$, R$(-5, -3)$.

Translate with vector $\begin{pmatrix} -2 \\ 2 \end{pmatrix}$ and reflect in line $y = -3 - x$.

9 (a) Give a rotation which produces the same result as -90°.
(b) What rotation is the same as $+100^\circ$?
(c) Which rotation gives the same result as $+200^\circ$?
(d) Give a rotation which is the same as -220°.

10 Plot each of these shapes on axes as shown here.

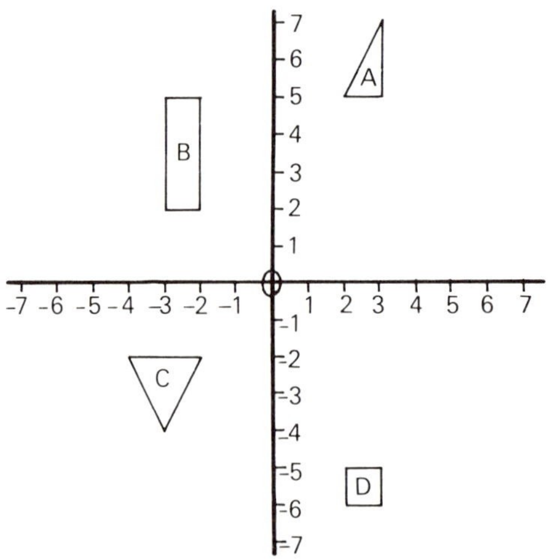

After each of these rotations, what is the significance of the resulting co-ordinates?

(a) Rotate shape A -90° about the origin (0, 0).
(b) Rotate shape B 180° about the origin (0, 0).
(c) Use (0, 0) as a centre to rotate shape C $+90^\circ$.
(d) Rotate shape D -270° about point (0, 0).

11 Draw axes numbered -8 to 8.

(a) Plot a capital L using points (3, 5), (3, 7), (4, 5).
(b) Rotate the shape $-90°$ about (0, 0).
(c) Rotate the original shape $180°$ about the origin.
(d) Rotate the original letter L $+90°$ about the origin.
(e) Refer back to the original letter L. Choose point (3, 5) as a centre of rotation. Rotate the shape $-90°$.
(f) Rotate the original shape $180°$ about point (3, 5).

12 You will require the following drawing for this question and for Question 13.

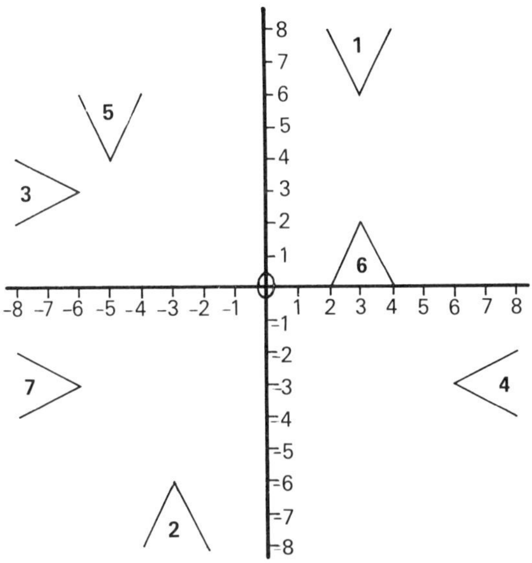

In each case give the angle and the centre of rotation.

(a) What rotation takes V1 to V2?
(b) How is V2 rotated to position V4?
(c) Give the rotation from V3 to V5.
(d) What is the rotation from V2 to V7?
(e) How would you rotate V1 to position V6?
(f) How could V3 be rotated to the position of V4?
(g) Rotate V7 to V4.
(h) How could V5 be rotated to position V2?

13 Use the diagram in the last question.

(a) What reflection takes V1 to V6?
(b) Name the reflection taking V4 to V7.
(c) Give the line of reflection taking V7 to V2.
(d) Name the vector which translates V6 to V2.
(e) Give the translation of V5 to V1.
(f) Give the glide reflection taking V1 to V2.
(g) Give the line of reflection to take V3 to V5.
(h) Give the glide reflection from V2 to V5.

Matrices

Revision notes

Information about routes in a network can be stored in a matrix.

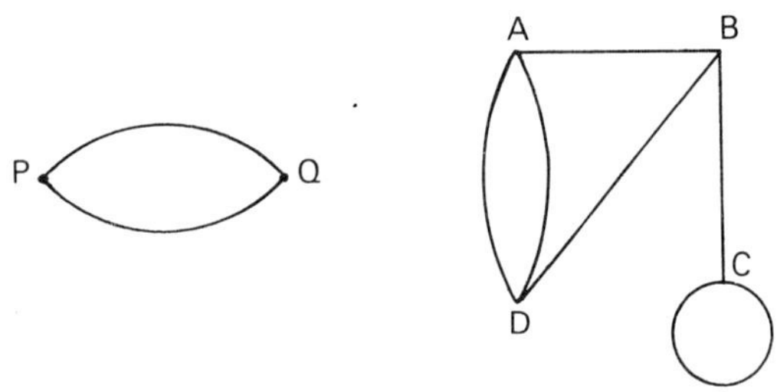

The first network shows two routes joining P and Q. The table explains the routes which are then written in matrix form.

From / To

	P	Q
P	0	2
Q	2	0

$$\begin{pmatrix} 0 & 2 \\ 2 & 0 \end{pmatrix}$$

In the second diagram there is a loop at point C. We can travel from C to C each way round the loop (2 routes).

From / To

	A	B	C	D
A	0	1	0	2
B	1	0	1	1
C	0	1	2	0
D	2	1	0	0

$$\begin{pmatrix} 0 & 1 & 0 & 2 \\ 1 & 0 & 1 & 1 \\ 0 & 1 & 2 & 0 \\ 2 & 1 & 0 & 0 \end{pmatrix}$$

The next network is *directed,* shown by the arrows on one-way streets. The loop at A is two-way, since it has no arrow.

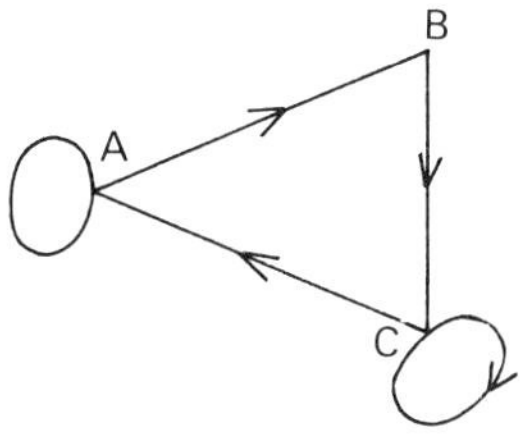

$$\begin{pmatrix} 2 & 1 & 0 \\ 0 & 0 & 1 \\ 1 & 0 & 1 \end{pmatrix}$$

Note. The matrix of a directed network is no longer symmetrical about its leading diagonal (top left to bottom right). The leading diagonal also contains an odd number.

A matrix of the order 2 by 3 has 2 rows and 3 columns.
A 1 by 4 matrix is therefore a row matrix.
A 4 by 1 matrix is a column matrix.
2 by 2 and 5 by 5 are square matrices.
Matrices of the same order may be added and subtracted.

▶ If $\mathbf{A} = \begin{pmatrix} 2 & 4 \\ 3 & 1 \end{pmatrix}$, $\mathbf{B} = \begin{pmatrix} 1 \\ 2 \\ 3 \end{pmatrix}$, $\mathbf{C} = \begin{pmatrix} -1 \\ 2 \\ 0 \end{pmatrix}$, $\mathbf{D} = \begin{pmatrix} -6 & 0 \\ 2 & -4 \end{pmatrix}$,

calculate (a) $\mathbf{A} + \mathbf{D}$ (b) $\mathbf{C} - \mathbf{B}$ (c) $2\mathbf{A} - \mathbf{D}$.

(a) $\begin{pmatrix} 2 & 4 \\ 3 & 1 \end{pmatrix} + \begin{pmatrix} -6 & 0 \\ 2 & -4 \end{pmatrix} = \begin{pmatrix} -4 & 4 \\ 5 & -3 \end{pmatrix}.$

(b) $\begin{pmatrix} -1 \\ 2 \\ 0 \end{pmatrix} - \begin{pmatrix} 1 \\ 2 \\ 3 \end{pmatrix} = \begin{pmatrix} -2 \\ 0 \\ -3 \end{pmatrix}.$

(c) $2\begin{pmatrix} 2 & 4 \\ 3 & 1 \end{pmatrix} - \begin{pmatrix} -6 & 0 \\ 2 & -4 \end{pmatrix} = \begin{pmatrix} 4 & 8 \\ 6 & 2 \end{pmatrix} - \begin{pmatrix} -6 & 0 \\ 2 & -4 \end{pmatrix}$

$$= \begin{pmatrix} 10 & 8 \\ 4 & 6 \end{pmatrix}.$$

Note. Addition is *commutative,* i.e. $\mathbf{A} + \mathbf{D} = \mathbf{D} + \mathbf{A}$

Multiplication

Matrices may be multiplied by each other, if the number of columns in the first matrix is the same as the number of rows in the second matrix.

▶ When $\mathbf{P} = \begin{pmatrix} 3 & 2 \\ 1 & 0 \\ -1 & 1 \end{pmatrix}$, $\mathbf{Q} = \begin{pmatrix} 2 & 1 \\ 0 & 1 \end{pmatrix}$, $\mathbf{R} = \begin{pmatrix} 3 \\ -1 \\ 0 \end{pmatrix}$

$\mathbf{S} = (-1 \quad 2 \quad 2)$, $\mathbf{T} = \begin{pmatrix} -1 \\ 4 \end{pmatrix}$,

calculate if possible (a) **PQ** (b) **RS** (c) **PS** (d) **SR**.

$$\text{(a)}\ \mathbf{PQ} = \begin{pmatrix} 3 & 2 \\ 1 & 0 \\ -1 & 1 \end{pmatrix}\begin{pmatrix} 2 & 1 \\ 0 & 1 \end{pmatrix} = \begin{pmatrix} 6 & 5 \\ 2 & 1 \\ -2 & 0 \end{pmatrix}.$$

$$\text{(b)}\ \mathbf{RS} = \begin{pmatrix} 3 \\ -1 \\ 0 \end{pmatrix}(-1 \quad 2 \quad 2) = \begin{pmatrix} -3 & 6 & 6 \\ 1 & -2 & -2 \\ 0 & 0 & 0 \end{pmatrix}.$$

$$\text{(c)}\ \mathbf{PS} = \begin{pmatrix} 3 & 2 \\ 1 & 0 \\ -1 & 1 \end{pmatrix}(-1 \quad 2 \quad 2).$$ 3 by 2 × 1 by 3: not possible.

Note. Multiplication is *non-commutative,* i.e. **SP** could be calculated.

$$\text{(d)}\ \mathbf{SR} = (-1 \quad 2 \quad 2)\begin{pmatrix} 3 \\ -1 \\ 0 \end{pmatrix} = -5.$$ Single figure answer.

Identity

The identity matrix used in an operation produces no change.

For addition and subtraction of 2 by 2 matrices, it is $\begin{pmatrix} 0 & 0 \\ 0 & 0 \end{pmatrix}$.

For multiplication of 2 by 2 matrices, it is $\begin{pmatrix} 1 & 0 \\ 0 & 1 \end{pmatrix}$.

The inverse is that matrix which in operation gives the identity.

For multiplication, obtain the inverse as follows:

Change the signs of elements top right and bottom left. Exchange positions of terms top left and bottom right. Divide by the determinant (if it is not 1).

▶ Find the inverse of (a) $\begin{pmatrix} 5 & 2 \\ 2 & 1 \end{pmatrix}$ (b) $\begin{pmatrix} 6 & 5 \\ 2 & 2 \end{pmatrix}$.

(a) Determinant $= (5 \times 1) - (2 \times 2) = 1$. Inverse of $\begin{pmatrix} 5 & 2 \\ 2 & 1 \end{pmatrix}$ is $\begin{pmatrix} 1 & -2 \\ -2 & 5 \end{pmatrix}$

(b) Determinant $= (6 \times 2) - (5 \times 2) = 2$. Inverse is $\frac{1}{2}\begin{pmatrix} 2 & -5 \\ -2 & 6 \end{pmatrix} = \begin{pmatrix} 1 & -2\frac{1}{2} \\ -1 & 3 \end{pmatrix}$.

Transformations

The coordinates of points to be transformed are first written in matrix form.

Coordinates (2, −2), (3, 4), (−5, 2) are written $\begin{pmatrix} 2 & 3 & -5 \\ -2 & 4 & 2 \end{pmatrix}$.

When such a matrix is multiplied by a suitable 2 by 2 matrix, a transformation takes place.

▶ Transform the above coordinates with matrix $\begin{pmatrix} 1 & 0 \\ 0 & -1 \end{pmatrix}$.

Multiplication gives $\begin{pmatrix} 1 & 0 \\ 0 & -1 \end{pmatrix}\begin{pmatrix} 2 & 3 & -5 \\ -2 & 4 & 2 \end{pmatrix} = \begin{pmatrix} 2 & 3 & -5 \\ 2 & -4 & -2 \end{pmatrix}$.

This gives the new coordinates (2, 2), (3, −4), (−5, −2).
A reflection in line $y = 0$ has taken place.

It is possible to reflect, rotate and enlarge using matrices. The revision exercises will illustrate those transformations.

Revision exercises

1 $\mathbf{P} = \begin{pmatrix} 3 & -1 \\ 2 & 0 \end{pmatrix}$, $\mathbf{Q} = \begin{pmatrix} 2 & -2 & 1 \\ 1 & -1 & 0 \end{pmatrix}$, $\mathbf{R} = \begin{pmatrix} -4 & 1 \\ 0 & -2 \\ 3 & -1 \end{pmatrix}$, $\mathbf{S} = \begin{pmatrix} -2 & -3 \\ 4 & 0 \end{pmatrix}$,

$\mathbf{T} = \begin{pmatrix} -1 & 2 \\ 3 & -2 \\ -1 & -1 \end{pmatrix}$.

Find an answer where you think a calculation is possible.
(a) 3**Q** (b) **P** + **S** (c) **T** − **R** (d) **R** − **T** (e) **Q** + **S** (f) 2**S** + 3**P**
(g) 3**R** − 3**T** (h) **P** − **R** (i) **P** − **Q** (j) **S** − 2**P**.

2 These are route-matrices giving information about networks. Make a drawing for each one using letters of the alphabet.

(a) $\begin{pmatrix} 0 & 1 & 2 \\ 1 & 0 & 1 \\ 2 & 1 & 0 \end{pmatrix}$ (b) $\begin{pmatrix} 0 & 2 \\ 2 & 2 \end{pmatrix}$ (c) $\begin{pmatrix} 0 & 1 & 3 \\ 1 & 2 & 1 \\ 3 & 1 & 0 \end{pmatrix}$

(d) $\begin{pmatrix} 2 & 1 & 0 & 1 \\ 1 & 2 & 1 & 0 \\ 0 & 1 & 2 & 1 \\ 1 & 0 & 1 & 2 \end{pmatrix}$ (e) $\begin{pmatrix} 0 & 2 & 0 & 1 \\ 2 & 0 & 1 & 1 \\ 0 & 1 & 0 & 2 \\ 1 & 1 & 2 & 0 \end{pmatrix}$ (f) $\begin{pmatrix} 0 & 2 & 2 & 0 & 1 \\ 2 & 0 & 1 & 0 & 0 \\ 2 & 1 & 0 & 1 & 1 \\ 0 & 0 & 1 & 0 & 1 \\ 1 & 0 & 1 & 1 & 0 \end{pmatrix}$

(g) $\begin{pmatrix} 0 & 0 & 2 \\ 0 & 2 & 0 \\ 2 & 0 & 0 \end{pmatrix}$ (h) $\begin{pmatrix} 2 & 0 & 0 & 0 & 1 \\ 0 & 2 & 0 & 0 & 1 \\ 0 & 0 & 2 & 0 & 1 \\ 0 & 0 & 0 & 2 & 1 \\ 1 & 1 & 1 & 1 & 0 \end{pmatrix}$

3 Draw directed networks using these matrices.

(a) $\begin{pmatrix} 0 & 1 & 0 \\ 0 & 0 & 1 \\ 1 & 0 & 0 \end{pmatrix}$ (b) $\begin{pmatrix} 0 & 1 & 1 & 0 \\ 1 & 0 & 0 & 0 \\ 0 & 0 & 2 & 1 \\ 1 & 0 & 0 & 0 \end{pmatrix}$ (c) $\begin{pmatrix} 1 & 1 & 1 \\ 1 & 0 & 0 \\ 1 & 1 & 1 \end{pmatrix}$

(d) $\begin{pmatrix} 0 & 1 & 0 & 1 \\ 0 & 1 & 0 & 0 \\ 0 & 1 & 0 & 0 \\ 0 & 0 & 1 & 0 \end{pmatrix}$ (e) $\begin{pmatrix} 0 & 1 & 1 \\ 2 & 0 & 1 \\ 2 & 2 & 0 \end{pmatrix}$ (f) $\begin{pmatrix} 0 & 1 & 0 & 0 \\ 0 & 0 & 1 & 0 \\ 0 & 0 & 2 & 0 \\ 1 & 0 & 0 & 1 \end{pmatrix}$

(g) $\begin{pmatrix} 0 & 1 & 0 & 2 \\ 1 & 0 & 1 & 0 \\ 0 & 1 & 2 & 0 \\ 1 & 0 & 0 & 0 \end{pmatrix}$ (h) $\begin{pmatrix} 2 & 1 & 0 & 1 \\ 1 & 0 & 1 & 2 \\ 0 & 1 & 0 & 1 \\ 0 & 1 & 1 & 1 \end{pmatrix}$

4 Make a route-matrix for each directed network.

(a)
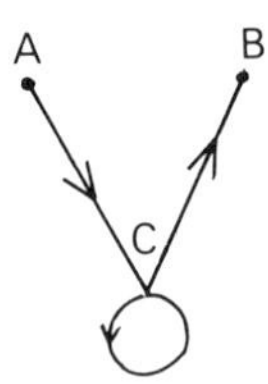

(b)
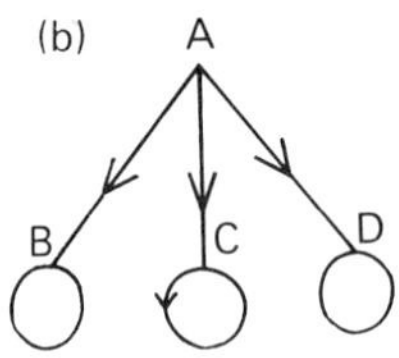

(c)
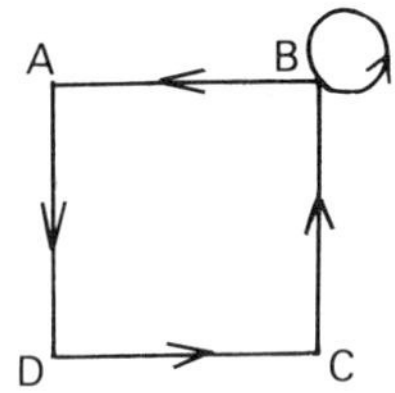

(d)
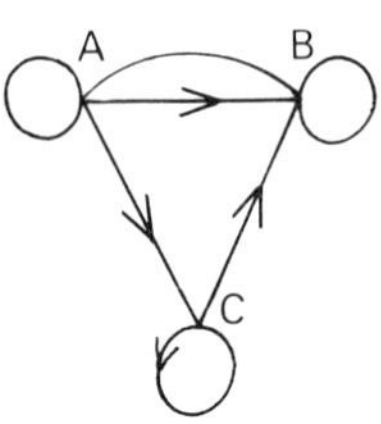

(e)

(f)
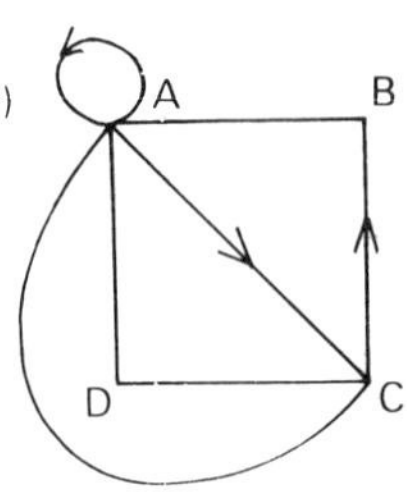

5 $\mathbf{A}=\begin{pmatrix}3\\1\\2\end{pmatrix}$, $\mathbf{B}=(1 \quad 2 \quad 1 \quad 3)$, $\mathbf{C}=(1 \quad 1 \quad 3)$, $\mathbf{D}=\begin{pmatrix}2\\1\\4\end{pmatrix}$, $\mathbf{E}=\begin{pmatrix}3\\1\\2\\1\end{pmatrix}$.

Where possible, work these multiplications.
(a) **CD** (b) **DC** (c) **BE** (d) **EB** (e) **AD** (f) **DA** (g) **BD** (h) **AC**
(i) **CA** (j) **DE**.

6 $\mathbf{P}=\begin{pmatrix}4 & 1\\1 & 2\end{pmatrix}$, $\mathbf{Q}=\begin{pmatrix}3 & -1\\-1 & 2\\-2 & 0\end{pmatrix}$, $\mathbf{R}=\begin{pmatrix}-1 & 2 & 1\\2 & 3 & 1\end{pmatrix}$, $\mathbf{S}=\begin{pmatrix}3 & 1 & 2\\-1 & 0 & 3\\2 & -2 & -1\end{pmatrix}$,

$\mathbf{T}=\begin{pmatrix}-2 & 1 & 3 & 4\\1 & 3 & 4 & -2\end{pmatrix}$.

Calculate if possible
(a) **QP** (b) **PQ** (c) **RS** (d) **SR** (e) **QT** (f) **TQ** (g) **SQ** (h) **RQ**
(i) **PT** (j) **PR**.

7 **A**, **B** and **C** are matrices such that

$\mathbf{A}=\begin{pmatrix}3 & 1 & 2\\0 & 2 & 1\end{pmatrix}$, $\mathbf{B}=\begin{pmatrix}2 & 1\\5 & 3\\0 & 4\end{pmatrix}$ $\mathbf{C}=\begin{pmatrix}3 & 0\\2 & 2\end{pmatrix}$.

(a) **ABC** means calculate **AB** first in that order, then multiply the result by **C**. Find the resulting matrix.
(b) **BCA** is multiplication **BC**, then the result by **A**. Find the result and compare it with **ABC**.
(c) Is it possible to calculate **ACB** and **BAC**?

8 Carry out these matrix multiplications.

(a) $\begin{pmatrix}4 & 7\\1 & 2\end{pmatrix}\begin{pmatrix}2 & -7\\-1 & 4\end{pmatrix}$ (b) $\begin{pmatrix}2 & 1\\5 & 3\end{pmatrix}\begin{pmatrix}3 & -1\\-5 & 2\end{pmatrix}$ (c) $\begin{pmatrix}9 & 2\\4 & 1\end{pmatrix}\begin{pmatrix}1 & -2\\-4 & 9\end{pmatrix}$

9 What are the inverse matrices under multiplication, for these 2 by 2 matrices?

(a) $\begin{pmatrix}2 & 5\\1 & 3\end{pmatrix}$ (b) $\begin{pmatrix}3 & 4\\2 & 3\end{pmatrix}$ (c) $\begin{pmatrix}5 & 3\\3 & 2\end{pmatrix}$ (d) $\begin{pmatrix}2 & 1\\1 & 1\end{pmatrix}$ (e) $\begin{pmatrix}4 & 3\\1 & 1\end{pmatrix}$

(f) $\begin{pmatrix}5 & 2\\2 & 1\end{pmatrix}$ (g) $\begin{pmatrix}7 & 3\\2 & 1\end{pmatrix}$ (h) $\begin{pmatrix}5 & 7\\2 & 3\end{pmatrix}$ (i) $\begin{pmatrix}4 & 3\\2 & 2\end{pmatrix}$ (j) $\begin{pmatrix}3 & 3\\2 & 3\end{pmatrix}$.

10 Give the inverse of each matrix under multiplication.

(a) $\begin{pmatrix}-3 & -7\\1 & 2\end{pmatrix}$ (b) $\begin{pmatrix}-2 & 1\\-5 & 2\end{pmatrix}$ (c) $\begin{pmatrix}-5 & -2\\3 & 1\end{pmatrix}$ (d) $\begin{pmatrix}4 & -3\\3 & -2\end{pmatrix}$.

Prove your answers by multiplication.

* **11** Take the coordinates of four points chosen by yourself and list as movements from the origin (0, 0) in the form of a 2 by 4 matrix. Multiply that matrix by

$$\begin{pmatrix} 1 & 0 \\ 0 & -1 \end{pmatrix}.$$

Plot the result as four points and check that you have carried out a reflection in $y = 0$.

* **12** Use the same four points and the original 2 by 4 matrix with which you started the last question. This time multiply the matrix by $\begin{pmatrix} -1 & 0 \\ 0 & 1 \end{pmatrix}$.

By plotting the result decide the transformation which that matrix has produced. Repeat with four more points.

* **13** (a) Under multiplication by a 2 by 2 matrix, what is the significance of the matrix $\begin{pmatrix} 1 & 0 \\ 0 & 1 \end{pmatrix}$?

(b) If you now take four points, stored as a 2 by 4 matrix and multiply by $\begin{pmatrix} 1 & 0 \\ 0 & 1 \end{pmatrix}$, what should be the result?

(c) Check that answer with four points.

* **14** (a) By using a 2 by 4 matrix, find the effect of multiplying by matrix

$$\begin{pmatrix} 0 & 1 \\ 1 & 0 \end{pmatrix}.$$

(b) Plot the original points and the result, to decide the line in which reflection occurs.

* **15** (a) Multiply your own 2 by 4 matrix by $\begin{pmatrix} 0 & -1 \\ -1 & 0 \end{pmatrix}$.

(b) What reflection does that matrix produce?

* **16** (a) Plot the points (2, 2), (4, 2), (2, 5).

(b) List the vector movements from (0, 0) as a 2 by 3 matrix.

(c) Find the results produced with a multiplication by the matrices

(i) $\begin{pmatrix} 0 & -1 \\ 1 & 0 \end{pmatrix}$ (ii) $\begin{pmatrix} 0 & 1 \\ -1 & 0 \end{pmatrix}$ (iii) $\begin{pmatrix} -1 & 0 \\ 0 & -1 \end{pmatrix}$.

* **17** All transformation matrices used in the previous questions are listed here.

$$\mathbf{B} = \begin{pmatrix} -1 & 0 \\ 0 & 1 \end{pmatrix} \qquad \mathbf{C} = \begin{pmatrix} 0 & 1 \\ 1 & 0 \end{pmatrix} \qquad \mathbf{D} = \begin{pmatrix} 0 & -1 \\ -1 & 0 \end{pmatrix}$$

$$\mathbf{E} = \begin{pmatrix} 0 & -1 \\ 1 & 0 \end{pmatrix} \qquad \mathbf{F} = \begin{pmatrix} 0 & 1 \\ -1 & 0 \end{pmatrix} \qquad \mathbf{G} = \begin{pmatrix} -1 & 0 \\ 0 & -1 \end{pmatrix}.$$

(a) Find the square of each matrix. Do any of those multiplications produce the identity matrix? If not, what is the result?

(b) If $\mathbf{A} = \begin{pmatrix} 1 & 0 \\ 0 & -1 \end{pmatrix}$, then $\mathbf{A}^3 = \begin{pmatrix} 1 & 0 \\ 0 & -1 \end{pmatrix}$ which is the same as **A**, the transformation matrix for a reflection in $y = 0$. Find the transformations given by $\mathbf{B}^3, \mathbf{C}^3, \mathbf{D}^3, \mathbf{E}^3, \mathbf{F}^3, \mathbf{G}^3$.

(c) If the fourth power of each matrix is calculated, which do you think will produce the identity?

* **18** You have discovered that a reflection followed by a reflection in the same line, gives the identity transformation and a rotation of 180°, followed by a similar rotation will produce the identity. What does a transformation by matrix $\begin{pmatrix} 0 & 1 \\ -1 & 0 \end{pmatrix}$, followed by a transformation using matrix $\begin{pmatrix} 0 & -1 \\ 1 & 0 \end{pmatrix}$ produce?

* **19** Plot the points A(−1, 4), B(−4, −3), C(4, −4), D(3, 2). Carry out a transformation using matrix $\begin{pmatrix} 2 & 0 \\ 0 & 2 \end{pmatrix}$.

* **20** (a) Plot any three points on new axes.

(b) What transformation would you expect by using matrix $\begin{pmatrix} 3 & 0 \\ 0 & 3 \end{pmatrix}$?

(c) Carry out the transformation. Check the lengths of lines and the centre of enlargement.

* **21** (a) What would you expect the transformation matrix $\begin{pmatrix} \frac{1}{2} & 0 \\ 0 & \frac{1}{2} \end{pmatrix}$ to produce?

(b) Carry out that transformation on three points of your own choice.

* **22** (a) Starting with points A(−3, 2), B(−3, −5), C(1, −1), carry out a transformation

with matrix $\begin{pmatrix} 2 & 0 \\ 0 & 1 \end{pmatrix}$,

to give points D, E and F.

$$\begin{pmatrix} 2 & 0 \\ 0 & 1 \end{pmatrix}\begin{pmatrix} -3 & -3 & 1 \\ 2 & -5 & -1 \end{pmatrix}$$

$$= \begin{pmatrix} -6 & -6 & 2 \\ 2 & -5 & -1 \end{pmatrix}.$$

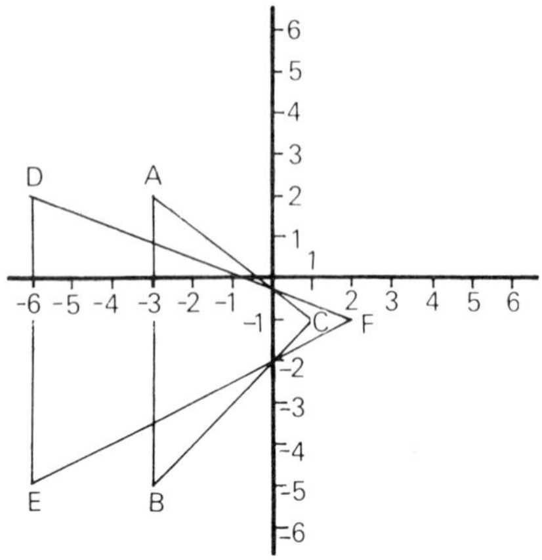

The side AB is the same length as side DE but other lengths are different. The triangle has been stretched in one direction. Distances from line $x = 0$ have been stretched twice the size. This is a one-way stretch.

(b) Use the same points A, B and C to produce a one-way stretch with transformation matrix $\begin{pmatrix} 3 & 0 \\ 0 & 1 \end{pmatrix}$.

* **23** (a) Plot the points A(−2, 2), B(1, 2), C(1, −3), D(−2, −3) to form rectangle ABCD.

(b) Produce a one-way stretch using matrix $\begin{pmatrix} 1 & 0 \\ 0 & 2 \end{pmatrix}$. What is different about that transformation?

(c) Try a one-way stretch with matrix $\begin{pmatrix} 1 & 0 \\ 0 & 3 \end{pmatrix}$.

* **24** (a) On suitable axes plot these shapes by using the coordinates given below.

(i) A(−3, 2), B(−3, −2)
(ii) C(−2, 5), D(2, 5)
(iii) E(−1, 3), F(3, 3), G(−1, 1), H(2, 1), I(−1, −1), J(3, −1).

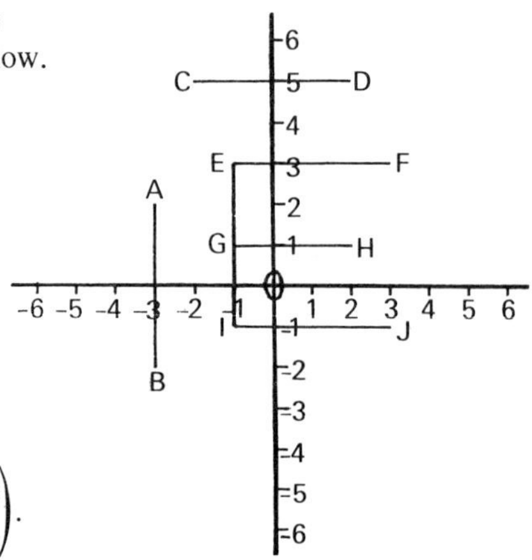

(b) Find the results of these transformations on each shape.

$$\begin{pmatrix} 2 & 0 \\ 0 & 2 \end{pmatrix}, \begin{pmatrix} \frac{1}{2} & 0 \\ 0 & \frac{1}{2} \end{pmatrix}, \begin{pmatrix} 1 & 0 \\ 0 & 2 \end{pmatrix}, \begin{pmatrix} 2 & 0 \\ 0 & 1 \end{pmatrix}.$$

* **25** On suitable axes start with rectangle ABCD given by points A(1, 0), B(3, 0), C(3, 5), D(1, 5).

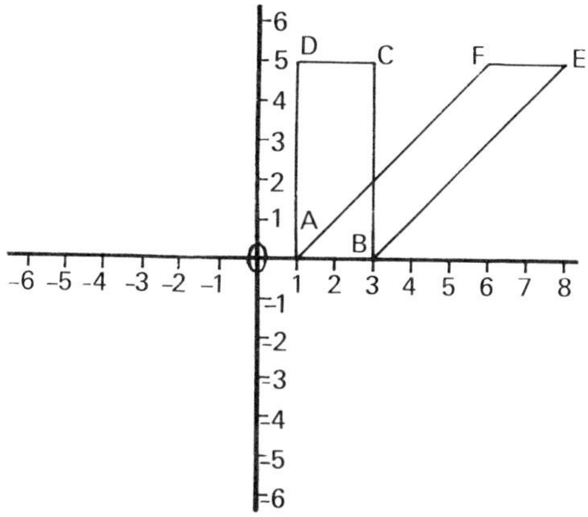

Carry out the transformation

$$\begin{pmatrix}1 & 1\\0 & 1\end{pmatrix}\begin{pmatrix}1 & 3 & 3 & 1\\0 & 0 & 5 & 5\end{pmatrix} = \begin{pmatrix}1 & 3 & 8 & 6\\0 & 0 & 5 & 5\end{pmatrix},$$

to give points A, B, E and F. The line CD has moved parallel to the line $y = 0$. The amount of movement from C to E is the same as the distance from C to the line $y = 0$ and similarly from D to F. A and B are on line $y = 0$ and have suffered no movement. This transformation is called a shear.

* **26** Use the points A, B, C, D from the last question. Transform with matrix $\begin{pmatrix}1 & -1\\0 & 1\end{pmatrix}$. This is another shear parallel to line $y = 0$.

* **27** (a) What kind of shear would you expect with matrix $\begin{pmatrix}1 & 0\\1 & 1\end{pmatrix}$?

Use the points P(0, 2), Q(0, 4), R(3, 2), S(3, 4) forming rectangle PQRS, to obtain a shear with that matrix.

(b) Starting with PQRS, transform with matrix $\begin{pmatrix}1 & 0\\-1 & 1\end{pmatrix}$.

* **28** (a) On suitable axes, plot a square using points A(0, 0), B(2, 0), C(2, 2) and D(0, 2).

(b) Use that square to produce shears with these matrices.

(i) $\begin{pmatrix}1 & 2\\0 & 1\end{pmatrix}$ (ii) $\begin{pmatrix}1 & -2\\0 & 1\end{pmatrix}$ (iii) $\begin{pmatrix}1 & 0\\2 & 1\end{pmatrix}$ (iv) $\begin{pmatrix}1 & 0\\-2 & 1\end{pmatrix}$.

(c) What is the area of the original square?

(d) What is the area of the resulting shear in each case?

Time and Distance

Revision notes

On a graph, time is usually horizontal and distance is vertical.
Since time cannot stop, a graph must always travel to the right.
Distance may not always be travelled, so a graph may not always move upwards.

Graph 1

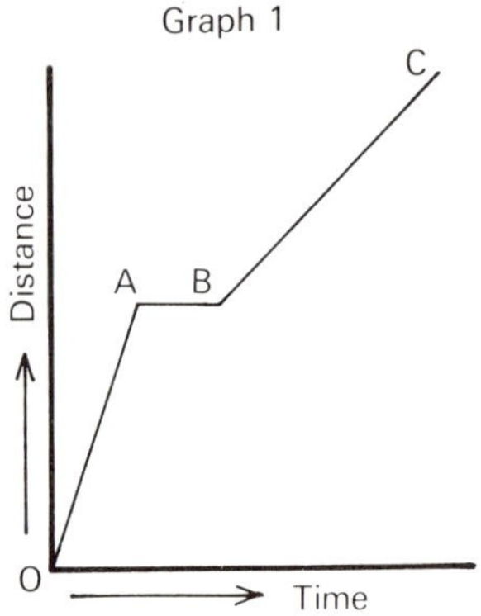

Graph 2

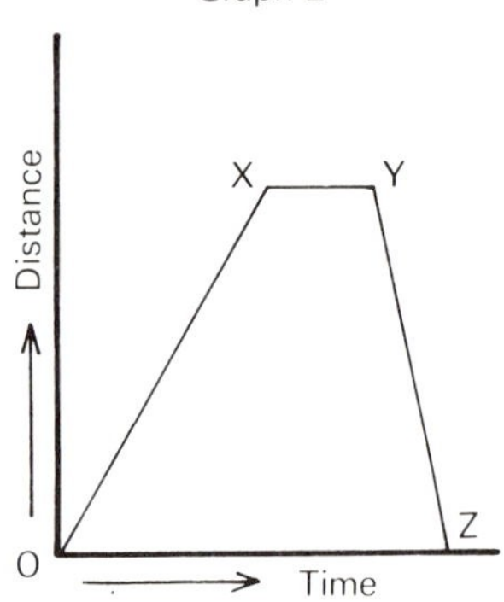

Graph 1
From O to A, some distance is travelled in a certain time and the amount moved in one unit of time gives the speed.
From A to B the traveller was stationary. Time moved on to the right, but there was no movement vertically.
From B to C the graph is not so steep, therefore the speed was less than between points O and A. The traveller was still moving away from the starting point.

Graph 2
As in the first graph, the traveller is stationary from X to Y.
From Y to Z shows a movement backwards, finally returning to O.
The graph indicates a journey out and back again.
Journey YZ is faster than journey OX because the gradient is greater. The same distance is travelled, but from Y to Z less time was taken, thus giving a greater speed.

Revision exercises

1 The graph shows the progress of a man walking for 5 hours.

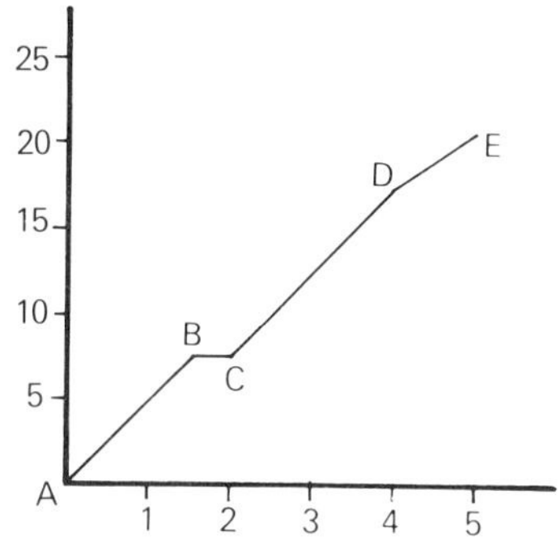

(a) Describe the journey represented by
(i) AB (ii) BC (iii) CD (iv) DE.

(b) From the graph, give the average speed over the whole journey.

2 The graph below represents the progress of a man jogging for 2 hours.

(a) What is represented by
(i) AB (ii) BC (iii) CD?

(b) Find his average speed over the whole journey.

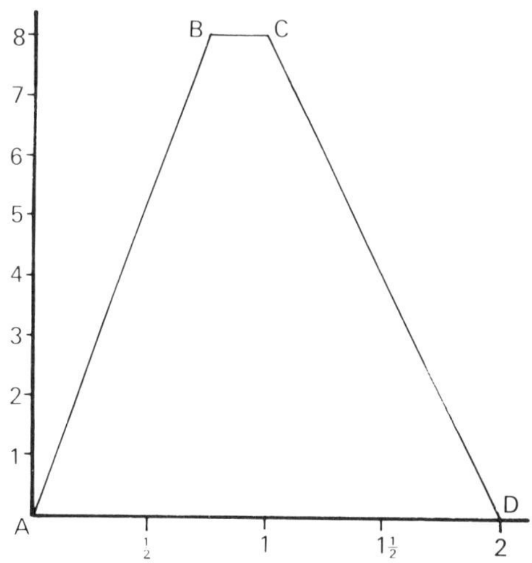

3 Draw a graph to show these stages in a car's progress:

AB 15 km at an average speed of 30 km/h.
BC 20 km travelled in 1 hour.
CD Rested for half an hour.
DE Averaged a speed of 30 km/h for a further $1\frac{1}{2}$ hours.

4 Illustrate these stages in a car's progress:

AB 30 km which took 1 hour 15 minutes.
BC Rested for 30 minutes.
CD Travelled for 2 hours at an average speed of 25 km/h.
DE Returned home in a time of 3 hours.

5 A cyclist travels for $1\frac{1}{2}$ hours at 14 km/h, then for $\frac{1}{2}$ hour at 16 km/h and finishes his journey in a further $2\frac{1}{2}$ hours at 12 km/h. Graph the journey and find

(a) how far he had travelled after $2\frac{1}{2}$ hours,
(b) how long it took him to travel 44 km,
(c) the total distance he had travelled.

6 A group on a charity walk averaged 7 km/h for 1 hour and 6 km/h for the next hour. After resting for $\frac{1}{4}$ hour, they finished the walk in two more hours at an average speed of 5 km/h. Construct a graph of that information and find

(a) how long the group took to travel $20\frac{1}{2}$ km,
(b) how far they had travelled after 3 hours had elapsed,
(c) how much a girl collected after finishing the walk, if she was sponsored for a total of 32 pence a kilometre.

7 A plane commences a journey at 09.00 and for half an hour averages 480 km/h, then travels at 560 km/h for one more hour, until it lands to take on fuel which takes $1\frac{1}{2}$ hours. It then completes its journey in $2\frac{1}{2}$ hours at an average speed of 500 km/h. Draw a graph of the whole journey.

(a) How far had the plane travelled at 13.30?
(b) What was the time when it had completed 925 km?
(c) Starting at the same time, it might have completed the journey without a stop at an average of 500 km/h. Draw a graph to find out when it would have arrived at the same destination.

8 A long-distance runner in training averages 20 km/h for 45 minutes, then 18 km/h for 30 minutes. After a rest of 15 minutes, he returns home at an average speed of 15 km/h.

(a) How far had he run after 2 hours?
(b) How long did it take him to cover 21 kilometres?
(c) How long was he away from home altogether?

9 A cyclist starts at 10.00, travelling at 12 km/h until 12.30, and then rests for half an hour. He continues at 10 km/h for the next 3 hours. A car starts from the same place at 11.00, travelling to the same destination at 35 km/h. Using the same axes, draw a graph of each journey.

(a) At what time did the car pass the cyclist?
(b) How far had they each travelled at that time?
(c) When did the car arrive at its destination?

10 A train started from town A at 09.00, travelled to town B 175 kilometres away, arriving at 11.30. Another train started from town B at 09.30 and travelled to town A arriving 12.15.

(a) At what time did the two trains pass?

(b) How far from town A were they at that time?

(c) At approximately what average speed did the second train travel?

11 Starting at 10.00, a man walks at 6 km/h for $2\frac{1}{2}$ hours, then rests for lunch until 13.15. He then continues at 5 km/h for 3 hours. A cyclist starts at 12.00 from the same place, travelling at 18 km/h.

(a) Where is the walker when he is passed by the cyclist?

(b) How far did the walker travel altogether?

(c) At what time does the cyclist arrive at the point the walker had reached at 16.15?

12 Two trains start from town A to travel to town B, a distance of 150 kilometres. The first starts at 09.00, averaging 60 km/h. The second starts at 10.30, arriving at 12.45.

(a) Looking at the graphs, which was the faster train?

(b) How long after the first train did the second train arrive at town B?

(c) What was the speed of the second train?

Navigation

Revision notes

Three-figure bearings indicate a clockwise rotation from North.

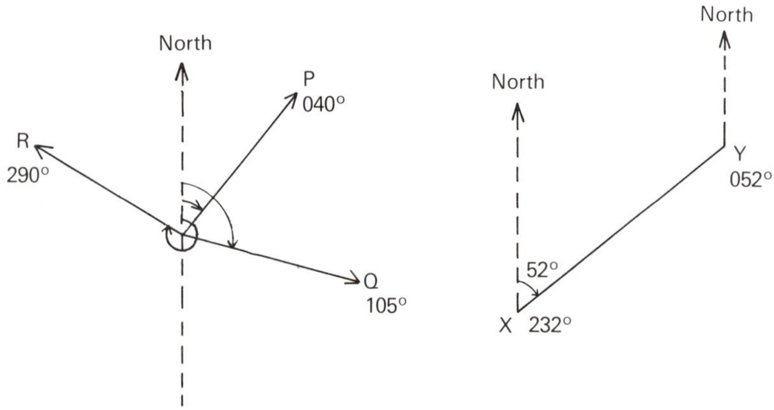

The direction of P is a rotation of 40° from North, bearing 040°.
Q is on an angle of 105° from North, giving a bearing of 105°.
A rotation of 290° (70° anticlockwise) gives R, bearing 290°.
Y is on a bearing *from* X of 052°.
X is on a bearing *from* Y of 232°. (*Note.* 52 + 180 = 232.)

Wind speed

When a plane wishes to fly to a destination, it must take the wind speed and its direction into account. Although a plane may fly directly to its destination at a particular speed, the pilot navigates another direction at a different speed. It has an air speed and sets a course for navigation, but in fact its final flight is in a different direction at a different ground speed.

▶ A plane's destination is on a bearing of 075°, at a distance of 605 km, which it must complete in 1 hour 15 minutes. The wind is blowing on a bearing of 300°, at a speed of 80 km/h. Find the air speed and navigating bearing
(a) by scale drawing (b) by calculation.

By drawing:

In $1\frac{1}{4}$ hours the plane will travel 605 km.

$$\text{Ground speed} = \frac{605}{5} \times 4 = 484 \text{ km/h.}$$

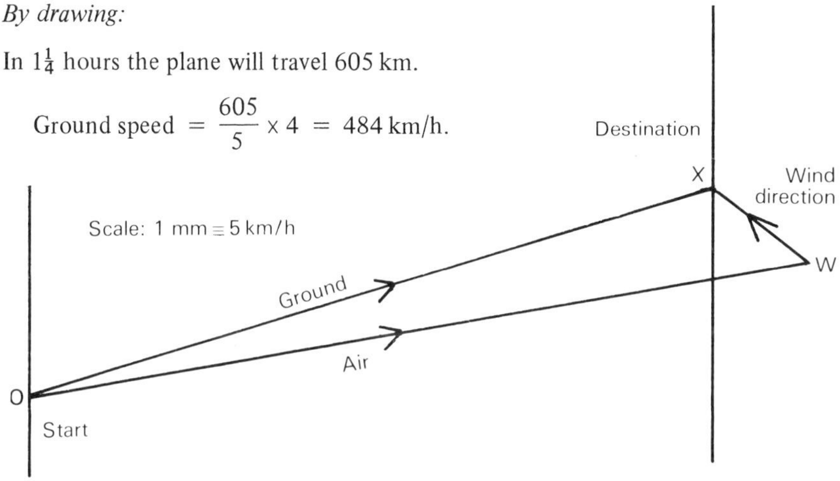

Lines are drawn to represent *speeds,* not distances.
OX is on bearing 075°, a length of 96.8 mm (484 ÷ 5). Wind bearing 300°.
Therefore W is on bearing 120° from X (300 − 180).
XW is a length of 16 mm (80 ÷ 5).
Join length OW.
Air speed and bearing are then taken from O.
OW measures 108.5 mm, giving a speed of 542.5 km/h (108.5 × 5).
Navigating bearing taken from O is 081°.

By calculation:

In the triangle OXW:
OX = 484 (speed), XW = 80 (speed), ∠OXW = 135° (75 + 60).

$$\begin{aligned}\text{Using the Cosine Rule, } OW^2 &= 484^2 + 80^2 - (2 \times 484 \times 80 \times \text{Cos } 135^\circ) \\ &= 234\,256 + 6400 + 54\,758.6 \\ &= 295\,414.6. \\ OW &= 543.5 \text{ km/h.}\end{aligned}$$

$$\begin{aligned}\text{Using the Sine Rule, Sin } \angle XOW &= \frac{80 \text{ Sin } 135^\circ}{543.5} \\ &= 0.1041 \\ \angle XOW &= 5^\circ\ 58'. \\ \text{Angle between North and OW} &= 75^\circ + 5^\circ\ 58' \\ &= 80^\circ\ 58'.\end{aligned}$$

Air speed 543.5 km/h, navigating bearing 080° 58′.
(Compare with answers obtained by drawing.)

Revision exercises

1 What is the three-figure bearing of
(a) South (b) North-West (c) South-East
(d) North-North-East (e) South-South-East (f) South-South-West?

2 Give the three-figure bearing of
(a) 60° E of N (b) 30° W of S (c) 25° W of N
(d) N 100° E (e) S 75° W (f) N 100° W.

3 Give the smaller angle between
(a) N and SW (b) SE and 300° (c) S 40° W and 350°
(d) 130° and 310° (e) SSW and 100° (f) 050° and 325°.

4 From a point O, draw radiating lines of any length to show bearings
(a) 135° (b) 064° (c) 260° (d) 305° (e) 198° (f) 203° (g) 312°.

5 In this exercise, all lines in the drawing will be 4.5 cm long. Starting from a point A, a plane flies to B on a bearing 145°, then to C, bearing 275°, then to D, bearing 025°, and finally to E, bearing due South. From the drawing, find the direct bearing from A to E and the bearing from E to A.

6 From a point A, draw a line 3.5 cm long on a bearing 065° to point B. Also from A, draw a line to C, 5 cm long on a bearing 136°. Find the bearing of B from C.

7 From point P, draw a line 4.8 cm long on a bearing 055° to point Q. Also from P, draw PR 10 cm long on a bearing 068°. Find the length RQ and the bearing of Q from R.

8 From A to B is 94 mm on a bearing of 122° and from A to C is 73 mm on a bearing of 140°. What is the length and the bearing from C to B?

9 From point A, the point B is 95 mm on a bearing of 262° and the point C is 110 mm on a bearing of 254°. Find the length and the bearing of C from B.

10 If 1 mm represents 1 kilometre per hour, draw lines to represent
(a) 15 km/h (b) 38 km/h (c) 49 km/h (d) 73 km/h (e) 68 km/h.

11 Use a scale of 1 mm to 5 km/h to represent these speeds.
(a) 95 km/h (b) 135 km/h (c) 180 km/h (d) 45 km/h (e) 325 km/h.

12 Use a scale of 1 mm to 4 km/h to represent these speeds.
(a) 76 km/h (b) 136 km/h (c) 204 km/h (d) 324 km/h (e) 254 km/h.

13 In these diagrams, the lines represent speeds. Use the scale which is given in each case, to find the speeds represented by the lines AB, BC and CA.

(a) 1 mm to 10 km/h.

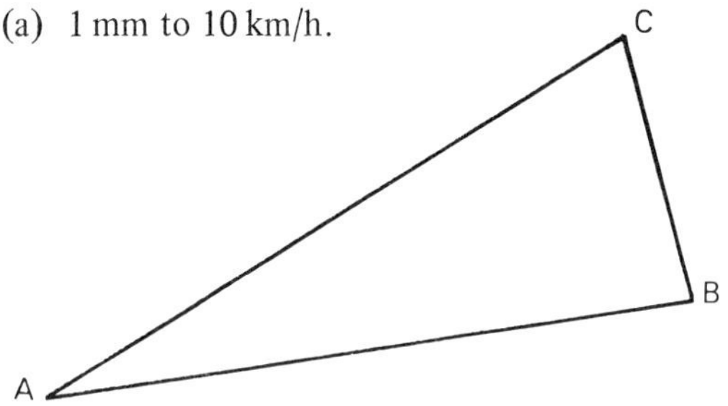

(b) 1 mm to 2 km/h.

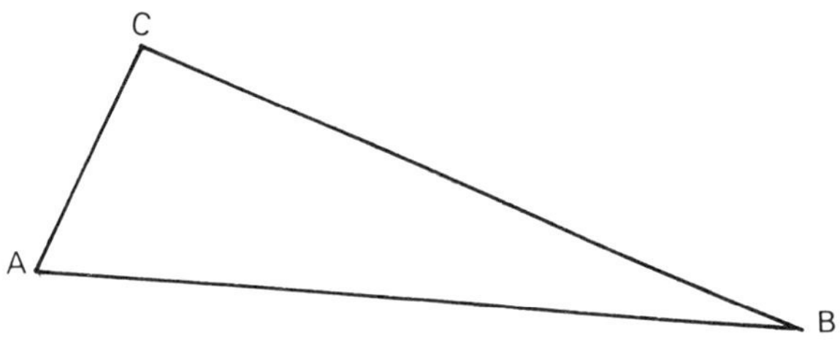

(c) 1 mm to 5 km/h.

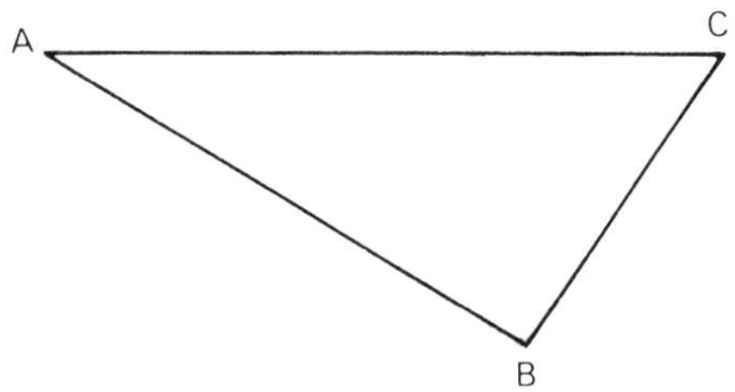

(d) 1 mm to $4\frac{1}{2}$ km/h.

14 Draw triangles ABC, using a suitable scale for the speeds.

(a) AB = 83 km/h, BC = 54 km/h, CA = 48 km/h.
(b) AB = 120 km/h, BC = 210 km/h, CA = 186 km/h.
(c) AB = 325 km/h, BC = 405 km/h, CA = 380 km/h.
(d) AB = 640 km/h, BC = 560 km/h, CA = 496 km/h.

15 Make rough drawings in each case to show, as a dotted line, the change in course caused by the wind, and say if the plane's speed will increase or decrease.

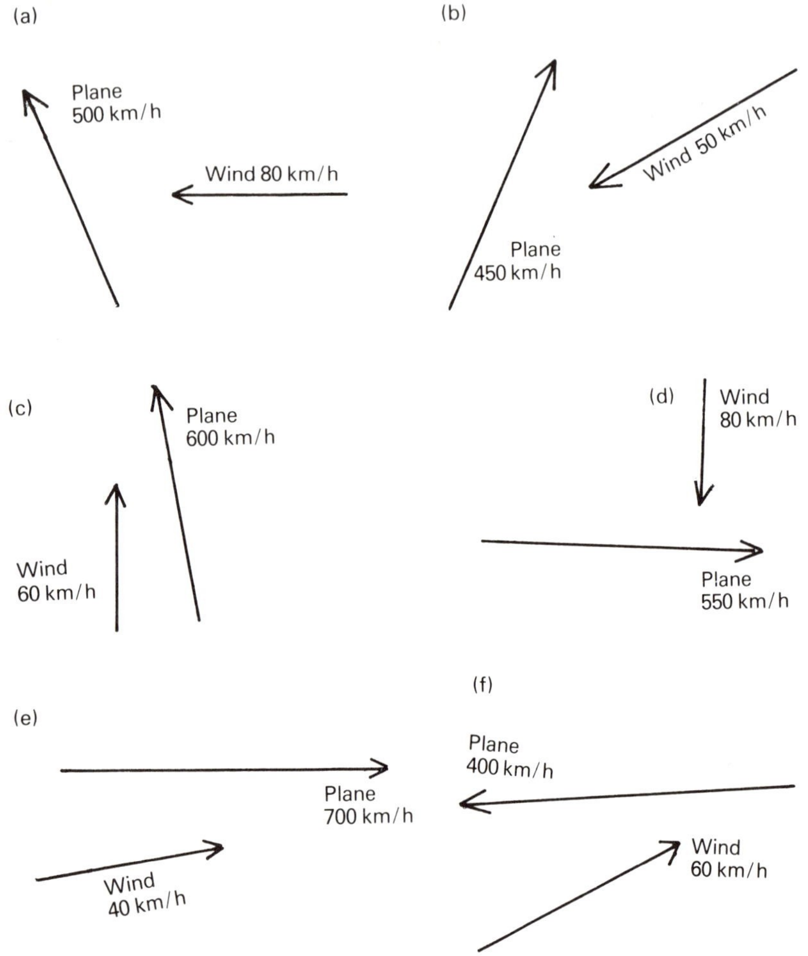

* **16** With a scale drawing, find the air speed and bearing a plane must use in each case.

(a) Ground speed 172 km/h, bearing 220°, wind 42 km/h, 236°.
(b) Ground speed 336 km/h, bearing 007°, wind 40 km/h, due East.
(c) Ground speed 320 km/h, bearing 141°, wind 90 km/h, 257°.

* **17** A plane wishes to fly from town A at 200 km/h to town B which is on a bearing 338°. If there is a wind of 60 km/h, bearing 350°, what will be the air speed and planned bearing of the plane?

* **18** Wind is blowing at 81 km/h due North. If a plane's ground speed is 252 km/h and its destination is on a bearing 315° from its departure point, what is its air speed and bearing?

* **19** In each case you have the air speed and planned bearing plus the necessary facts about the wind. Use a suitable scale to find the ground speed and the bearing of the destination.
(a) Air speed 332 km/h, bearing 334°, wind 76 km/h, 290°.
(b) Air speed 280 km/h, bearing due West, wind 91 km/h, 205°.
(c) Air speed 380 km/h, bearing 173°, wind 125 km/h, 295°.

* **20** A plane plots a course of 058° with an air speed of 504 km/h and there is a 42 km/h wind, bearing 340°. Find the plane's ground speed and the bearing of its destination.

* **21** Helped by a 72 km/h wind, bearing 156°, a plane sets course on bearing 123°, with an air speed of 306 km/h. Find the ground speed and the bearing of its destination.

* **22** A plane's air speed is 285 km/h and its planned course is 262°. Its destination is on a bearing 254° and it maintains a ground speed of 330 km/h. Find the wind speed and direction.

* **23** A plane flies to a town on a bearing 122° and with a ground speed of 188 km/h. To do so, it has an air speed of 146 km/h and plots a course of 140°. Find the speed and bearing of the wind.

* **24** The ground speed of a plane is 312 km/h, when it flies to a town on a bearing 244°. If it plans a course of 233° at an air speed of 260 km/h, what is the wind bearing and speed?

* **25** A plane plots a course of 104° and an air speed of 215 km/h, to achieve a ground speed 185 km/h and fly to its destination on a bearing 117°. Find the speed and bearing of the wind.

* **26** Examine these three situations, in which the pilots of the planes maintain the same air speed and bearing, but with differing wind conditions. Find the ground speed and the bearing on which the plane actually moves.
(a) Air speed 250 km/h, bearing 060°, wind 50 km/h, 100°.
(b) Air speed 250 km/h, bearing 060°, wind 50 km/h, 010°.
(c) Air speed 250 km/h, bearing 060°, wind 50 km/h, 330°.

* **27** Paris is 340 km from London on a bearing 150°, and the journey takes one hour. Find the navigating speed and bearing for a pilot when the wind is (a) 117 km/h due North (b) 117 km/h bearing 200°.

* **28** Moscow lies on a bearing 063° from London, a distance of 2400 km. A plane completes the journey in 4 hours. Calculate the air speed and navigating bearing to achieve the journey with a wind of
(a) 128 km/h blowing due South (b) 128 km/h bearing 100°.

* **29** Gloucester is on a bearing 285° from London and the distance is 148 km, a journey which takes a plane 20 minutes in a 80 km/h wind, bearing 230°. The plane then changes course and travels to Leicester on a bearing 040°, a distance of 112 kilometres, in 15 minutes. The wind remains constant. Find the necessary flight plan details for the whole journey.

* **30** A plane flies from Bristol to London, bearing 085°, a distance of 168 kilometres, in 20 minutes. It then changes course to fly to Northampton on a bearing 325°, a distance of 96 kilometres, in 15 minutes. There is a 64 km/h wind, blowing on a bearing of 040° for the whole journey. Work out the air speeds and bearings for the flight plan.

Answers

Part 1 Basic Revision

Revision 1. Number Page 9

1 (a) $\frac{6}{12}$ (b) $\frac{5}{15}$ (c) $\frac{6}{48}$ (d) $\frac{10}{100}$ (e) $\frac{8}{12}$ (f) $\frac{15}{40}$ (g) $\frac{12}{30}$ (h) $\frac{21}{28}$.

2 (a) $\frac{6}{8}$ (b) $\frac{6}{10}$ (c) $\frac{8}{16}$ (d) $\frac{12}{16}$ (e) $\frac{15}{4}$ (f) $\frac{47}{8}$ (g) $\frac{43}{5}$ (h) $\frac{47}{6}$.

3 (a) $1\frac{7}{12}$ (b) $1\frac{1}{20}$ (c) $\frac{7}{24}$ (d) $\frac{11}{24}$ (e) $6\frac{1}{12}$ (f) $7\frac{19}{20}$ (g) $1\frac{17}{24}$ (h) $2\frac{13}{24}$.

4 (a) $\frac{5}{24}$ (b) $\frac{2}{5}$ (c) $\frac{1}{16}$ (d) $\frac{1}{32}$ (e) 6 (f) $3\frac{1}{5}$ (g) $1\frac{9}{10}$ (h) $2\frac{1}{2}$ (i) 7 (j) 15.

5 (a) $\frac{2}{3}$ (b) $\frac{4}{5}$ (c) $\frac{3}{4}$ (d) $\frac{2}{3}$ (e) $\frac{1}{8}$ (f) $\frac{1}{4}$.

6 (a) £9, £6 (b) £20, £4 (c) 9h, 3h (d) 21 cm, 9 cm (e) 12 cm, 9 cm, 6 cm
(f) £1, £1.50, £2.50.

7 (a) 12 cm (b) 18 cm (c) $4\frac{1}{2}$ cm.

8 (a) (i) $\{1, 4\}$, (ii) $\{1, 3, 4, 6, 9, 12, 16\}$, (iii) $\emptyset$
(b) (i) No, (ii) Yes, (iii) No, (iv) No, (v) Yes.

9 (a) $2 \times 2 \times 5$
(b) $2 \times 3 \times 5$
(c) $2 \times 2 \times 2 \times 2 \times 2$
(d) $3 \times 3 \times 5$
(e) $2 \times 2 \times 5 \times 5$.

10 (a) 13 (b) 11 (c) 24 (d) 59 (e) 47 (f) 51.

11 (a) 1001_2 (b) 1110_2 (c) 10110_2 (d) 11010_2 (e) 11111_2 (f) 110000_2
(g) 111001_2 (h) 111110_2.

12 (a) 1110_2 (b) 10100_2 (c) 1100_2 (d) 10100_2 (e) 11_2 (f) 100_2 (g) 101_2
(h) 1101_2.

13 (a) 293 (b) 8 (c) 6435 (d) 125 (e) 661 (f) 1962.

14 (a) 151 (b) 126 (c) 18 (d) 76432 (e) 79532.

15 (a) 6, 12, 18, 24, 30, 36
(b) 4, 9, 16, 25, 36, 49, 64, 81
(c) 12, 24, 36, 48, 60, 72, 84, 96
(d) 10, 20, 30, 40, 50, 60, 70, 80, 90, 100, 110, 120.

16 (a) 0.7 (b) 0.08 (c) 0.35 (d) 0.76 (e) 0.6 (f) 0.22.

17 (a) $\frac{19}{20}$ (b) $\frac{4}{5}$ (c) $\frac{9}{20}$ (d) $\frac{9}{25}$ (e) $\frac{23}{50}$ (f) $\frac{1}{5}$.

18 (a) 19.6 (b) 4.16 (c) 6.14 (d) 39.505 (e) 6.48 (f) 9.09.

19 (a) 13.6 (b) 2470 (c) 150.7 (d) 3.87 (e) 0.0109 (f) 0.124 (g) 27 (h) 112.7
(i) 297.5 (j) 13.7 (k) 1.61 (l) 22.3.

20 (a) 0.9 cm (b) 0.8 cm (c) 0.3 cm (d) 2.5 cm (e) 7.9 cm (f) 8.2 cm.

Revision 2. Number Page 11

1 (a) A6, B4, C7, D7 (b) P3, Q5, R8, S2 (c) A7, B4, P7, Q0, R6, S1, T9, U3, V6 (d) A8, B3, C1, D7, E9, F4, P1, Q4, R4 (e) A6, B11, C8, D9, E14 (f) A−1, B3, C0, D5, E−2 (g) A36, B63, C125.

2 (a) 9 (b) 8 (c) 16 (d) 10.

3 (a) 126, 567 (b) 53, 61, 73 (c) $2^2 \times 13$ (d) 26 (e) 9, 18, 27, 36, 45, 54, 63, 72, 81, 90, 99 (f) 3 and 47, 7 and 43, 13 and 37, 19 and 31.

4 (a) 48 (b) $4\frac{1}{24}$ (c) $1\frac{8}{17}$ (d) $1\frac{9}{16}$ (e) 0.143 (f) 14.3 (g) 36.5 (h) 0.6615.

5 (a) 36 (b) 3, 29 (c) 20 (d) $87 = 3 \times 29$ (e) 36.

6 (a) 9 (b) 0.2 (c) 1.1 (d) 0.7 (e) 0.03.

7 (a) 6.2 (b) 8.9 (c) 3.9 (d) 2.9 (e) 3.2.

8 (a) 43_5 (b) 104_5 (c) 120_5 (d) 210_5 (e) 240_5.

9 (a) 15 (b) 27 (c) 53 (d) 59 (e) 101.

10 (a) 69.6 kg, 46.4 kg (b) £3.25, £9.75, £13 (c) \$11.10, \$16.65, \$27.75 (d) 5.06 kg, 0.275 kg, 0.165 kg.

11 (a) 1 (b) −2 (c) −2 (d) 2 (e) 3 (f) −5 (g) 4 (h) −2.

12 Mode 15, Median 18, Mean 19.5.

13 (a) 1 in 5 (b) 4 in 5 (c) 1 in 6 (d) (i) 1 in 8, (ii) 3 in 16, (iii) 1 in 4.

14 (a) 14004 (b) 1.368×10^2 (c) 14.

15 (a) 5.26 (b) 1.89 (c) 6.37 (d) 0.189 (e) 0.0561.

16 95.

17 (a) {2, 3, 5, 7, 11, 13, 17, 19}
(b) (i) {2, 3, 4, 5, 7, 8, 11, 12, 13, 16, 17, 19, 20},
(ii) {3}, (iii) ∅
(d) (i) {1, 2, 5, 7, 10, 11, 13, 14, 17, 19}, (ii) {1, 10, 14}
(e) (i) False, (ii) False, (iii) True, (iv) True.

18 (a) 10000111_2 (b) 1021_3 (c) 0.001_2 (d) Base 4.

19 (a) $\frac{61.6}{7}$, $\sqrt{81}$, (0.07×130) (b) 120_4, 100_5, 11010_2, 1001_3
(c) $\frac{5}{8}, \frac{4}{5}, \frac{17}{20}$ (d) 0.35, 37%, $\frac{3}{8}$, $(\frac{2}{3})^2$.

20 (b) (i) {1, 9}, (ii) {9}, (iii) {1, 3, 5, 7, 11, 13}, (iv) ∅, (v) {2}.

Revision 3. Number and Money Page 19

1 (a) 47 (b) 930 (c) 52.6 (d) 308 (e) 22 500 (f) 57.6 (g) 475 (h) 9820.

2 (a) 14.1 (b) 46.5 (c) 21.04 (d) 21.56 (e) 202.5 (f) 46.08 (g) 28.5 (h) 88.38.

3 (a) 141 (b) 4650 (c) 210.4 (d) 2156 (e) 202 500 (f) 460.8 (g) 2850 (h) 88 380.

4 (a) 120 (b) 5.2p.

5 (a) £145 (b) \$2.60.

6 (a) £6.25 (b) £7.50 (c) £12.50.

7 (a) £27 500 (b) £22 500.

8 (a) £20.40 (b) £23.80.

9 (a) £321 (b) £7.38.

10 (a) £4020 (b) £4576.

11 (a) £84 (b) £23.10.

12 (a) 1.59 (b) 0.75 (c) 6.79 (d) 6.54 (e) 19.82 (f) 143.

13 (a) 55% (b) 40% (c) 52% (d) 7% (e) $47\frac{1}{2}$% (f) $93\frac{3}{4}$% (g) 37.5% (h) 26.5% (i) 7.6% (j) 85% (k) 36% (l) $61\frac{2}{3}$%.

14 (a) 45% (b) 37% (c) 32% (d) 35% (e) 64% (f) 1% (g) $23\frac{1}{3}$% (h) 27% (i) 4%.

15 (a) £3.75 (b) £10.20 (c) £6.24 (d) £205 (e) £26.64 (f) £105.

16 9%.

17 (a) £22 (b) £13.80 (c) £170.20 (d) £53.24 (e) £16.79 (f) £35.86.
18 (a) £12.36 (b) £172.50 (c) £115.50 (d) £645 (e) £1540 (f) £2321.
19 £8.50 and £9.20.
20 (a) £289.80 (b) £260.82 (c) £21.

Revision 4. Money and Measures Page 20

1 (a) £20.06 (b) £53.77 (c) £13.75 (d) £157.63 (e) £8.50 (f) £15.35 (g) £3.26 (h) £5.85.
2 (a) 3.058 m (b) 25 cm (c) 0.095 kg.
3 (a) £9 (b) £6.
4 (a) 250 for £1.45 (b) 60 for £1.50 (c) 75 for £6.60.
5 £29.40 + £7.65 + £2.25 + £2.40 = £41.70.
6 £40.50 and £37.50.
7 (a) April, June, September, November (b) 1816, 1936, 1976 (c) 165 days.
8 (a) 250 m (b) 900 m (c) 750 m (d) 1 m (e) 700 m (f) 350 m (g) 3100 m (h) 2650 m (i) 5800 m.
9 (a) 250 g (b) 150 g (c) 500 g (d) 190 g (e) 300 g (f) 600 g (g) 4750 g (h) 5060 g (i) 3700 g.
10 (a) £43.20 (b) £54.40 (c) £82.35 (d) £86.40 (e) £114.75 (f) £105.
11 (a) £1.67 (b) £1.75 (c) £1.86.
12 (a) £3144 (b) £4500 (c) £3006 (d) £5001 (e) £4239.
13 (a) £2.76 (b) £2.67 (c) £1.86 (d) £2.82.
14 (a) 4 hours (b) 3 hours 45 minutes (c) 4 hours 30 minutes (d) 4 hours 45 minutes (e) 4 hours 45 minutes (f) 6 hours 45 minutes.
15 £75.53.
16 (a) 03.54 (b) 10.51.
17 (a) 17.6 m (b) 6.6 m (c) 24.2 m (d) 66 m.
18 (a) £55 (b) £1037.40 (c) £328.54.
19 08.55.
20 (a) 300 m (b) $\frac{1}{2}$ of £7.58 (c) 0.9 kg (d) $\frac{1}{5}$ of £22.40 (e) 20 minutes (f) $\frac{1}{10}$ of £85.50.

Revision 5. Money Page 23

1 (a) £5.50 (b) £52.50 (c) £16.24.
2 £124.62.
3 (a) 8% (b) £96.99.
4 £4.50, $12\frac{1}{2}$%.
5 £120.75, £15.75.
6 £38, 14%.
7 £35, £21.
8 (a) £173.25 (b) £3.15.
9 (a) £230 (b) £216.20 (c) £15.
10 (a) £233.33 (b) £1080.
11 £32.94.
12 (a) £52.50 (b) £20.80 (c) $247.20.
13 $6\frac{1}{2}$%.
14 (a) £61.80 (b) £86.94 (c) £157.50.
15 £171.20.
16 (a) £297.50 (b) £343 (c) £476 (d) £1356.25 (e) £1433.25.
17 (a) £5520 (b) £20.70 (c) £331.20 (d) £788.22.
18 (a) £110.40 (b) £36 025 000 (c) £56 460 500.
19 (a) (i) $6.24, (ii) $8.28, (iii) $37.80 (b) (i) £5.25, (ii) £12.55, (iii) £118.75.
20 British £33.33, foreign £37.50, difference £4.17.

Revision 6. Shapes Page 30

2 $a = 85°$, $b = 79°$, $c = 147°$, $d = 30°$, $e = 75°$, $f = 75°$.
5 (d) the circle passes through point D
(e) centre at midpoint AC, radius half AC.
6 (a) 3 cm^2 (b) 625 m^2 (c) 114 cm^2 (d) 111.6 cm^2 (e) 66 m^2 (f) 212 cm^2.
7 (a) 15 m (b) 7.8 cm.
8 (a) parallelogram (b) rectangle (c) square.
9 (a) 135° (b) 90° (c) (i) 10, (ii) 12, (iii) 6, (iv) 9, (v) 1
(d) (i) 180°, (ii) 120°, (iii) 210°, (iv) 240°.
10 (a) 225° (b) 180° (c) 135° (d) 315° (e) 045°.
11 (a) 60° (b) 145° (c) 100° (d) 190° (e) 185° (f) 260°.
12 B 065°, C 115°, D 210°, E 270°, F 320°.
13 (a) 25° (b) 45°, 45°, 90° (c) 84°.
14 (a) 171 cm^2 (b) 4000 m^2 (c) $4\frac{1}{2}$ cm^2 (d) $25\frac{1}{2}$ m^2.
15 (a) 15 cm (b) 3.5 cm (c) 16 cm (d) 16 cm.
16 (a) 57.2 cm^2 (b) 187 cm^2.
17 (a) A(2, 3), B(4, 5), C(4, 6), D(6, 10), E(8, 6), F(6, 3), G(4, 1), H(4, 0)
(c) square (d) parallelogram (e) isosceles (f) rhombus.
18 (a) (3, 5) (b) (5, 3) (c) (4, 3) (d) ($2\frac{1}{2}$, 5) (e) ($3\frac{1}{2}$, $3\frac{1}{2}$) (f) ($5\frac{1}{2}$, $6\frac{1}{2}$).
19 (a) A(12, 1), B(13, 6), C(9, 5)
(b) X(13, 2), Y(8, 3), Z(10, 0)
(c) P(12, 12), Q(11, 15), R(8, 10).
20 (c) A(4, 10), B(5, 6), C(6, 8) (d) X($5\frac{1}{2}$, 5), Y($3\frac{1}{2}$, 1), Z($1\frac{1}{2}$, 7).

Revision 7. Shapes Page 33

1 (b) Saturday (c) (i) 20%, (ii) $13\frac{1}{3}$%.
2 (c) parallelogram (d) A(−2, −5), B(1, −5), C(3, −1), D(0, −1)
(e) A(−5, −5), B(−8, −5), C(−10, −1), D(−7, −1).
3 (a) parallelogram (b) rhombus (c) rectangle.
4 $a = 35°$, $b = 55°$, $c = 65°$, $d = 115°$, $e = 40°$, $f = 75°$.
5 (a) (i) 2, (ii) 2 (b) (i) 5, (ii) 5 (c) (i) 0, (ii) 1 (d) (i) 0, (ii) 4.
7 (a) 98 m^2 (b) 570 cm^2 (c) 930 m^2 (d) 82.5 cm^2 (e) 146 cm^2 (f) 28.8 cm^2.
8 *a* and *f*, *b* and *h*, *c* and *d*, *e* and *g*.
9 *a* and *d*.
10 (a) $\begin{pmatrix}1\\9\end{pmatrix}$ (b) $\begin{pmatrix}-3\\8\end{pmatrix}$ (c) $\begin{pmatrix}-4\\6\end{pmatrix}$.
11 (a) $\frac{5}{8}$ (b) $\frac{3}{2}$ (c) $3\frac{3}{4}$ (d) 8 (e) 9 (f) 12 (g) 43°.
12 All networks.
13 (a) 90 mm (b) 175 mm (c) 92.5 mm (d) 146 mm (e) 318.5 mm (f) 626.5 mm.
15 (b) 322 km (c) 213°.
16 (a) ∠ACD = 55°, ∠DOC = 70°
(b) ∠ACE = 55°, ∠EBC = 35°, ∠AOE = 110°,
∠EDC = 145°.
19 (a) (ii) 222 cm^2, (iii) 180 cm^3, (b) (ii) 344 cm^2, (iii) 448 cm^3.
20 (a) 1.825 m^3 (b) 5.76 m^3 (c) 20 cm^3.

Revision 8. Shapes Page 37

1 (a) $a = 20°$ (b) $b = 25°$ (c) $c = 45°$, $d = 45°$.
3 (a) 72° (b) 54° (c) 108°.
4 $a = 6\frac{1}{4}$ cm, $b = 3$ cm, $c = 2\frac{1}{4}$ cm, $d = 3\frac{3}{4}$ cm.
5 (a) 085° (b) 215° (c) 305° (d) 265°.
6 By calculation DB = 71.4 m, DC = 64.7 m, BC = 30.17 m, area 2761 m^2.
7 (a) (i) 135°, (ii) 165°, (iii) 140°, (iv) 170°
(b) (i) 12, (ii) 10, (iii) 15, (iv) 60.
8 (a) (i) $\begin{pmatrix}4\\1\end{pmatrix}$, (ii) $\begin{pmatrix}-2\\-3\end{pmatrix}$ (b) $\frac{1}{2}\mathbf{b}$ (c) $\mathbf{b}+\mathbf{c}$ (d) $\mathbf{a}+\mathbf{b}$ (e) $\mathbf{a}+\mathbf{b}+\mathbf{c}$.
9 (a) 1 (b) 39° (c) 192° (d) 162°.
10 (a) obtuse (b) right (c) right (d) acute.
11 3.33 cm.
12 (a) 60° (b) 216 cm^2 (c) 2200 cm^3 (d) 8.66 cm^3.
13 XY = 56 m, YZ = 53 m.
14 (a) 1810 m^3 (b) 1 810 000 litres.
15 1077.02 cm^3.
16 $5062\frac{1}{2}$ m^2.
17 (a) 15 cm (b) 120 cm^2 (c) 14.1 cm.
18 $a = 82°$, $b = 64°$, $c = 29°$, $d = 122°$, $e = 29°$.
19 (a) 1080 cm^3 (c) 828 cm^2.
20 (b) Midpoints AB $(-2\frac{1}{2}, 2)$, BC $(1\frac{1}{4}, 2)$, DC $(1\frac{1}{4}, -2\frac{1}{2})$, DA $(-2\frac{1}{2}, -2\frac{1}{2})$
(d) parallelogram (rectangle).

Revision 9. Algebra Page 47

1 (a) −1 (b) −9 (c) 3 (d) 5 (e) −5 (f) 2 (g) −6 (h) 8 (i) 1.
2 (a) 5 (b) 9 (c) 83 (d) 26 (e) 54 (f) −210 (g) −114 (h) 326 (i) −64.
3 (a) A number of pence equals one hundred times a number of pounds
(b) A number of millimetres equals ten times a number of centimetres
(c) A number of centimetres equals a hundred times a number of metres
(d) A number of grams equals a thousand times a number of kilograms
(e) The area of a rectangle equals length times breadth.
4 (a) 6 (b) 35 (c) 33 (d) 36 (e) 8 (f) 6 (g) 10 (h) 1 (i) 2.
5 (a) ± 8 (b) −10 (c) −30 (d) 1 (e) ± 1 (f) 21 (g) 4 (h) 19 (i) ± 7 (j) 12
(k) 50 (l) 8.
6 (a) $2x + y = 15$ (b) $\frac{x}{2y} = 10$ (c) $\frac{12}{x} = y$ (d) $x^2 = y$
(e) $5x + 8 = y$ (f) $\frac{x}{3} + 2 = 6$.
7 (a) $S = M - 25$ (b) $m = 1000M$ (c) $L = \frac{P}{100}$ (d) $P = a + b + c$
(e) $P = 3a$ (f) $P = AV$ (g) $L = \frac{A}{B}$.
8 (a) 15 (b) 0 (c) $1\frac{2}{3}$ (d) $37\frac{1}{2}$ (e) $12\frac{1}{2}$ (f) 0 (g) 16 (h) $2\frac{1}{2}$.
9 (a) 2 (b) 450 (c) $37\frac{1}{2}$ (d) 0.045 (e) 0.3 (f) 30 (g) 40 (h) 1.

10 (a) $5a - 5c$ (b) $3x - 6y$ (c) $ax + ay$ (d) $6a - 4c$ (e) $a^2 + ac$ (f) $32x - 24y$ (g) $20x + 8a - 12c$ (h) $2cx - cb + 3ac$ (i) $a^2 + 3ab - 4ac$.
11 (a) 42 (b) 44 (c) 20 (d) 20 (e) 28 (f) 0.
12 (a) $a = b - c$ (b) $a = c - b$ (c) $a = c - b$ (d) $a = b/c$ (e) $a = bc$ (f) $a = b + c$ (g) $a = (b - c)/2$ (h) $a = c + 3b$ (i) $a = c/b$.
13 (a) 14 (b) 6 (c) -6 (d) 40 (e) 0.4 (f) 22 (g) 30 (h) -3 (i) 0.
14 (a) -3 (b) -4 (c) -5 (d) -4 (e) -6 (f) 8 (g) -14 (h) 50.
15 (a) -56 (b) -100 (c) -81 (d) $-1\frac{1}{2}$ (e) 90 (f) 15 (g) $\frac{1}{4}$ (h) -4 (i) -21.
16 (a) -6 (b) -28 (c) -36 (d) 30 (e) -15 (f) 50 (g) -14 (h) 2 (i) 20.
17 (a) 14 (b) -13 (c) -17 (d) -17 (e) -8 (f) $-1\frac{1}{4}$ (g) $3\frac{3}{4}$ (h) -1 (i) $\frac{2}{3}$.
18 (a) 4 (b) -1 (c) 13 (d) -3 (e) 14 (f) -36.
19 (a) 10 (b) 3 (c) $-1\frac{1}{2}$ (d) 10 (e) -5 (f) $12\frac{1}{2}$.
20 (a) 121 (b) 28 (c) 33 (d) 20 (e) 12.

Revision 10. Algebra Page 50

1 (a) $2x - 13$ (b) $2a - 9b - 2c$ (c) $2a - 5b - 1$ (d) $10a - 15b - 20$ (e) $18x - 13y$ (f) $12a - 17b$.
2 (a) 72 (b) 192 (c) $6\frac{1}{4}$ (d) ± 6 (e) ± 2 (f) ± 20 (g) ± 1 (h) $\pm\frac{1}{2}$ (i) $\pm 4\frac{1}{6}$.
3 (a) a^5b^3 (b) $a^5b^4c^3$ (c) $\dfrac{a^3c}{b}$ (d) $\dfrac{a^4}{bc}$ (e) $15a^3b^6c^6$ (f) $\dfrac{2a^2}{3b^4c}$ (g) $\dfrac{a}{4bc^2}$ (h) $\dfrac{2b^2}{3ac^3}$.
4 (a) a^2b^{-1} (b) ab (c) $a^{-5}b^2$ (d) $a^{5/2}b$ (e) $a^{-3/2}b^{-1/2}$ (f) $a^{3/2}b^{1/2}$ (g) $a^{3/2}$ (h) $a^{5/2}b^{3/2}$ (i) $a^{-5/2}b^{3/2}$ (j) $a^{3/2}$.
5 (a) 6 (b) 4 (c) 3 (d) 6 (e) 2 (f) -2.
6 (a) 2.845 (b) 3.602 (c) 1.079 (d) 1.447 (e) 1.799 (f) 0.243 (g) 0.829 (h) 2.535.
7 (a) $2x$ (b) $2y$ (c) $x + y$ (d) $x - y$ (e) $2x + y$.
8 (a) 5 (b) 3 (c) $6x^2 + 15x$ (d) $2\frac{1}{2}$ (e) $135°$.
9 (a) $T - b$ (b) $\dfrac{100b}{T}$ (c) $T = \dfrac{9b}{5}$.
10 (a) 4 (b) 11 (c) $-1\frac{1}{3}$ (d) -8 (e) $-\frac{3}{4}$ (f) 4 (g) $3\frac{3}{4}$ (h) -1 (i) 2.
11 (a) -16 (b) $-4\frac{1}{2}$ (c) -54 (d) -3 (e) 4 (f) -15 (g) -15 (h) -24 (i) $\frac{2}{3}$.
12 (a) $4C - 4D$ (b) $C = D$ (c) Yes (d) Yes (e) Yes (f) $C = \frac{1}{2}, D = 0$.
13 (a) $x = 3, y = -3$ (b) $x = 4, y = 1$ (c) $x = 0, y = 2$ (d) $x = 2, y = 4$ (e) $x = 3, y = 5$ (f) $x = -10, y = -8$.
14 (a) 81 (b) 5^4 (c) $\pm\frac{8}{3}$ (d) 23 or -31 (e) $1\frac{1}{4}$ or $-2\frac{3}{4}$ (f) 2^{-2}.
15 (a) $a^2 + a - 12$ (b) $2a^2 + 8a - 10$ (c) $4a^2 - 9$ (d) $6a^2 - 11a + 3$ (e) $-8a^2 - 14a + 15$ (f) $9a^2 - 16$ (g) $6a^2 - 17a - 14$ (h) $25a^2 + 20a + 3$ (i) $16a^2 - 25$.
16 (a) 39.09 (b) 6.369 (c) 18.31 (d) 7.099 (e) 3.249 (f) 3.599 (g) 22.53 (h) 6.386.
17 (a) $(x + 1)(x + 2)$ (b) $(x - 3)(x + 2)$ (c) $(x - 5)(x - 2)$ (d) $(2x + 1)(x - 1)$ (e) $(x - 3)(2x + 3)$ (f) $(3x + 1)(x + 2)$ (g) $(2x - 2)(3x - 4)$ (h) $(2x + 5)(2x - 3)$ (i) $(3x - 4)(4x + 3)$.
18 (a) $5x^2 + 6x - 8$ (b) $x^2 + 4x + 4$ (c) $x^2 - 4$.
19 (a) 1 (b) $10x + 2$ (c) $x = 2$.
20 (a) 2 (b) 2 (c) 6 (d) 4.

Part 2 Selective Revision

Financial Matters Page 59

1 (a) £13.20 (b) £2.60.
2 (a) £162 (b) £20.25.
3 (a) £222 (b) £9.25.
4 £512 250.
5 £4 912 900.
6 50p in £.
7 £19.60.
8 (a) 60p (b) 54p (c) £6.37 (d) £443.75.
9 (b) 20% (c) (i) D, (ii) F (d) 16%.
10 (a) £102 (b) £111 (c) £468 (d) 4 months at £53 and final £10.
11 (a) £576, £500, £4924 (b) £624, £528, £4704 (c) £768, £675, £7407 (d) £1176, £1100, £9924 (e) £936, £861, £8125.
12 (a) £4426 (b) £4427 (c) £2374.
13 £3414.
14 (a) £2250 (b) £3500.
15 (a) £29.76 (b) £34.72 (c) £11.78 (d) £100.44.
16 £14 000.
17 (a) £3780 (b) £4440.
18 (a) £297.60, £31.25, £23, Total £351.85 (b) £4464 (c) £13 400.
19 (a) £9.49 (b) £28.91 (c) £41.84 (d) £248.96 (e) £126.49.
20 £945.
21 (a) £6264 (b) £1461.57.
22 (a) £8304 (b) £5980 (c) £2117.
23 (a) £1118.70 (b) £21.51.
24 (a) £15 000 (b) £1260.62.
25 £4.26.
26 (a) £11.91 (b) £18.90 (c) £27.15 (d) £37.59.
27 £170.75.
28 £136.70.
29 £46.72.
30 (a) £172.80 (b) £192 (c) £150 (d) £12 (e) 8%.
31 £102.30.
32 (a) £31 500 000 (b) £1 480 000 (c) 52p in £.
33 (a) $141.30 (b) £7.60.
34 (a) £128.52 (b) £4880.

Probability Page 65

1 (a) $\frac{1}{2}$ (b) $\frac{1}{3}$ (c) 3.
2 (a) $\frac{1}{3}$ (b) $\frac{2}{3}$ (c) $\frac{1}{2}$.
3 (a) $\frac{1}{2}$ (b) 1/7 (c) 5.
4 (a) 8 (b) 16.
5 (a) 9 (b) 27.
6 256.
7 (a) 1/8 (b) 3/8 (c) 1/4 (d) 3/8 (e) 7/8 (f) 1/2.
8 (a) 3/8 (b) 1/8 (c) 1/4 (d) 11/16 (e) 1/2 (f) 1/2 (g) 5/16 (h) 15/16.
9 (a) 1/9 (b) 2/9 (c) 2/3 (d) 7/9 (e) 19/27 (f) 7/27.
10 (a) 1/4 (b) 7/16 (c) 1/8 (d) 1/8 (e) 1/8 (f) 3/16 (g) 3/4.
11 (a) 2/5 (b) 3/5 (c) 1/2 (d) 1/5.
12 (a) 1/6 (b) 1/4 (c) 3/4 (d) 2/3.
13 (a) 5/16 (b) 1/4 (c) 5/24 (d) 11/16 (e) 11/24.
14 (a) 1/13 (b) 2/13 (c) 1/26 (d) 9/13.
15 (a) 1/5 (b) 2/5 (c) 3/5 (d) 1/5 (e) 2/5.
16 (a) 4/15 (b) 4/15 (c) 1/3 Blue/Blue has the best chance.
17 (a) 1/11 (b) 5/33 (c) 1/22 (d) 1/22.
18 (a) 5/72 (b) 5/72 (c) 5/24 (d) 5/168 (e) 5/84 (f) 5/42 (g) 5/504 (h) 1/504.
19 (a) (i) 5/22, (ii) 1/11, (iii) 1/66, (b) 1/3.
20 (a) 3/11 (b) 8/165 (c) 16/55.
21 (a) 1/12 (b) 1/12 (c) 1/4 (d) 1/84 (e) 3/56.
22 (a) 1/20 (b) 11/20 (c) 2/5 (d) 9/70 (e) 1/1820.
23 (a) 6/35 (b) 1/10 (c) 1/21 (d) 3/10 (e) 1/6 (f) 1/133 (g) 9/38.

Algebra Page 71

1 (a) 4 (b) 3 (c) 2 (d) $2\frac{1}{2}$ (e) $-\frac{2}{5}$ (f) $1\frac{5}{6}$ (g) $1\frac{4}{5}$ (h) -3.
2 (a) 9 (b) $-\frac{4}{9}$ (c) $-\frac{1}{4}$ (d) -14 (e) $1\frac{1}{2}$ (f) $6\frac{7}{11}$.
3 (a) 3 (b) 2 (c) 3 (d) 4 (e) -2 (f) -3 (g) $\frac{1}{2}$ (h) $-\frac{1}{3}$ (i) $1\frac{1}{2}$.
4 (a) 0 (b) 0 (c) -1 (d) 1 (e) -4 (f) 2 (g) -4 (h) 2 (i) -3 (j) 3 (k) 8 (l) -3.
5 (a) 0 (b) 0 (c) 1 (d) $-\frac{1}{2}$ (e) 4 (f) $\frac{1}{3}$ (g) $\frac{2}{5}$ (h) -2 (i) 6 (j) -12 (k) 6 (l) $-\frac{1}{4}$.
6 (a) a^5b^2 (b) b^5c^3 (c) b^8y^3 (d) a^4c^2 (e) yd (f) a^2d^4 (g) $10b^6y^4c^3$ (h) $\dfrac{5ba}{c^3}$ (i) $\dfrac{4byc^3}{3}$.
7 (a) $\dfrac{2d^2e}{5ac}$ (b) $\dfrac{3d^2}{4b^2e}$ (c) $\dfrac{4c^2}{3ab}$ (d) $\dfrac{3b^2e^2}{2d^3}$.
8 (a) $\frac{1}{2}$ (b) ± 2 (c) ± 5 (d) $\frac{1}{3}$ (e) $\frac{1}{4}$ (f) ± 10 (g) 1 (h) $\frac{1}{16}$ (i) 1 (j) 1 (k) $\pm\frac{1}{2}$ (l) $\pm\frac{1}{4}$.
9 (a) ab^3 (b) b^3 (c) a^4b^3 (d) $a^{-1}b^{-1}$ (e) a^2b^{-3} (f) $a^{-1/2}b^{-3/2}$.
10 (a) ± 8 (b) 4 (c) ± 1 (d) $\frac{1}{3}$ (e) $\pm\frac{1}{1000}$ (f) 1 (g) $\pm\frac{1}{2}$ (h) $\pm\frac{3}{4}$.
11 (a) $x = 2, y = 2$ (b) $x = 2, y = 6$ (c) $x = -7, y = 8$ (d) $x = 3, y = 2$ (e) $x = 1, y = 5$ (f) $x = -1, y = 1$ (g) $x = -4, y = 5$ (h) $x = -1\frac{1}{4}, y = 2\frac{1}{2}$ (i) $x = -1\frac{1}{2}, y = 1\frac{1}{2}$.
12 (a) $x = -3, y = -2$ (b) $x = -3, y = -2$.
13 (a) $A + B = 7x - y$ (b) $A - B = 6x$ (c) $x = -2, y = -3$.

14 (a) $2A - B = -11$ (b) $2A - 2B = -9C$ (c) $\frac{A}{B} = 4$ (d) $C = -3, D = -4$.

15 (a) $x(6x + 5)$ (b) $y(3 - y)$ (c) $2y(2y - 5)$ (d) $2xy(4x + 1 - 3y)$ (e) $3xy^2(3 - 4x)$ (f) $5y(x^2 - 2xy - y)$ (g) $xy(xy + 3x - 4y)$ (h) $5y^2(x - 2x^2 - y)$ (i) $3x^2(4x - 2y + 3y^2)$.

16 (a) $(x + 3)(x - 3)$ (b) $(x + 6)(x - 6)$ (c) $(3x + 7)(3x - 7)$ (d) $(5y + 8)(5y - 8)$ (e) $2(3x + 2y)(3x - 2y)$ (f) $3(2x + 5y)(2x - 5y)$ (g) $3(3a + 4b)(3a - 4b)$ (h) $6(3x + 2y)(3x - 2y)$.

17 (a) $(x - 3)(x + 4)$ (b) $(x + 2)(x - 5)$ (c) $(x - 4)(x - 5)$ (d) $(2x - 1)(x + 1)$ (e) $(2x + 1)(x - 1)$ (f) $(2x - 1)(x - 1)$.

18 (a) $(2x - 2)(x - 1)$ (b) $(2x + 3)(x - 1)$ (c) $(3x - 3)(2x + 1)$ (d) $(3x - 2)(2x + 4)$ (e) $(3x + 1)(2x + 4)$ (f) $(3x + 4)(x - 2)$ (g) $(5x - 2)(x - 5)$ (h) $(6x - 2)(x + 4)$ (i) $(5x - 3)(2x + 4)$.

19 (a) (0, 0) Minimum (b) Maximum. **20** (0, −2) Maximum. **21** (0, 2) Minimum. **23** −3 or $\frac{1}{2}$. **24** $1\frac{1}{2}$ or −3. **25** 2 or −4.

26 (a) 4 or −4 (b) $\frac{2}{3}$ or $-\frac{2}{3}$ (c) $\frac{1}{3}$ or $\frac{1}{2}$ (d) 4 or $\frac{2}{3}$ (e) 9 or −4 (f) −1 or 2 (g) $1\frac{1}{2}$ or −3 (h) $\frac{1}{2}$ or $-\frac{1}{2}$ (i) −3 or $2\frac{1}{2}$ (j) $\frac{1}{2}$ or $-3\frac{1}{2}$ (k) $\frac{1}{3}$ (l) $1\frac{1}{2}$.

27 Values of *a*, *b* and *c* respectively:
(a) 3, 2, −2 (b) 5, −6, 3 (c) −2, 5, −2 (d) −1, −3, 8 (e) −1, 6, 3 (f) 1, 0, −6 (g) 3, −8, 0 (h) −3, 0, 15 (i) −2, 5, 0.

28 (a) 9 or −4 (b) $\frac{1}{3}$ or $\frac{1}{2}$ (c) $1\frac{2}{3}$ or −3 (d) 2 or −1 (e) 4 or $\frac{2}{3}$ (f) $\frac{2}{5}$ or −2 (g) $1\frac{1}{4}$ or $-1\frac{1}{4}$ (h) 5 or −4 (i) $\frac{1}{2}$ or $-\frac{2}{5}$.

29 (a) 2.76 or 0.24 (b) 0.29 or −2.29 (c) 5 or 1.5 (d) 0.25 or −3.5 (e) 0.54 or −1.87 (f) 1.71 or 0.29 (g) 1.72 or −0.12 (h) 0.19 or −1.48 (i) 1.1 or −0.6.

30 Real roots in *c, d, f, g, h, i*.

Pythagoras Page 78

2 (a) acute (b) obtuse (c) right (d) right (e) acute (f) obtuse (g) right (h) obtuse (i) right.

3 (a) $b^2 = a^2 - c^2$ (b) $c^2 = a^2 - b^2$.

4 (a) 11.3 cm (b) 8.14 cm (c) 12.1 cm (d) 8.44 cm (e) 10.6 cm (f) 4.05 cm.

5 (a) 13.5 (b) 17.2 (c) 1.73 (d) 2.00 (e) 15.4 (f) 9.38.

6 5.37 cm. **7** (a) 3.32 m (b) 6.86 m. **8** 7.13 cm. **9** 9.33 cm. **10** 7.28 cm.

11 8.09 m. **12** 4.24 m. **13** 27.5 km. **14** 65.2 km.

15 (a) 45° (b) 90° (c) 67.9 km (d) 73.4 km.

16 (a) 18.4 cm (b) 8.94 cm.

17 (a) 7.27 cm (b) 5.83 cm.

18 (a) 3.91 cm (b) 3.01 cm.

19 (a) 8.92 m (b) 0.88 m.

20 56 cm.

Statistics Page 84

1 5 and 6.

2 English 9, Mathematics 11.

3 (a) 4 (b) 8 (c) $10\frac{1}{2}$ (d) 6 (e) $14\frac{1}{2}$.

4 (a) 120 (b) $102\frac{1}{2}$.
5 English 11, Mathematics 10.
6 105.9.
7 (a) $12\frac{2}{11}$ (b) 12 (c) 12.
8 (a) 1 (b) 0.5 (c) -0.5 (d) -2.5 (e) -3.5 (f) 4.1 (g) $\frac{1}{2}$.
9 (a) 143 (b) $-26, 14, 28, -34, -4, 43, -37, -33, 35, 48, -6, -16$ (c) 1 (d) -5, 137.
10 (a) 53.4 (b) 52 (c) 52.
11 (a) Average (b) Below average.
12 (d) 1, 2, 1, 6, 7, 7, 7, 5, 3, 1.
13 (a) Mean 65.2, Median 64, Mode 64 (b) 0, 0, 2, 2, 4, 4, 7, 3, 4, 2, 2, 0.
14 (a) 55.9 (b) 1, 0, 1, 4, 6, 3, 5, 0, 1, 1 (d) 55.7.
15 (a) Mode 3.8, Median 5.6 (b) 5.7 (c) 1, 3, 3, 5, 1, 4, 3, 2, 4, 3, 2 (d) 5.6.
16 (a) 4, 1, 2, 4, 3, 2, 4, 2, 5, 2, 2, 5 (b) 5, 6, 5, 6, 7, 7 (c) 62.6 (d) 62.2.

Trigonometry Page 90

1 (a) $57^\circ\ 48'$ (b) $34^\circ\ 48'$ (c) $41^\circ\ 37'$.
2 (a) AB 6.63 cm, BC 7.54 cm (b) AB 17.6 cm, BC 15.47 cm (c) AB 4.06 cm, BC 3.72 cm.
3 1.97 m.
4 BC 4.45 m, AC 6.92 m, BD 3.41 m.
5 22.6 cm.
6 9.18 cm.
7 7.1 cm.
8 (a) 6.44 cm (b) 9.1 cm (c) 11.8 cm.
9 664 cm^3.
10 5.52 cm.
11 (a) 4.5 cm (b) 1.2 cm (c) 7.425 cm^2.
12 (a) 20.22 m (b) 15.86 m (c) 14.36 m.
13 (a) 26.96 cm (b) 39.95 cm (c) 35.99 cm.
14 17.57 m. **15** 13.76 m. **16** 38.88 m. **17** 32°. **18** 9.79 m.
19 212.4 m. **20** 9.62 cm. **21** $54^\circ\ 42'$.
22 (a) 18.68 cm (b) $15^\circ\ 31'$ (c) $13^\circ\ 32'$ (d) 19.2 cm.
23 7.95 cm. **25** (a) 71° (b) 53° (c) 6.17 cm.
26 (a) $51^\circ\ 52'$ (b) $56^\circ\ 8'$ (c) 4.54 cm.
27 (a) 34° (b) 7.63 cm (c) 4.74 cm.
28 (a) 8.65 cm (b) 15.1 cm (c) 8.83 cm.
29 (a) $44^\circ\ 30'$, $42^\circ\ 30'$ (b) 22°, 126° (c) $121^\circ\ 30'$, 17°.
30 (a) 54°, 74°, 52° (b) 50°, 63°, 67° (c) $77^\circ\ 30'$, 48°, $54^\circ\ 30'$ (d) 67°, $63^\circ\ 30'$, $49^\circ\ 30'$.
31 (a) 6.055 cm (b) 7.2 cm (c) 14.37 cm (d) 19.55 cm.
32 (a) $127^\circ\ 30'$ (b) 144° (c) $112^\circ\ 30'$ (d) 123°.
33 (a) $\angle A = 55^\circ\ 30'$, $\angle B = 41^\circ\ 30'$, $\angle C = 83^\circ$
(b) AB = 4.82 cm, $\angle A = 26^\circ$, $\angle B = 40^\circ$
(c) $\angle C = 87^\circ$, AB = 7.92 cm, AC = 6.25 cm.
34 (a) 73.5 km (b) 73.2 km.
35 (b) $47^\circ\ 30'$, $262^\circ\ 30'$ (c) 85.6 km.

Area and Volume Page 99

1 (a) 3 cm^2 (b) 8 cm (c) $17\frac{1}{2}$ m (d) 8 m (e) 84 cm^2 (f) 34 m (g) $10\frac{1}{2}$ cm^2 (h) $7\frac{1}{2}$ m.
2 (a) $1\frac{1}{2}$ cm^2 (b) $7\frac{1}{2}$ mm^2 (c) 10 mm^2 (d) $11\frac{1}{4}$ m^2 (e) 8 m^2 (f) 24 cm^2.
3 (a) 425.5 m^2 (b) $29\frac{1}{4}$ cm^2 (c) $6\frac{2}{5}$ m^2 (d) 126 m^2 (e) 211 m^2 (f) 21 cm^2 (g) 5934.5 m^2 (h) 39 cm^2.
4 (a) 18 m (b) 15.6 cm (c) $1\frac{1}{3}$ m (d) $1\frac{4}{5}$ cm.
5 (a) $10\frac{1}{2}$ cm (b) 15.3 cm (c) $5\frac{1}{3}$ cm (d) 9.5 cm.
6 (a) 3.12 (b) 3.14 (c) 3.13 (d) 3.13 (e) 3.14 (f) 3.14.
7 (a) 44 cm (b) 22 cm (c) $15\frac{5}{7}$ m (d) 132 mm (e) $8\frac{4}{5}$ cm.
8 (a) 37.68 m (b) 113.04 mm (c) 314 cm (d) 10.676 cm (e) 4.71 m (f) 23.864 cm (g) 32.97 m (h) 20.41 cm (i) 23.236 cm.
9 400 m.
10 71 cm.
11 (a) 154 cm^2 (b) 616 m^2 (c) $38\frac{1}{2}$ cm^2 (d) 1386 m^2 (e) $9\frac{5}{8}$ m^2 (f) $346\frac{1}{2}$ cm^2.
12 (a) 3.1 cm^2 (b) 28.3 cm^2 (c) 78.5 cm^2 (d) 254.3 m^2 (e) 13.8 cm^2 (f) 88.2 m^2 (g) 66.4 cm^2 (h) 176.6 m^2 (i) 128.6 cm^2 (j) 333.1 m^2.
13 (a) $278\frac{1}{2}$ m^2 (b) $6\frac{1}{2}$ cm^2 (c) 59 cm^2.
14 (a) 77 mm^3 (b) 154 cm^3 (c) 77 cm^3 (d) $49\frac{1}{2}$ cm^3 (e) $61\frac{3}{5}$ m^3 (f) $563\frac{1}{5}$ cm^3
15 (a) 565.2 m^3 (b) 492.4 cm^3 (c) 27.59 m^3 (d) 0.2543 cm^3 (e) 140.7 cm^3 (f) 65.39 m^3.
16 (a) 408 cm^3 (b) 44 cm^3 (c) 478 cm^3 (d) 5245 cm^3.
17 (a) 1712.2 cm^3 (b) 608.6 m^3.
18 (a) 6 cm^2 (b) 30 cm^2 (c) 3 cm^2 (d) 0.615 cm^2 (e) 11.22 cm^2.
19 (a) 347 cm^2 (b) 7.65 cm^2 (c) 0.267 cm^2.
20 (b) $A = \frac{1}{2} \times 7 \times 3.75 = 13.125$ cm^2 (c) $s = 8.65$ and area = 13.16 cm^2.
21 (a) 6.64 cm^2 (b) 21.18 cm^2 (c) 4.3 cm^2 (d) 5.04 cm^2 (e) 21.5 cm^2 (f) 24.8 cm^2.
22 (a) 27.2 cm^2 (b) 27.2 cm^2 (c) 27.2 cm^2 (d) 27.3 cm^2 (e) 27.1 cm^2 (f) 27.3 cm^2.
23 (a) $7\frac{1}{3}$ cm (b) $1\frac{5}{6}$ cm (c) $4\frac{8}{9}$ cm (d) $49\frac{1}{2}$ cm (e) $7\frac{1}{3}$ cm (f) $7\frac{1}{3}$ cm.
24 (a) 2.09 cm (b) 3.14 cm (c) 2.79 cm (d) 10.99 cm (e) 6.98 cm (f) 9.42 cm.
25 $2\frac{4}{5}$ cm.
26 72°.
27 350 km.
28 52.8 m, 1663.2 m^2.
29 5.5 cm, 12.375 cm^2.
30 35.2 cm, 316.8 cm^2.
31 99 m, 2004.75 m^2.
32 16.5 cm, 144.375 cm^2.
33 (a) 4.07 cm (b) 3.01 cm (c) 8.09 cm (d) 6.09 cm (e) 9.91 cm.
34 (a) 10.81 cm (b) 3.11 cm (c) 6.62 cm (d) 5 cm.
35 5.28 cm and 5.32 cm.
36 $1\frac{3}{4}$ cm.
37 (a) 785 cm^3 (b) 10 cm (c) 15.10 cm.
38 (a) 3.375 litres (b) 0.125 litres (c) 0.234 litres (d) 1.13 litres.
39 (a) 17 250 kg (b) 1.152 kg (c) 34.65 kg.
40 (a) 3.44 litres (b) 2.752 kg.
41 (a) 6.28 litres (b) 2.669 kg.
42 (a) 140.94 cm^3 (b) $\frac{3}{20}$ m^3 (c) 62 500 cm^3 (d) 7380 cm^3 (e) $3307\frac{1}{2}$ cm^3 (f) $57\frac{3}{4}$ m^3.
43 (a) 126.72 m^2 (b) 336 cm^2 (c) 422.4 cm^2 (d) 17.2 m^2 (e) 42.39 m^2.
44 (a) 77.19 cm^3 (b) 41 cm^3 (c) 192.5 cm^3 (d) 172.38 cm^3.

45 (a) 22 cm (b) 1877 cm^3.
46 (a) 21 cm (b) 17 248 cm^3.
47 (a) 6.6 litres (b) 4.4 cm.
48 (a) 0.0335 m^3 (b) 1440 cm^3 (c) 4.19 m^3 (d) 14.1 cm^3.
49 2.09 kg. **50** 1%. **51** 2420 kg.
52 (a) 66 cm^2 (b) 66 cm^2 (c) 616 cm^2 (d) 1260 cm^2 (e) 84.9 cm^2 (f) 47.1 cm^2 (g) 10 010 cm^2 (h) 322 cm^2.
53 3925 m^2. **54** 2833.6 cm^2.

Latitude and Longitude Page 110

1 (a) 8250 km (b) 13 750 km (c) 7700 km (d) 4730 km (e) 12 980 km (f) 2090 km (g) 5720 km (h) 17 490 km.
2 (a) 8517 km (b) 2102 km (c) 13 826 km (d) 11 946 km (e) 9734 km (f) 18 472 km.
3 (a) 5500 km (b) 2750 km (c) 6820 km (d) 8140 km (e) 4840 km (f) 7810 km.
4 (a) 4048 km (b) 3598 km (c) 7984 km (d) 8096 km (e) 3486 km (f) 4948 km.
5 (a) 4697 km, 29 497 km (b) 4964 km, 31 174 km (c) 3317 km, 20 831 km (d) 1799 km, 11 298 km (e) 2768 km, 17 383 km (f) 6083 km, 38 201 km.
6 (a) 4171 km (b) 4025 km (c) 6664 km (d) 10 541 km (e) 17 069 km (f) 3549 km.
7 (a) 8543 km (b) 8090 km (c) 17 131 km (d) 3152 km (e) 11 695 km (f) 9041 km.
8 2334 km. **9** 3590 km. **10** 2952 km.
11 (a) 6667 km (b) 3146 km. **12** (a) 5000 km (b) 29°.
13 5778 + 6129 + 1778 = 13 685 km.
14 (a) 9350 km (b) 7920 km (c) 6300 km.

Transformations Page 114

1 (2, 0), (3, −2), (4, 0), (3, −1).
2 (b) (−2, 0), (0, 0), (−2, −1), (−1, −1), (−2, −2), (0, −2) (c) (−6, −1), (−4, −1), (−6, −2), (−5, −2), (−6, −3), (−4, −3).
3 (a) (−4, −5), (−2, −5), (−4, −4), (−3, −4), (−4, −3), (−2, −3) (b) (−2, −5), (0, −5), (−2, −4), (−1, −4), (−2, −3), (0, −3).
4 (a) Reflection $x = \frac{1}{2}$

(b) Reflection $y = 1\frac{1}{2}$, Translation $\begin{pmatrix} 1\frac{1}{2} \\ 0 \end{pmatrix}$

(c) Reflection $y = 0$, Reflection $x = -\frac{1}{4}$, or Single Rotation 180° about $(-\frac{3}{4}, 0)$

(d) Reflection $y = 0$, Translation $\begin{pmatrix} 1\frac{1}{2} \\ 0 \end{pmatrix}$

(e) Reflection $x = \frac{1}{2}$, Translation $\begin{pmatrix} 0 \\ -3 \end{pmatrix}$.

6 (c) Reflection $y = 1$, Vector $\begin{pmatrix}-3\\0\end{pmatrix}$.

7 (a) Reflection $x = -\frac{1}{2}$, Vector $\begin{pmatrix}0\\4\frac{1}{2}\end{pmatrix}$ (b) Reflection $x = \frac{1}{2}$, Vector $\begin{pmatrix}0\\-5\end{pmatrix}$

(c) Reflection $y = -1\frac{1}{2}$, Vector $\begin{pmatrix}5\\0\end{pmatrix}$ (d) Reflection $y = -1\frac{1}{2}$, Vector $\begin{pmatrix}-5\\0\end{pmatrix}$.

8 (a) (−1, 3), (0, 4), (−2, 4), (−2, 3) (b) (2, 1), (4, 0), (4, 1) (c) (−6, 1) (d) (4, −1), (3, 0), (3, −1), (4, −2) (e) (−2, 2), (0, 1), (−2, 4).

9 (a) $+270°$ (b) $-260°$ (c) $-160°$ (d) $+140°$.

10 (a) (5, −2), (5, −3), (7, −3)
(b) (2, −2), (3, −2), (2, −5), (3, −5)
(c) (2, −2), (2, −4), (4, −3)
(d) (5, 2), (5, 3), (6, 2), (6, 3).

11 (b) (5, −3), (7, −3), (5, −4)
(c) (−3, −5), (−3, −7), (−4, −5)
(d) (−5, 3), (−7, 3), (−5, 4)
(e) (3, 5), (5, 5), (3, 4)
(f) (3, 5), (3, 3), (2, 5).

12 (a) 180°, (0, 0) (b) +90°, (0, 0) (c) −90°, (−5, 3) (d) −90°, (−3, −3) (e) 180°, (3, 4) (f) 180°, (0, 0) (g) 180°, (0, −3) (h) 180°, (−4, −1).

13 (a) $y = 4$ (b) $x = 0$ (c) $y = x$
(d) $\begin{pmatrix}-6\\-8\end{pmatrix}$ (e) $\begin{pmatrix}8\\2\end{pmatrix}$ (f) $y = 0$ and $\begin{pmatrix}-6\\0\end{pmatrix}$ (g) $y = -x - 2$ (h) $y = -1$ and $\begin{pmatrix}-2\\0\end{pmatrix}$.

Matrices Page 120

1 (a) $\begin{pmatrix}6 & -6 & 3\\3 & -3 & 0\end{pmatrix}$ (b) $\begin{pmatrix}1 & -4\\6 & 0\end{pmatrix}$ (c) $\begin{pmatrix}3 & 1\\3 & 0\\-4 & 0\end{pmatrix}$ (d) $\begin{pmatrix}-3 & -1\\-3 & 0\\4 & 0\end{pmatrix}$

(e) Not possible (f) $\begin{pmatrix}5 & -9\\14 & 0\end{pmatrix}$ (g) $\begin{pmatrix}-9 & -3\\-9 & 0\\12 & 0\end{pmatrix}$ (h) Not possible

(i) Not possible (j) $\begin{pmatrix}-8 & -1\\0 & 0\end{pmatrix}$.

4 (a) $\begin{pmatrix}0 & 0 & 1\\0 & 0 & 0\\0 & 1 & 1\end{pmatrix}$ (b) $\begin{pmatrix}0 & 1 & 1 & 1\\0 & 2 & 0 & 0\\0 & 0 & 1 & 0\\0 & 0 & 0 & 2\end{pmatrix}$ (c) $\begin{pmatrix}0 & 0 & 0 & 1\\1 & 1 & 0 & 0\\0 & 1 & 0 & 0\\0 & 0 & 1 & 0\end{pmatrix}$

(d) $\begin{pmatrix}2 & 2 & 1\\1 & 2 & 0\\0 & 1 & 1\end{pmatrix}$ (e) $\begin{pmatrix}1 & 2\\1 & 0\end{pmatrix}$ (f) $\begin{pmatrix}1 & 1 & 2 & 1\\1 & 0 & 0 & 0\\1 & 1 & 0 & 1\\1 & 0 & 1 & 0\end{pmatrix}$

5 (a) 15 (b) $\begin{pmatrix} 2 & 2 & 6 \\ 1 & 1 & 3 \\ 4 & 4 & 12 \end{pmatrix}$ (c) 10 (d) $\begin{pmatrix} 3 & 6 & 3 & 9 \\ 1 & 2 & 1 & 3 \\ 2 & 4 & 2 & 6 \\ 1 & 2 & 1 & 3 \end{pmatrix}$

(e) Not possible (f) Not possible (g) Not possible

(h) $\begin{pmatrix} 3 & 3 & 9 \\ 1 & 1 & 3 \\ 2 & 2 & 6 \end{pmatrix}$ (i) 10 (j) Not possible.

6 (a) $\begin{pmatrix} 11 & 1 \\ -2 & 3 \\ -8 & -2 \end{pmatrix}$ (b) Not possible (c) $\begin{pmatrix} -3 & -3 & 3 \\ 5 & 0 & 12 \end{pmatrix}$ (d) Not possible

(e) $\begin{pmatrix} -7 & 0 & 5 & 14 \\ 4 & 5 & 5 & -8 \\ 4 & -2 & -6 & -8 \end{pmatrix}$ (f) Not possible (g) $\begin{pmatrix} 4 & -1 \\ -9 & 1 \\ 10 & -6 \end{pmatrix}$

(h) $\begin{pmatrix} -7 & 5 \\ 1 & 4 \end{pmatrix}$ (i) $\begin{pmatrix} -7 & 7 & 16 & 14 \\ 0 & 7 & 11 & 0 \end{pmatrix}$ (j) $\begin{pmatrix} -2 & 11 & 5 \\ 3 & 8 & 3 \end{pmatrix}$.

7 (a) $\begin{pmatrix} 61 & 28 \\ 50 & 20 \end{pmatrix}$ (b) $\begin{pmatrix} 24 & 12 & 18 \\ 63 & 33 & 48 \\ 24 & 24 & 24 \end{pmatrix}$ (c) Not possible.

8 (a) $\begin{pmatrix} 1 & 0 \\ 0 & 1 \end{pmatrix}$ (b) $\begin{pmatrix} 1 & 0 \\ 0 & 1 \end{pmatrix}$ (c) $\begin{pmatrix} 1 & 0 \\ 0 & 1 \end{pmatrix}$.

9 (a) $\begin{pmatrix} 3 & -5 \\ -1 & 2 \end{pmatrix}$ (b) $\begin{pmatrix} 3 & -4 \\ -2 & 3 \end{pmatrix}$ (c) $\begin{pmatrix} 2 & -3 \\ -3 & 5 \end{pmatrix}$ (d) $\begin{pmatrix} 1 & -1 \\ -1 & 2 \end{pmatrix}$

(e) $\begin{pmatrix} 1 & -3 \\ -1 & 4 \end{pmatrix}$ (f) $\begin{pmatrix} 1 & -2 \\ -2 & 5 \end{pmatrix}$ (g) $\begin{pmatrix} 1 & -3 \\ -2 & 7 \end{pmatrix}$ (h) $\begin{pmatrix} 3 & -7 \\ -2 & 5 \end{pmatrix}$

(i) $\begin{pmatrix} 1 & -1\frac{1}{2} \\ -1 & 2 \end{pmatrix}$ (j) $\begin{pmatrix} 1 & -1 \\ -\frac{2}{3} & 1 \end{pmatrix}$.

10 (a) $\begin{pmatrix} 2 & 7 \\ -1 & -3 \end{pmatrix}$ (b) $\begin{pmatrix} 2 & -1 \\ 5 & -2 \end{pmatrix}$ (c) $\begin{pmatrix} 1 & 2 \\ -3 & -5 \end{pmatrix}$ (d) $\begin{pmatrix} -2 & 3 \\ -3 & 4 \end{pmatrix}$.

12 Reflection $x = 0$.

13 (a) Identity (b) No change.

14 Reflection $y = x$.

15 Reflection $y = -x$.

16 (i) Rotation $+90^\circ$, (ii) Rotation -90°, (iii) Rotation 180°.

17 (a) $\mathbf{B}^2, \mathbf{C}^2, \mathbf{D}^2, \mathbf{G}^2$ produce identity, $\mathbf{E}^2, \mathbf{F}^2$ give $\begin{pmatrix} -1 & 0 \\ 0 & -1 \end{pmatrix}$ Rotation 180°

(b) $\mathbf{B}^3 = \mathbf{B}$, $\mathbf{C}^3 = \mathbf{C}$, $\mathbf{D}^3 = \mathbf{D}$, $\mathbf{E}^3 = \mathbf{F}$, $\mathbf{F}^3 = \mathbf{E}$, $\mathbf{G}^3 = \mathbf{G}$

(c) **A, B, C, D, G**.

18 Identity. Clockwise 90° followed by anticlockwise 90°.

19 Enlargement +2. **20** Enlargement +3.
21 Enlargement $+\frac{1}{2}$. **23** One-way stretch from $y = 0$.
27 (a) Shear parallel to $x = 0$ in a positive direction
(b) Shear parallel to $x = 0$ in a negative direction.
28 Area is unchanged.

Time and Distance Page 130

1 (b) 4.1 km/h.
2 (b) 8 km/h.
5 (a) 35 km (b) $3\frac{1}{4}$ h (c) 59 km.
6 (a) $3\frac{3}{4}$ h (b) $16\frac{3}{4}$ km (c) £7.36.
7 (a) 1550 km (b) 12.15 (c) 13.06.
8 (a) $31\frac{1}{2}$ km (b) 1 h 5 min (c) 3 h 6 min.
9 (a) 11.32 (b) $18\frac{1}{2}$ km (c) 12.43.
10 (a) 10.33 (b) $108\frac{1}{2}$ km (c) 64 km/h.
11 (a) Having lunch (b) 30 km (c) 13.40.
12 (a) Second train (b) 1 h 15 min (c) $66\frac{2}{3}$ km/h.

Navigation Page 134

1 (a) 180° (b) 315° (c) 135° (d) $022\frac{1}{2}$ (e) $157\frac{1}{2}$° (f) $202\frac{1}{2}$°.
2 (a) 060° (b) 210° (c) 335° (d) 100° (e) 255° (f) 260°.
3 (a) 135° (b) 165° (c) 130° (d) 180° (e) $102\frac{1}{2}$° (f) 85°.
5 178° and 358°. **6** 357°. **7** 5.4 cm, 260°. **8** 33 mm, 080°.
9 20 mm, 218°.
10 Lines (a) 15 mm (b) 38 mm (c) 49 mm (d) 73 mm (e) 68 mm.
11 Lines (a) 19 mm (b) 27 mm (c) 36 mm (d) 9 mm (e) 65 mm.
12 Lines (a) 19 mm (b) 34 mm (c) 51 mm (d) 81 mm (e) $63\frac{1}{2}$ mm.
13 (a) AB 630 km/h, BC 250 km/h, CA 650 km/h
(b) AB 144 km/h, BC 134 km/h, CA 46 km/h
(c) AB 235 km/h, BC 145 km/h, CA 285 km/h
(d) AB 90 km/h, BC $274\frac{1}{2}$ km/h, CA 360 km/h.

(Answers **16** to **30** are by calculation. Reasonable allowance should be made for answers obtained by construction.)

16 (a) 132 km/h, 215° (b) 333 km/h, due N (c) 368.4 km/h, 129°.
17 142 km/h, 333°.
18 203 km/h, 298°.
19 (a) 390 km/h, 326° (b) 329 km/h, 256° (c) 331 km/h, 192°.
20 514 km/h, 054°. **21** 368.5 km/h, 129°. **22** 62.1 km/h, 214° 30′.
23 66.7 km/h, 080° 30′. **24** 75.4 km/h, 285° 30′. **25** 54.2 km/h, 234°.
26 (a) 290 km/h, 066° 30′ (b) 285 km/h, 052° (c) 255 km/h, 049°.
27 (a) 452 km/h, 155° (b) 280 km/h, 132°.
28 (a) 668 km/h, 053° (b) 504 km/h, 054°.
29 403.5 km/h, 295°, then 527 km/h, 041° 30′.
30 461 km/h, 090°, then 373 km/h, 315° 30′.

160
150
170
85
30
70
40
27
20
427
789

150
170
140
70
40
20
27
617

721

289
140
139

170
140
150
100
70
40
20
27
717

165
135

280
125